The Coming Antichrist

The Coming Antichrist

by

Walter K. Price

MOODY PRESS
CHICAGO

In grateful memory of
Otis C. Amis,
1904-71

© 1974 by
THE MOODY BIBLE INSTITUTE
OF CHICAGO

All scripture quotations in this book are from
the American Standard Version of 1901.

Library of Congress Catalog Card Number: 73-15088

ISBN: 0-8024-1602-0

Printed in the United States of America

Contents

Introduction

THE BIBLE DOCTRINE of the Antichrist appears within a clearly defined scheme of prophetic events which will unfold upon the earth in the last days. The Antichrist is presented in Scripture as a *spirit of evil* which appears periodically during the course of history. However, this spirit of evil will be climaxed in one *person of evil* at the end of time. The person of the Antichrist and the events of the last days will be inseparable. Furthermore, the Antichrist has a vital role in the biblical division of history called the times of the gentiles. This is a period of time which the Lord has determined upon Israel and the nations.

The New Testament church begins, develops, and concludes in a parenthetical way within the times of the gentiles. This great parenthesis in which the church exists upon earth is a segment of time bounded by Pentecost and the rapture. It occurs within the larger context of the times of the gentiles. The Antichrist will be uniquely related to Israel and to the nations, but the church will be removed from the world before the Antichrist is revealed.

To understand the person and activity of the Antichrist, an understanding of the events that take place within the times of the gentiles is necessary. While the spirit of the Antichrist pervades the whole of the times of the gentiles, it is the actual person of the Antichrist who climaxes and brings to a close this prophetic period.

THE TIMES OF THE GENTILES

The term *times of the gentiles* was first used by Jesus in Luke 21:24, when he predicted that the holy city would be under gentile control until the second coming of Christ. Though there have been periodic episodes in which Jerusalem has been free from this gentile domination, these have been relatively few and very short-lived. Jerusalem will not be completely free of gentile dominion until the end of the tribulation period. It was revealed to Daniel that the times of the gentiles would last for seventy weeks, or 490 years (Dan 9:24-27). Subsequent discussion demonstrates that a long delay occurs between the sixty-ninth and the seventieth week and that the seventieth week of seven years will be fulfilled after the church is raptured.

The times of the gentiles began in 605 B.C. with the first conquest of Judah by the Babylonians. During the last phase of the Babylonian conquest, around 587 B.C., King Zedekiah was blinded and taken into Babylonian captivity. There has not been a king in the line of David upon the throne of Israel since that time. Other Jewish kings were to reign between the Maccabean revolt and the coming of the Romans. But these were of the Hasmonean family, a priestly family, not from the tribe of Judah or the royal family of David.

The times of the gentiles began with the Babylonian exile and has been running its course for the last twenty-five hundred years. We are still in the times of the gentiles. After the return from Babylon in the sixth and fifth centuries B.C., the Jews were again in the land, but still under gentile overlords. Successively they were ruled by Persians, Alexander the Great, Ptolemies of Egypt, and Seleucids of Syria. Then after a brief period of self-determination, the Romans came and the Jews were under the imperial rule of Rome until the city of Jerusalem fell in A.D. 70. After another brief revolt against the Romans, ending in A.D. 135, the Jews were to be scattered from their homeland during the next two thousand years. They were ruled by almost every nation upon the face of the earth. Wherever the wandering Jew went, he found himself under gentile dominion.

Zionism called the Jews back to the land during the twentieth century. But even while Israel was coming to the land, gentiles ruled in Jerusalem. The Turks remained until World War I ended their control of the Holy Land. Then the League of Nations enforced a mandate upon Palestine, and the British administered this manifestation of gentile dominion. Even when Israel was declared a nation in 1948 and the British left, the Arabs would not relinquish control of Jerusalem until they were forced to do so by the Six-Day War in 1967. Since then, Jerusalem has found itself free from gentile dominion. But this is only for a moment. When the tribulation period begins and the reign of the Antichrist is established, Israel and Jerusalem will again be brought under the dominion of the nations.

The events which bring to a close the times of the gentiles develop in the following way. The church age, which began at Pentecost, will end when the last soul to be added to the body of Christ is won. Immediately thereafter, the rapture will occur. This is a phase of the second coming of Christ which is separate, but not separable from it, for the rapture will be followed after seven years by the second coming of Jesus Christ in glory. At the time of the rapture the Lord Jesus does not return to the earth, nor is his coming public. The church is snatched away secretly to meet him in the air. With the church absent, the Holy Spirit, whom Paul calls the restrainer in 2 Thessalonians 2:7, also changes his relationship to this earthly scene.

It is then that the Antichrist is revealed not as an antagonist of the church, for the true church is gone, but as an antagonist of the saints of God who will be saved during the tribulation period. The Antichrist will also conflict with the nation Israel, as well as with the gentile nations.

Soon after the rapture the Antichrist will succeed in forming a ten-nation confederation within the boundary of the
ancient Roman empire. During this time he will permit
Israel to rest and to re-establish herself in the land in all her
pristine glory. The temple will be rebuilt, and the ancient
Levitical system of sacrifices and offerings, along with the
various feasts and holidays, will be reinstituted. This re-
surgence of preexilic sacrifice and worship will bring about a
revival of Old Testament religion in Israel. Perhaps it will
be relieved of all the trappings that Rabbinic and Talmudic
Judaism have added to it, and the religion of Israel will appear again as it was in the days of the first temple.

Apparently the Jews and their religion, along with an
apostate church, will further the ambitions of the Antichrist
for world political dominion. This apostate church is the institutional church which will be left upon earth after the true
church, the body of Christ, is caught out of the world at the
rapture. However, at midtribulation, the political ambitions
of the Antichrist are fulfilled, as the last resistance is smashed.
This occurs when Russia, the foe from the far north, will be
defeated as she attempts to invade Israel. The Antichrist has
further ambitions, however. These are ambitions not only to
rule the world but to be deified and worshiped as God. His
ambition to rule the world will be fulfilled during the first
half of the tribulation period. The second ambition to be
worshiped as god will be realized during the last three and
one-half years of the tribulation period. Judaism and the
apostate world church will have aided the political ambitions
of the Antichrist early in the tribulation. However, they now
hinder his religious ambitions and therefore must be liqui-
dated. The apostate church will be destroyed immediately at
midtribulation, and the remaining three and one-half years
of the great tribulation will find Israel severely persecuted,
for many of the Jews will refuse to worship the Antichrist.

The great tribulation period, along with the career of the Antichrist, will come to an end when the Antichrist is attacked by kings from the East. Apparently a vast army from the Orient will round the Fertile Crescent and descend upon the armies of the Antichrist which are in the Holy Land. The conflict will not be between Israel and the Antichrist at this point. However, the armies of the Orient and the armies of the Antichrist do meet in the land of Israel. Though Zechariah's second oracle concerning Israel (12:1—14:21) indicates that Israel is involved in the hostilities, the two belligerents are the Oriental forces of the kings of the East and the forces of the Antichrist. Israel is caught, as in a vise, between these two contending forces.

Because these hostilities occur in the Holy Land, the elect nation Israel will be jeopardized by this conflagration. It is then that the War of Armageddon will take place as the Lord moves to end the hostilities for Israel's sake. This occurs at the second coming of Christ. At this time the career of the Antichrist will be brought to an end as he is cast alive into the abyss. Also at this time the nation Israel will receive the Lord Jesus Christ as Messiah. In contrast to the tyrannical and chaotic world rule of the Antichrist, the Lord Jesus Christ will establish a kingdom, and for a thousand years the earth will bask in the light of his glorious reign. This will be the earthly kingdom of God in Israel, which the Old Testament prophets foresaw, and which is literally fulfilled upon the earth.

The career of the Antichrist is therefore an inseparable part of the events of the last days. It is he who leads the nations into direct conflict with the God of Israel. His severe persecution of the Jews will prepare Israel to receive Jesus as Messiah. His dominion over the nations will lead them into the final conflict with God. The Lord will punish the nations in the judgment of Armageddon because of their treatment of the Jewish people during the entire course of the times of the gentiles.

The Antichrist is presented in Scripture as a literal person who will be revealed to this world scene immediately after the rapture of the church. Therefore, all of the prophetic context in which the Antichrist appears in Scripture is also to be taken literally. The warnings and promises of God to Israel, presented in the Old Testament, are not to be spiritualized and reapplied to the church. Israel is a literal nation with which God will yet deal in judgment, as well as in glorious restoration. All of this occurs within the context of the misanthropic reign of the Antichrist, which immediately precedes the glorious reign of the Messiah in Israel.

THE LITERAL INTERPRETATION OF PROPHECY

Many years ago David L. Cooper set out what he called the Golden Rule of Interpretation: "When the plain sense of Scripture makes common sense, seek no other sense; therefore, take every word at its primary, ordinary, usual, literal meaning unless the facts of the immediate context, studied in the light of related passages and axiomatic and fundamental truths, indicate clearly otherwise."

Because the prophetic word is to be taken literally in most cases, the most literally accurate translation of the Bible is the best to use when studying prophecy. Therefore, the Scripture text which will be used throughout this book is that of the American Standard Version of 1901. It does not flow with the poetic beauty of the Authorized Version. But neither does it take the liberties with the text in order to make it more palatable to the modern reader, as do the Revised Standard Version and the New English Bible. It is a literal and an accurate translation of the Hebrew and the Greek of the original texts. For those who hold a high view of the inspiration of the Bible and believe that the original text was verbally inspired (though admitting individual differences in literary style), this literal accuracy of the American Standard Version is important. The text of the American Standard Version has not been emended so as to alter substantially its reading, as the case in the Revised Standard Version, for example. In some of the more recent translations the received text of the Old Testament has been so altered that the meaning is entirely changed. In many instances this alteration—or "emendation" as the scholars call it—has been done at the subjective whim of some liberal critic whose understanding of the Word is purely academic.

The only objection that many have to the American Standard Version is its use of the name *Jehovah* where the King James Version follows the LXX and uses Lord. The covenant name for the God of Israel in the Old Testament is *Yahweh*. This name was so sacred that by the second century B.C. the Jews refused to pronounce it. (Orthodox Jews will not pronounce this sacred name even today.) When the ancient Jewish scholar came across the name *Yahweh* he would pronounce it "Adonai," which means "my Lord." The Hebrew at that time had no vowels. The system of vowel points had not yet been invented, and therefore *Yahweh* was written YHVH, which is called the Tetragrammaton—the Four-Letter Word. No one really knows how it was pronounced. When the Masoretic scholars added to the consonantal word YHVH the vowels from the word Adonai, the name turned out to be "YaHoVaH." However, this is a hybrid word. Therefore, Jehovah has been dropped from all modern translations in favor of Lord. We actually follow the respectful attitude of ancient Israel when we substitute the word Lord for Jehovah, for we are figuratively pronouncing the word *Yahweh* as "Adonai"—"Lord" in our language.

1

History's Futile Attempts to Identify the Antichrist

SINCE THE CHURCH is to be taken out of the world before the Antichrist is revealed (2 Th 2:1-7), it will never be possible for the Bible expositor living during the age which extends from Pentecost to the rapture, to identify the Antichrist with certainty. His identification will only become known during the tribulation period. Even then the Antichrist will possibly not be revealed with certainty until toward the beginning of the last three and one-half years of the period.

Though positive identification is never possible during this present age, much data is given in the prophetic Word which will enable us to define the person and the mission of the Antichrist with some degree of accuracy. Even the abortive attempts that have been made during the last two thousand years to identify the Antichrist are helpful, for they have kept the Bible doctrine of the Antichrist alive in the imagination of believers. This has made eschatology a relevant issue during every era of the age of the church, for behind the appearance of some potential Antichrist is the blessed hope—the anticipation of the Lord's return.

FOUR BASIC VIEWS OF THE ANTICHRIST

Historically there are four basic views concerning the identity of Antichrist. First, the idea of Antichrist has been con-

15

sidered as a *principle of evil,* an ideal personification of the evil powers of the world. Just as Uncle Sam is the personification of all that is American, so the Antichrist will be the personification of all that is evil. *The Assumption of Moses* (ca. A.D. 30) identifies the Antichrist, or anti-Messiah in this case, as a tyrant who possesses the evil-ideal traits of Antiochus Epiphanes plus those of Herod the Great. In this view intangible evil is made explicit in the Antichrist.

Second, the Antichrist has been considered an *institution of evil.* During the Reformation the papacy was more often identified as Antichrist than was any particular pope. Those who take a preterist view of the book of the Revelation, considering it to have been written to encourage the suffering saints of God during the first-century persecutions of the church at the hands of Rome, interpret the Antichrist as the institution of the Roman empire.

Third, the Antichrist has been viewed as a *person of evil.* Historically, a large number of persons have been identified as the Antichrist. This chapter will note many of them. Even in pre-Christian times the author of *The Psalms of Solomon* (ca. 60 B.C.) identified the Roman general Pompey as the anti-Messiah.

However, these three views tend to be static and consider the Antichrist to be but a personification, or an institution, or a person. There is a fourth view that includes all the previous ones and combines them in a *dynamic view* of the Antichrist. First John 2:18 says, "Little children, it is the last hour: and as ye heard that antichrist cometh, even now have there arisen many anti-christs; whereby we know that it is the last hour." And again in 1 John 4:3, John writes, "And every spirit that confesseth not Jesus is not of God: and this is the spirit of the anti-christ, whereof ye have heard that it cometh; and now it is in the world already."

There is no definite article in the Greek of 1 John 2:18. John actually says, "it is *a* last hour." It is *an* hour of crisis that has in it some of the characteristics of *the* last hour; however, the crisis of John's day is not *the* last hour, merely *a* last hour. Just as the last hour is preceded in history by various hours of crisis, so the Antichrist will be preceded in history by many persons and institutions that will have some or many, but not all, of his characteristics. Only the Antichrist will consummate in himself, at the end of the age, all the evil that has appeared periodically in various historical institutions and persons.

These verses in 1 John indicate that the Antichrist is something more than just one unique person who appears on the stage of history at the end of the age. Though this is not to deny that the final Antichrist is a person who will dominate the world during the end-time, the dynamic view also takes into consideration the fact that there are many partial manifestations of the Antichrist during the course of world history which will lead up to his final revelation during the last days. It is for this reason that in many historical instances, when some person or institution has been identified as Antichrist, this identification was not totally false. Such attempts were in error when they said that a certain historical person was the Antichrist—which most of them did. However, there was a measure of truth in these identifications when we recognize that these historical persons actually did have some of the characteristics of the Antichrist.

In all periods of human history there have been representatives of both good and evil. These have appeared in both persons and institutions. All that has been partially manifest of good and of evil during the course of history will have its final climax in one person who will sum up in himself all these partial manifestations of good or evil. All that is good has been summed up in the historical manifestation of the Person of Jesus Christ. Just so, all the evil, which has been partially manifest in persons and institutions that have appeared in the course of history, will be finally summed up at the end of the age in the person of the Antichrist.

HISTORICAL ATTEMPTS TO IDENTIFY THE ANTICHRIST

Before the New Testament canon had closed, two Roman emperors had already been identified as the Antichrist. Though the idea that some historical person was anti-Messiah did occur during the interbiblical period, these were the first attempts in the Christian era to identify some person as Antichrist. The emperor Caligula, whose reign began in A.D. 37, attempted to place his image in the holy sanctuary. Because this was the very thing that Antiochus IV had done, many believed that Caligula was the Antichrist. Even though he died in A.D. 41, he was expected to revive from his death stroke, and many believed that he would live again to establish his image in the temple.

However, the most famous Antichrist theory of the first century was that of "Nero Redivivus." In A.D. 68, when the Roman Senate condemned Nero to death for his hideous crimes, he fled to a suburban villa and there put an end to his life. Because he died almost alone and in an obscure place, rumors began to circulate that he had fled to the Parthians from which he would come at the head of a great army to revenge himself upon the Roman world. The rumors which had spread into the provinces persisted for many years into the following century. There were two impostors who actually arose, claiming to be Nero. One gained a large following among the Parthians and the news of this coming one threw Asia Minor into great terror (Suetonius, *Nero* 57; Tacitus, *History* 1.2, 2.8,9; *Dio Cassius* 64.9.) .

As time passed, the returning Nero grew more ghostly, and he was invested with supernatural powers. At first he had been nothing more than a deposed ruler, returning to regain his throne and to heap vengeance upon those who had deposed him. However, as too many years passed for him to retain natural life, and as the legend persisted, he was thought of as being revived from the dead. The apocalyptic *Ascension of Isaiah* makes mention of this. "And after it has come to its consummation, Beliar the great prince, the King of this world who has ruled it since it came into being shall descend; he will come down from his firmament in the form of a man, a lawless king, a slayer of his mother, who himself (even) this king will persecute" (4.2). In this work from the end of the first century, it is said that Beliar, the Antichrist, would come in the person of an unrighteous king who murdered his mother. Nero was often identified as a matricidal monster.

The belief that Nero would return was still in existence in the fifth century A.D., for Augustine makes reference to it saying, "Others, again suppose that he [Nero] is not even dead, but that he was concealed that he might be supposed to have been killed, and that he *now* lives in concealment in the vigor of that same age which he had reached when he was believed to have perished, and will live until he is revealed in his own time and restored to his kingdom." (*The City of God* 20.19). Augustine wrote these words between 412 and 426 A.D., three hundred and fifty years after Nero's death.

THE ANTICHRIST IN SECOND AND THIRD CENTURY PATRISTIC WRITINGS

The writings of the apostolic Fathers form a valuable supplement to the New Testament, for they give witness to the life and thought of the church in the early second century A.D. From the first half of this second century there comes to us in fragmentary form the writings of these men who were successors to the original apostles, and whom we call the apostolic Fathers. The struggle between Christianity and the pagan empire had not assumed the proportions it would assume in a few decades, therefore literary activity at this time was not as extensive as it would later be. The writings that are preserved from this era are not histories, or apologies, or expositions, but merely epistles or homilies. Though the church had suffered persecutions under Nero and Domitian, these were neither intense enough, nor were they widespread enough, to cause the almost universal expectation of the Antichrist that would emerge during the official persecutions of the next century.

Included in the writings of the apostolic Fathers is *The Epistle of Barnabas.* The unknown author of this epistle—almost certainly was not the Barnabas who was Paul's companion—indicates his belief that the Roman empire is the fourth beast of Daniel's vision and that it will be followed by ten kingdoms out of which the Antichrist will arise. The Antichrist is called the Black One, and in this epistle the writer admonishes his readers, "Take heed in these last days. For the whole time of our faith shall profit us nothing, unless we now, in the season of lawlessness and in the offenses that shall be, as becometh sons of God, offer resistance, that the Black One may not effect an entrance."[1]

In the days of the apostolic Fathers there developed an influential theory concerning the time of the Antichrist's advent. During the second century A.D. many writers agreed that the fourth kingdom in Daniel's vision was the contemporary Roman empire. They also believed that the Roman empire would come to its end by being broken up into ten kingdoms. Because the idea of a revived Roman empire was not developed until the time of Hippolytus, almost a century later, many early writers believed that the existent Roman empire—the legs of iron—would move directly into the next stage of Daniel's image, and that the next form of world government would be that which was symbolized by the feet and ten toes, composed of a mixture of iron and clay.

Since we have a much larger historical perspective, we now see that the ancient Roman empire and the revived Roman empire are separated by the age of the church, already of two thousand years' duration. However, in this early age, prophetic interpreters believed that the next form of world government would immediately follow the fall of Rome. Therefore, they taught that when the Roman empire fell it would be followed immediately by the ten-toed kingdom, out of which the Antichrist, the "little horn" of Daniel 7, would arise. As long as Rome stood, therefore, the ten-kingdom confederation remained in the future, and the advent of the Antichrist was forestalled. Hence the Roman empire was seen as the restrainer of 2 Thessalonians 2:7.

The ante-Nicene era of church history is dated from A.D. 150 until the emperor Constantine called the first general council of the church. This was the Council of Nicaea, which convened in May, A.D. 325, to settle the Arian controversy. This 175-year period, which led up to the reign of Constantine, covers the time when the gospel spread throughout the Roman world, and the subsequent persecutions of the church at the hands of the Roman emperors occurred. During this time, Rome continued to be identified as the fourth of Daniel's four world empires, and as we have noted, it was assumed that the Roman empire restrained the revelation of the Antichrist.

The consensus of interpretation was that Rome would soon be divided into ten kingdoms and the Antichrist would arise out of them. Indeed, Hippolytus, called by some the bishop of Rome, fearlessly made the point in his writings that Rome would fall. This was a dangerous prediction in his day, for Roman authorities would not look passively upon such a public declaration. Many early Christians prayed for the preservation of the empire, for as long as it remained intact, the ten kingdoms could not form, and the Antichrist was held at bay. But most felt that it would only be a matter of time until the Antichrist would appear and cause the church to flee into the wilderness.

Daniel's "little horn," Paul's "man of sin," and John's

Antichrist, were all viewed as the same person: the sinister persecutor of the saints whose coming was imminent and whose career would be ended only by the second coming of Christ. Most of the writers in the ante-Nicene period who mention the subject at all, viewed the second coming of Christ as personal, literal, and premillennial. Though there is not an overabundance of extant prophetic material from this early era, Justin Martyr (ca. 100-ca. 165), for example, taught the appearance of the Antichrist, whom he called "the man of apostasy," and that his advent would occur just before the second coming.

Irenaeus (ca. A.D. 200) surmised that the Antichrist would be a Jew. He believed that the mention of Dan in Jeremiah 8:16 and the omission of the name of Dan in the list of tribes found in Revelation 7 indicates the Antichrist's tribe. Though Irenaeus does not explain further why he believes that the Antichrist would come from the tribe of Dan, it is true that the Midrash on Genesis 49:14-17 declared that from Dan darkness would spread over the earth. Dan was the northern-most tribe, and the north was always considered the seat of darkness and evil. Dan was also the first of Israel's tribes to accept idolatry. In addition, the tribal insignia of Dan ac-tually bore the sign of a serpent and the serpent was ac-cepted as a sign of Antichrist. These may have been the things that influenced Irenaeus' interpretation.

During the Middle Ages, this supposed identity of the Anti-christ as a Jew was to cause many anti-Semitic outbreaks. Dramas were written and produced which showed how Jewish demons would help the Antichrist to conquer the world, until the second coming would annihilate both the Jews and the Antichrist together. When these mystery plays were enacted, armed forces were needed to protect the Jews and their quarters from the fury of the mob. Though the pope and his councils had insisted that Jews should not be killed—merely isolated and degraded until they became converted—

this made little impression on mobs that had been stirred into hysterical fear by these Antichrist plays.

Irenaeus also believed that the Antichrist would appear three and one-half years before the second coming, and that the second coming would occur at the beginning of a seventh thousand-year period. This means, of course, that Irenaeus accepted the old Jewish theory that the first six thousand years of history are analogous to the first six days of creation. And just as the seventh day was a sabbath, so the seventh thousand-year period will be the millennial Sabbath in which the Messiah will reign upon earth. Therefore, the Antichrist will appear just before the millennial reign is ushered in by the second coming.

We must remember that neither Irenaeus, nor any other of these early writers, had any conception of the vast amount of time that would elapse between the first and second coming of Christ. All of them expected his advent immediately. In addition, Irenaeus believed that the church was spiritual Israel, and therefore his idea of the millennial reign of Christ was a confusion of this temporal reign and the eternal state. However, the point remains that Irenaeus expected a personal Antichrist to appear just before these imminent end-time events.

Tertullian (ca. 150-ca. 225) was one of the most prolific writers of that era. Though he had thoroughly mastered Greek, he was the first ecclesiastical writer of prominence to use Latin. Like Irenaeus, Tertullian—the father of Latin theology—believed in a personal Antichrist. Though he also identified Marcion and his followers as having the spirit of Antichrist, Tertullian did not believe that the Antichrist would necessarily be a Jew. He expected the Antichrist to appear soon, his delay being only because the Roman empire remained intact. When Rome, the restrainer, broke up into its prophesied ten kingdom successors, then Antichrist would appear. In his *Apology*, Tertullian writes, "There is also

another and a greater necessity for our offering prayer in
behalf of the emperors, nay, for the complete stability of the
empire, and for Roman interests in general. For we know
that a mighty shock impending over the whole earth—in fact,
the very end of all things threatening dreadful woes—is only
retarded by the continued existence of the Roman empire.
We have no desire, then, to be overtaken by these dire events;
and in praying that their coming may be delayed, we are lend-
ing our aid to Rome's duration."

Hippolytus (ca. 160-ca. 235), who lived in the vicinity of
Rome, was one of the most learned and prolific writers of his
day. He was the last of the important theologians to write in
Greek. His writings spread eastward from Italy and were
translated into many different languages. He seems to be the
first to have conceived the idea that when the Roman empire
falls, it will revive again. In a work entitled *Treatise on Christ
and Antichrist,* he interpreted the first beast of Revelation 13
as the existent Roman empire. The second beast (Rev
13:11ff.) he interpreted as the kingdom of the Antichrist, the
two horns representing the Antichrist and the false prophet.
However, the two empires are separate. The original Roman
Empire when it falls, will live again, and its deadly wound
will be healed in the revived spirit of Roman imperialism.
Hippolytus is also believed to be the first to propose that a
gap—the church age—exists between the sixty-ninth and the
seventieth week of Daniel, and that the seventieth week runs
its course just before the second coming of Christ.

Cyprian (ca. 200-ca. 258), bishop of Carthage, lived when
the Emperor Decius issued the edict of 250 A.D. which initiated the most intense, universal, and systematic persecution
of the church up to that time. There had been other persecutions, but none so thorough as this one. Many Christians
suffered martyrdom. But the intent of the persecution was
not to inflict death upon believers, but rather by imprison-
ment and torture, force Christians to sacrifice to the old gods.

During this time Bishop Fabian of Rome and Babylas of Antioch died as martyrs. Origen and hosts of others were tortured. Cyprian was hidden during this time and from his concealment he wrote his epistles to the clergy. This severe persecution—which continued on into the reigns of two succeeding emperors, Gallus (251-253) and Valerian (253-260) — caused Cyprian to conclude that the end was near and that the reign of Antichrist was upon them.

He wrote, "For you ought to know and to believe, and hold it for certain, that the day of affliction has begun to hang over our heads, and the end of the world and the time of Antichrist to draw near, so that we must all stand prepared for the battle." (Epistle 55). In this same epistle he says

> Nor let any one of you, beloved brethren, be so terrified by the fear of future persecution, or the coming of the threatening Antichrist, as not to be found armed for all things by the evangelical exhortations and precepts, and by the heavenly warnings. Antichrist is coming, but above him comes Christ also. The enemy goeth above and rageth, but immediately the Lord follows to avenge our sufferings and our wounds. The adversary is enraged and threatens, but there is One who can deliver us from his hands. . . . And in the Apocalypse He instructs and forewarns, saying, 'If any man worship the beast and his image, and receive his mark in his forehead or in his hand, the same also shall drink of the wine of the wrath of God mixed in the cup of his indignation, and he shall be tormented with fire and brimstone in the presence of the holy angels, and in the presence of the Lamb; and the smoke of their torments shall ascend up forever and ever; and they shall have no rest day or night, who worship the beast and his image.'

Having been banished, Cyprian himself suffered martyrdom in Carthage in 258. When the sentence of death was read to him he said, "I heartily thank Almighty God who is pleased to set me free from the chains of the body."

During the persecution of Diocletian (ca. 304), Victorinus, who was bishop of Pettau (near modern Vienna) was put to death. He was the first systematic interpreter of the book of Revelation. Though his commentary is lost, fragments of it remain. In it he identified the Antichrist as coming out of the Roman caesars.

The time of the ante-Nicene Fathers was a time of increasing persecution. Because Christians were suffering at the hands of the Roman emperors and because they also believed that the Roman empire was the restrainer of the man of sin, there was a certain ambivalence that grew up about Rome in the ante-Nicene church. They believed that the terrible things they suffered at the hands of Rome were but precursers of what was to come under the Antichrist. However, it was this same Roman empire which also kept the Antichrist from bursting upon the world scene. The ten kingdom confederation out of which Antichrist would emerge could not arise until the "legs of iron"—Rome—were gone. Hence, the Roman Empire, while it was the source of persecution was also the source of protection, and was therefore the lesser of two evils; for when Rome was gone a greater persecution of the saints could be expected under the Antichrist. However, the final hope that shone through this frustrating ambivalence which saw Rome as both persecutor and protector, was the belief that the reign of the Antichrist would last only three and one-half years and immediately be followed by the second coming of Christ.

It was this belief in the personal, premillennial advent of the Lord Jesus Christ that sent the church of this era forth to be martyred. In the midst of intense persecution the blessed hope shone brightly. Although some of the believers lapsed, others stood firm in the belief that even if the darkness of persecution continued to deepen, climaxing in the appearance of the Antichrist, the coming of Jesus was just beyond this darkest hour. In no other period of church history was the blessed hope more meaningful, or the belief in the impending rise of the Antichrist more animated, than in the time of Roman persecution before Constantine ascended the imperial throne of the empire.

With the coming reign of Constantine things changed rapidly. The belief in the literal and premillennial return of Christ in order to establish his millennial kingdom upon earth changed into the belief that the Catholic church, in its earthly dominion, was the fulfillment of the promised earthly reign of Christ. Such was the thesis of Augustine's *The City of God*. In fact, the doctrine of the millennium was outlawed by the Council of Ephesus in A.D. 431.

However, it was actually Origen who, in the third century made the first attempt to discredit the idea of an earthly millennium. He conceived of the kingdom, not in terms of time and space, but in terms of an inward reality. He substituted for a collective millennial eschatology one in which each soul was the kingdom of God.

ANTICHRIST EXPECTATION IN THE POST-NICENE ERA

From the time that Constantine became emperor and espoused Christianity, attitudes toward the prophetic word were radically changed. This was due primarily to the change of attitude Rome showed toward the church. Where it had previously persecuted the church by official edict, now the church was given legal recognition and would soon be given preference by the state. This atmosphere gave rise to a whole new method of understanding prophecy. This complete reversal of attitude toward the church on the part of the Roman empire encouraged many to believe that the kingdom prophecies were not to find fulfillment in a literal kingdom established by the second coming of Christ, but in a temporal kingdom established by the rule of the church on earth. At first the church was tolerated by the government, along with paganism. Then, because the emperor himself had been "con-

verted," the church was favored. Finally, by the time of Theo-
dosius II, a half century later, Christianity was the only recognized religion of the empire.

Though many no longer identified the Roman emperor
with the coming Antichrist, when an emperor took sides on an
issue within the church, he was inevitably branded by the
opposing side as having something to do with the coming
Antichrist. The Council of Nicaea, for example, had ruled in
favor of Athanasius in the controversy over the nature of
Christ. However, Constantine's son, Constantius, who followed his father upon the throne, favored the Arian view
which had been denounced by the Nicaean council, over
which Constantine had presided. This caused Athanasius to
believe that Constantius was the forerunner of the Antichrist.
Said he, "The practices of Constantius are a prelude to the
coming of Antichrist." He even identified the Roman emperor with Daniel's little horn, calling him the "image of
Antichrist," for he had made war with the saints, humbled
kings, spoke words of blasphemy against the Most High, and
had changed times and laws.

During the time of this threat which Constantius presented
to orthodox Christianity, there appeared a work called the
Tiburtina which predicted that Constans I would soon reappear and take the throne of the empire from Constantius.
Constans I had been assassinated in 350 and the throne of the
empire taken by Constantius, the Arian heretic. This gave
orthodox Christians much concern. Out of this trauma there
arose a new series of Sibylline oracles which predicted the
triumphant return of Constans who would reign for more
than a century. His reign would be a time of material prosperity and abundance in which the prices of foods—all carefully enumerated—would be very low. Upon his return the
pagans would be defeated and the Jews would be converted to
Christianity, climaxing with the emperor's pilgrimage to Jerusalem, there to turn over the crown of the empire to God. The

Roman Empire would come to an end in a golden age. However, before the end of all things would be a time of tribulation. The Antichrist would come upon the scene and establish his reign in the temple in Jerusalem. But for the elect's sake, his reign would be shortened and the Archangel Michael dispatched to destroy the Antichrist. This would open the way for the second coming of Christ.

This idea that Constantius, the anti-Trinitarian ruler of the Roman empire, was the forerunner of the Antichrist opened a new trend in the interpretation of the prophetic word during the fourth and fifth centuries. While the apostolic Fathers saw the Antichrist coming only after the Roman Empire had broken up into the ten kingdoms, some like Athanasius and Hilary now began to teach that the coming Antichrist was imminent and that his forerunner could be found within the church. Like Athanasius, Hilary, who was bishop of Poitiers, was an avowed advocate of the doctrine of the Trinity taught by the Western church. He also believed that out of Arianism, which denied the deity of Christ, Antichrist would come. He was the first to link the priesthood with Antichrist, and to indicate his belief that the Antichrist would arise from within the church rather than from without.

Jerome, in the fifth century, testified that with the current breakup of the Roman empire the Antichrist must be very near. However, it was not until the year A.D. 1000 that there was an almost universal expectation of the end of the world, and the rise of the Antichrist just before the end was to come. Though this has been contested by some modern historians, Canon R. H. Charles in his *Studies in the Apocalypse* says that there were multitudes of people who gave all their possessions to the church. Churches were filled with worshipers, and a religious revival occurred around the year 1000. This expectation of the end of the world is also the reason why there was an abundance of churches built at the beginning of the eleventh century. Augustine had taught that Satan was

bound at the death of Christ and that a thousand years was
to follow, according to Revelation 20:2; in which his diabolical activity was curtailed. The years between the first
coming of Christ and the year A.D. 1000 were considered to
be the millennium.

Though Augustine had left the termination of this thousand-year period unidentified—for he took it to be a symbolic
representation of the Christian era—the idea seems to have
first been preached in Paris that the end was near and that the
Antichrist would appear at the end of the tenth century A.D.
The Abbot of Fleury writes, "In my youth, I heard a sermon
preached in church before the people of Paris, about the end
of the world. In that sermon, it was said that as soon as the
thousand years had ended, Antichrist would come, and soon
afterwards the universal judgment would follow."

The Queen of France—Gerberga, wife of Louis IV—was
much impressed with this teaching that the end of the world
would come around A.D. 1000. She asked her court chaplain Adso (later abbot of the monastery of Montier-en-Der,
France), to assemble all the information on this subject that
he could find. He wrote a pamphlet entitled *Libellus de
Antichristo* (little work on Antichrist). Though the spirit
of Antichrist had already appeared in such men as Antiochus, Nero, and Domitian, he said, the Antichrist himself
would be a person. In this work, Adso identified the birth-
place of the Antichrist as Babylon, and indicated that he
would come out of the tribe of Dan. However, the Antichrist
would not come until the Roman Empire had passed away.

Even in A.D. 954 when this work was written, the empire
was still considered to be sufficiently intact to restrain the
Antichrist. When he came, he would reign in the Jewish
temple or in the church, one or the other, for three and one-
half years, and would be finally killed by Christ when He
comes again. In his pamphlet, Adso characterized the Antichrist by drawing contrasts between Antichrist's character and

the character of Jesus Christ. Everything that Jesus is, the Antichrist is not. This little booklet was to influence the interpretation of the Antichrist's character for many years to come.

There were three books which did most to influence medieval thinking about the Antichrist. One was Adso's essay on the Antichrist.* The second is the *Tiburtina,* which has already been noted. The third book to influence the medieval doctrine of the Antichrist is another group of prophecies, set in Sibylline oracle form, called *Psuedo-Methodius.* It was written when the church faced the great crisis of Islam. It was so named because it had been falsely ascribed to a fourth-century bishop of Patara named Methodius. Its actual date is the late seventh century, for it was written to comfort Syrian Christians who were suffering under Muslim rule. It predicts the rise of a mighty emperor who will defeat the Muslims and ravage their land with fire and sword. He will usher in a time of peace and joy. Like the emperor Constans in the *Tiburtina,* this mighty emperor will journey to Jerusalem, there to await the advent of the Antichrist. When the Antichrist appears, the mighty emperor will die and the reign of the Antichrist begin. But soon Christ himself will appear in the clouds of heaven with power and great glory, and the Antichrist will be slain with the breath of his mouth.

Throughout the Middle Ages, the eschatology of these two Sibyllines, plus the pamphlet of Adso, influenced the interpretation of the Antichrist. Cohn says, "In the eighth century the *Pseudo-Methodius* was translated into Latin in Paris and in the tenth century the *Tiburtina* was incorporated by the French monk Adso in the treatise on Antichrist which he composed for the Queen of France. Both of these works were

---

°A full text of this work may be found in John Wright's *The Play of Antichrist,* (Toronto: The Pontifical Institute of Medieval Studies, 1967), pp. 100-110, and in Karl Young's *The Drama of the Medieval Church,* (Oxford: 1962), vol. 2, pp. 496-500.

widely disseminated and had great influence."[2] Cohn also observes

> For uncanonical and often downright heterodox though they were, the Sibyllines had enormous influence. They proved infinitely adaptable: constantly edited and reinterpreted to fit the conditions and appeal to the preoccupations of the moment, they catered at all times to the perennial craving of anxious mortals for an unquestionable forecast of the future. Already when the only versions known to the West were in Latin and therefore accessible only to clerics, some knowledge of their purport penetrated even to the lowest straits of the laity. From the fourteenth century onwards vernacular versions began to appear and when printing was invented such versions were amongst the first books to be printed. At the very close of the Middle Ages, when the fears and hopes which first shaped the Sibylline prophecies lay a thousand years and more in the past, these books were being read and studied everywhere.[3]

The year A.D. 1000 came and passed uneventfully. Peasants all over Europe were greatly relieved. The minds of the scholars, which had been preoccupied with that other world which was to force itself upon this one around A.D. 1000, were now freed to turn their thoughts to the present world. With this new orientation came the dawn of the Renaissance.

During the Crusades the Muslims were identified with the spirit of Antichrist. Pope Urban even justified the Crusaders going to Palestine, saying, "It is the will of God that through the labours of the crusaders Christianity shall flourish again at Jerusalem in these last times, so that when Antichrist begins his reign there—as he shortly must—he will find enough Christians to fight!"[4] The victorious advance of Islam had led many to believe that out of the Muslim religion Antichrist would arise. Throughout the Middle Ages the Muslim threat, through Spain, to Europe, caused this uneasy speculation to persist.

Between the years 1290 and 1335 there was a new flurry of Antichrist expectation, due to the year-day interpretation of such passages as Daniel 12:11-12; and Revelation 11:3. Also during this era the Waldensians said that any opposition to their teachings was Antichrist. The Hussites later held similar views.

However, it was not until the Reformation that Antichrist accusations again flew without restraint. Others, before the Reformation, had branded the pope as Antichrist. For example, as far back as A.D. 991, Arnulf, bishop of Orleans, had said, "What, in your eyes reverend fathers, is that Pontiff, seated on a throne, and clad in purple and gold? If he hath not charity, and be puffed up with his learning only, he is Antichrist sitting in the temple of God, and demeaning himself as a god; he is like unto a statue in the temple, like a dumb idol, and to ask of him a reply, is to appeal to a figure of stone."[5] St. Bernard in the twelfth century called Pope Leo, whom he regarded as a usurper of St. Peter's chair, the beast of the Apocalypse. In the thirteenth century, Frederick II, ruler of the Holy Roman empire, accused Pope Gregory IX of being Antichrist. The view that the pope was the Antichrist was first cultivated by the Franciscans themselves, who had remained true to the original ideals of poverty. From them the idea spread to the pre-Reformation sects. Wycliffe and John Huss were both convinced that the pope was the Antichrist.

THE REFORMATION AND AFTER

However, it was during the Reformation that the papal system and/or the pope himself were consistently identified as Antichrist. And this was done by the largest host of imminent writers ever to express a unified view as a responsible interpretation of current spiritual history. Martin Luther (1483-1546), leader of the Reformation in Germany and herald of the entire movement; Philip Melanchthon (1497-

1560), German Reformer; John Calvin (1509-1564), French Reformer in Geneva; Huldreich Zwingli (1484-1531), Swiss Reformation leader; Nicholas Ridley (1500?-1555), English Reformer and martyr; Hugh Latimer (1485?-1555), English Protestant martyr; William Tyndale (1492?-1536), English Reformer, Bible translator, and martyr; Thomas Cranmer (1489-1556), English Reformer and Archbishop of Canterbury; John Foxe (1516-1597), English martyrologist; John Knox (1505-1572), Scottish Reformer; along with many others in the Reformation movement, identified the papal office and/or the pope himself as Antichrist. Never in the history of the church were so many responsible scholars, preachers, linguists, theologians, expositors, and spiritual statesmen convinced that the Antichrist was alive and living in Rome.

John Whitgift, who later lectured on the Antichrist while serving as Lady Margaret Professor of Divinity in Cambridge University, presented his doctoral thesis to the faculty of the University in which he proved that the pope was the Antichrist. He was awarded a Doctor of Divinity degree on the basis of this work. The attack against Catholic countries by Protestant governments was justified on the grounds that it was an attack against Antichrist. In 1548 the government of King Edward VI of England so justified an invasion of Scotland as a blow against Antichrist. A few decades later Sir Francis Drake took his stand against Spain as a stand against Antichrist.

The designation of the papal system as Antichrist is also found in several of the confessions of the reformed churches. The Westminster Confession written in 1646, for example, says, "There is no other head of the church but the Lord Jesus Christ: nor can the Pope of Rome in any sense be the head thereof; but is that Antichrist, that man of sin and son of perdition, that exalteth himself in the church against Christ, and all that is called God" (*The Westminster Confession of*

Faith 25.6). King James I of England, who authorized the greatest of all the English translations of the Bible, also got into the controversy. While only twenty years of age he wrote *A Paraphrase Upon the Revelation of the Apostle S. John,* in which he set forth the view that the locusts mentioned in the book of Revelation were different orders of monks, and their king was the pope. He also identified the Beast of Revelation 13 with the pope. The pope himself complained that James "called him Antichrist at every word" when the king was at dinner conversation with his guests.

In 1612 a work entitled *The Mystery of Iniquitie* was translated into English by Samson Lennard. Its entire six hundred pages were dedicated to proving that the pope was the Antichrist. It long remained popular in Puritan England and was often quoted. In 1581 John Field wrote, "To prove the Pope is Antichrist is needless considering how it is a beaten argument in every book."[6] In 1642 Francis Potter, a Fellow of the Royal Society, published a book in which he proved by mathematics that the number 666 represented the pope. Samuel Pepys read the book in the precarious year of the Great London Fire, making reference to it on three occasions in his famous diary, February 18, November 4 and 10, 1666. He thought it "mighty ingenious."

English poets also identified the pope with Antichrist. The idea appears in Spenser's *The Faerie Queene*. The great poet John Donne, who was also Dean of St. Paul's and one of the greatest preachers of his age, believed that the pope was the Antichrist. George Herbert, English divine and poet, wrote, "As new and old Rome did one empire twist, So both together are one Antichrist."[7] Though John Milton does not make the identification in any of his poetical works, his prose abounds with the idea that the pope is Antichrist. Other English poets such as Phineas Fletcher, William Alabaster, and George Wither also identify the pope as Antichrist.

In his Riddle Lectures on the Antichrist, delivered before

the University of Newcastle upon Tyne, Professor Hill of Oxford summarizes the era by saying,

> Throughout the period 1530-1640 . . . the identification of Pope and Antichrist won very general support in the Church of England. One possible reason for the emergence of the noun "animal" in English at the beginning of the seventeenth century, to replace the hitherto universal "beast," is that the latter was acquiring too specific a sense as the equivalent of Antichrist. "Animal" as a noun does not appear in the Authorized Version, based as it is on earlier sixteenth-century translations; but in the decade before 1611 Shakespeare, for instance, was beginning to use "animal" where the A.V. would have said "beast."[8]

Of course, to all of this the Roman Catholic Church counter-attacked by branding the Reformers and their movement as Antichrist. However, it is interesting that they resorted to another weapon of counterattack. They revived the old theory that the Antichrist would be a Jew. If this were sustained it would relieve the Pope of any Antichrist guilt. However, this revival of the theory which associated the Jew with Antichrist also gave the anti-Semitic overtones to the Inquisition.

Puritan expositors of the seventeenth century, such as John Carter, William Ames, John Trapp, Thomas Goodwin, John Cotton, and Jeremiah Burroughs, were to continue the identification. In seventeenth-century America, the Massachusetts Bay Company was founded in order to create in New England "a bulwark against the kingdom of Antichrist." Though the pope was generally conceded to be the Antichrist against whom this bulwark was erected, others, like Mrs. Hutchinson, believed that the Antichrist was resident in the clergy of the Church of England because it denied the new covenant. John Eliot, the apostle to the Indians, identified Rome with the Antichrist, as did the American Puritan preacher John Cotton.

This identification continued among the leaders of the

Great Awakening and the Evangelical Revival in the eighteenth century. John Wesley, for example, identified the first beast of Revelation 13 as the "Romish papacy." In his *Explanatory Notes upon the New Testament* he even predicted that the papal Antichrist would be overthrown in the year 1836. He got this strange chronology from Bengel.

After the French Revolution, many believed that Napoleon was the Antichrist. On the opening page of Tolstoy's famous novel *War and Peace,* there is an interesting reference to this belief that Napoleon is the Antichrist. Later on in the novel, the central character of the story, Pierre (Count Bezukhov), finds the name *L 'Empereus Napoleon* to have the numerical equivalent 666 (including the "e" of "Le"). This he does by equating a,b,c with 1,2,3, etc. When he comes to k,l,m he equates them to 10,20,30. T is 100, u is 110, v is 120, and z is 160. Moreover, by the same process, since Pierre's own name has the numerical equivalent of 666, he believes that he is destined to put an end to the emperor's reign and thus plans later to kill him. Professor Salmon said,

> Any name, with sufficient ingenuity, can be made to yield the number 666. There are three rules by the help of which, I believe, an ingenious man could find the required sum in any given name. First, if the proper name by itself will not yield it; add a title; secondly, if the sum cannot be found in Greek, try Hebrew, or even Latin; thirdly, do not be too particular about the spelling. The use of a language different from that to which the name properly belongs allows a good deal of latitude in the transliteration.[9]

The British historian and statesman, Thomas Macaulay, tells the story of an encounter with someone who also held the view that Napoleon was the Antichrist:

> "Pray, Mr. Macaulay, do you think that Buonaparte was the Beast?" "No, sir, I cannot say that I do."
> "Sir, he was the Beast. I can prove it. I have found the

number 666 in his name. Why, sir, if he was not the Beast, who was?" This was a puzzling question, and I am not a little vain of my answer. "Sir," said I, "the House of Commons is the Beast. There are six hundred fifty eight members of the House and these with their chief officers—the three clerks, the Sergeant and his deputy, the Chaplain, the doorkeeper and the librarian—make 666." "Well, sir, that is strange. But I can assure you that, if you write Napoleon Buonaparte in Arabic, leaving out only two letters, it will give 666." "And, pray, sir, what right have you to leave out two letters? And, as St. John was writing Greek, and to Greeks, is it not likely that he would use the Greek rather than the Arabic notations?" "But sir," said this learned divine, "everybody knows that the Greek letters were never used to mark numbers." I answered with the meekest look and voice possible: "I do not think that everybody knows that. Indeed I have reason to believe that a different opinion—erroneous no doubt—is universally embraced by all who happen to know any Greek." So ended the controversy. The man looked at me as if he thought me a very wicked fellow; and, I dare say, has by this time discovered that, if you write my name in Tamil, leaving out T in Thomas, B in Babington, and M in Macaulay, it will give the number of this unfortunate Beast.[10]

Just as St. Martin, bishop of Tours, was certain that the Antichrist was already alive in his day and made a grave announcement to that effect in A.D. 380; and just as bishop Ranieri of Florence in 1080 expressed certainty that the Antichrist had already been born; and just as Vincens Ferrer in 1412 wrote Pope Benedict XIII that Antichrist was already nine years old, and that others had seen the vision, and therefore the Vatican should sound the warning, "so that the faithful might be prepared for the fearful battle immediately impending"; and just as Josephine Lamartine, a prophetess of Lorraine, predicted that the Antichrist was born in 1900; so many of our contemporaries have been certain that his advent is immediate.

Selma Lagerlöf declared that socialism is the Antichrist. The German philosopher Nietzsche declared that he himself was the Antichrist, for he posed as the only radical opponent of Christ in his belief that his philosophy would usher in a new and final age for mankind.

During the time that led up to, and included the second World War, Hitler and Mussolini were ripe for this identification, especially Mussolini because of his relationship to Rome. Oswald J. Smith, writing in 1926 in a book entitled *Is the Antichrist at Hand?*, calculated that the times of the gentiles would be 2520 years in duration. He then dated the captivity of Jerusalem by Nebuchadnezzar at 604 B.C., along with the final fall of the city which he dated 588 B.C. If 2520 years were added to 604 B.C., it would come out 1917. This date had already passed—but Smith found it significant because it was in that year that the Balfour Declaration was issued. But if 2520 were added to the year 588 B.C., Smith's date for Jerusalem's fall, the date for the end of the times of the gentiles turned out to be 1933. That date was still future —in fact, just seven years future when Smith wrote in 1926! So he said, "If our chronology is correct it means that all these things, including the great tribulation, the revival of the Roman empire, the reign of the Antichrist, and the battle of Armageddon must take place before the year 1933."[11] This, plus the fact that Mussolini was on the rise in Italy, caused Smith to hint strongly that the Italian dictator, whose avowed intention was to revive the Roman empire, might be the Antichrist.

The noted Bible teacher Dr. H. A. Ironside also predicted that the rise to power of Benito Mussolini, and his plans for Italy had deep prophetic implication for the last days. In an address delivered to the Bible Institute of Los Angeles on

January 8, 1930, which was entitled, "Looking Backward over a Third of a Century of Prophetic Fulfillment," he spoke of Mussolini.

> His bombastic utterances backed up by tremendous ability to perform have astonished the world. He declares himself the Man of Destiny, chosen to revive the Roman Empire and restore it to its pristine glory. The Mediterranean, he declares, shall yet become a Roman lake surrounded by nations in alliance with Italy. His grandiose plans move on to fulfillment in spite of all opposition. At least six powers already are in alliance with Italy, and that the remaining ones will join the confederation seems to be just a question of time.

During the late 1930's and early 1940's many pamphlets appeared identifying Adolph Hitler as the Antichrist. From a tract entitled "The Beast, the False Prophet, and Hitler," published in 1941, we find this serious suggestion:

> "Hitler himself is spelled out in the puzzle given in Rev. 16:18. This puzzle, when worked out, will indicate a certain man. We have only three numerals, 666, but through them we must find the man's name. So we must numeralize the alphabet. To do this we will let 100 stand for "A." It must be three figures to stand for the three digits 666.

A - 100	N - 113
B - 101	O - 114
C - 102	P - 115
D - 103	Q - 116
E - 104	R - 117
F - 105	S - 118
G - 106	T - 119
H - 107	U - 120
I - 108	V - 121
J - 109	W - 122
K - 110	X - 123
L - 111	Y - 124
M - 112	Z - 125

H - 107
I - 108
T - 119
L - 111
E - 104
R - 117

666

Hitler is 666![12]

Jeane Dixon, the popular clairvoyant and newspaper astrologer, is convinced that she has had a vision which indicates that the Antichrist (though she does not use this name) was born on February 5, 1962. In her book *My Life and Prophecies* she tells of this revelation.

> I gazed out my window and, although the sun was still in hiding, what I saw was almost beyond description.
>
> The bare-limbed trees of the city had given way to an endless desert scene, broiled by a relentless sun. Glowing like an enormous ball of fire, the sun had cracked the horizon, emitting brilliant rays of scintillating light which seemed to attract the earth like a magic wand.
>
> The sun's rays parted, facilitating the appearance of an Egyptian Pharaoh and his queen. I immediately recognized her as Queen Nefertiti; the man with her I took to be her husband, reported by history to be Ikhnaton, the so-called "heretic" Pharaoh. Holding hands as lovers do, they emerged from the brilliant rays, majestic in their bearing; Ikhnaton's royal headdress was a sign of his power under the sun . . . not of power under the Son.
>
> But my eyes were drawn to Nefertiti and the child she tenderly cradled in her other arm. It was a newborn babe, wrapped in soiled, ragged swaddling clothes. He was in stark contrast to the magnificently arrayed royal couple.
>
> Not a sound broke the unearthly silence as they issued forth with the child. I then became aware of a multitude of people that appeared between the child and me. It seemed as though the entire world was watching the royal couple

present the baby. Watching the baby over their heads, I witnessed Nefertiti hand the child to the people. Instantly rays of sunlight burst forth from the little boy, carefully blending themselves with the brilliance of the sun, blotting out everything but him.

Ikhnaton disappeared from the scene. Nefertiti remained. I observed her walking away from the child and the people, into the past, into the secret past of the ancients. Thirsty and tired, she rested beside a water jug, and just as she cupped her hands to drink, a sudden thrust of a dagger in her back ended her life. Her death scream, piercing and mournful, faded out with her.

My eyes once again focused on the baby. By now he had grown to manhood, and a small cross which had formed above his head enlarged and expanded until it covered the earth in all directions. Simultaneously, suffering people, of all races, knelt in worshipful adoration, lifting their arms and offering their hearts to the man. For a fleeting moment I felt as though I were one of them, but the channel that emanated from him was not that of the Holy Trinity. I knew within my heart that this revelation was to signify the beginning of wisdom, but whose wisdom and for whom? An overpowering feeling of love surrounded me, but the look I had seen in the man when he was still a babe—a look of serene wisdom and knowledge—made me sense that here was something God allowed me to see without my becoming a part of it.

I also sensed that I was once again safe within the protective arms of my Creator.

I glanced at my bedside clock. It was still early—7:17 A.M.

What does this revelation signify? I am convinced that this revelation indicates a child, born somewhere in the Middle East shortly after 7:00 A.M. on February 5, 1962—possibly a direct descendant of the royal line of Pharoah Ikhnaton and Queen Nefertiti—will revolutionize the world. There is no doubt that he will fuse multitudes into one all-embracing doctrine. He will form a new "Christianity," based on his "almighty power," but leading man in a direction far removed from the teachings and life of Christ, the Son.[13]

When Arnold of Villanova, a thirteenth-century Spanish doctor and theologian, predicted that the Antichrist was then alive, although Arnold was the physician who had cured Pope Boniface VIII of gout and "the stone," he was sentenced to prison for this presumption. He even appealed to the pope whom he had cured, but Boniface refused his request for clemency. Though this presumption is still as serious today, the attempt to identify the Antichrist as some sinister and mysterious contemporary goes on; but it can do nothing but bring discredit to biblical truth. The Antichrist, the lawless one, Paul says, cannot be revealed until the Holy Spirit is removed from his permanent residence on earth in the church. This will not happen until the church itself is taken out of the world when Jesus comes again for his own.

2

The Regal Character of the Antichrist

ALL THESE ABORTIVE ATTEMPTS to identify the Antichrist as a contemporary person can lead to but one conclusion: the Lord never intended the church to know who the Antichrist is to be. The church may experience the *spirit* of Antichrist (1 Jn 2:18) but not the *person* of Antichrist. Neither did the Lord intend the world to know who the Antichrist is until after the church is taken out at the rapture. Only then will he be revealed. The reason is that the Antichrist has primarily to do with Israel and the nations, not the church. However, one of the persistent errors of interpretation has been to view the Antichrist as a persecutor of the church. This is a mistake. To be sure, he will persecute the saints (Dan 7:25; Rev 13:15) but these are the tribulation saints, composed of those gentiles who accept Christ during the tribulation and those in Israel who do the same. But the Antichrist has nothing to do with the church, for he will not be revealed until the church is gone.

In 2 Thessalonians 2, Paul speaks of the revelation of the Antichrist *after* the church and the restrainer have been removed. He relates this revelation to a distinctive group: "them that perish" (v. 10). "Because they received not the love of the truth, that they might be saved. And for this cause God sendeth them a working of error, that they should believe a lie: that they all might be judged who believed not

44

the truth, but had pleasure in unrighteousness" (2 Th 2:10-12). Paul refers here to the nations, not the church. Moreover, when we turn to the nation Israel we find that the specific relationship between the Antichrist and Israel is even more clearly noted; especially in Daniel, Zechariah, and in the Olivet discourse of Jesus. The church is not even in the picture in these prophecies of the Antichrist.

Since all attempts to positively identify the Antichrist in this age are futile, what then can be known about the Antichrist? Are there no clues in Scripture as to his identity? The answer is yes, for just as there were many clues given in the prophets about the coming Messiah, yet Jesus of Nazareth was never positively identified in any of them, so the Antichrist is never positively identified. However, just as the Messianic prophecies of the Old Testament presented a cumulative picture of the Person and work of the Messiah to enable the discerning to identify Him when He came, the prophetic passages of both the Old and New Testament give a cumulative picture of the person and work of the Anti-Messiah which will enable the discerning to identify him when he is come upon the world scene.

The King of Fierce Countenance

"And in the latter time of their kingdom, when the transgressors are come to the full, a king of fierce countenance, and understanding dark sentences, shall stand up" (Dan 8:23). In this verse the Antichrist is called a "king of fierce countenance." However, before the significance of this name is examined, we must consider a prior question. Is the reference here to the Antichrist, or is the subject Antiochus IV, who is clearly in view as the little horn of verse 9? In Daniel 8 there seems to be a movement in verses 9 through 27 in which Daniel at first sees Antiochus IV as a type of Antichrist and then moves on to a vision of the prototype—the Antichrist himself. Perhaps the transition occurs at 8:23 where Anti-

ochus IV, the Greek little horn, becomes the king of fierce
countenance, the Antichrist.

Moreover, there is another evidence that a transition from
Antiochus to Antichrist occurs in this vision, for the vision
which Daniel had of the little horn in verses 9-14 is a clear
reference to the reign of Antiochus IV. But the interpretation which Gabriel gives to this vision carries the subject far
beyond Antiochus IV and the second century B.C., to the end-
time reign of the Antichrist. In fact, in these verses which
follow the vision of Daniel in verses 9-14, the "time of the
end," or its equivalent, is mentioned three times, verses 17,
19, and 26. So it is not a question of who is in view in Daniel
8, *either* Antiochus IV *or* the Antichrist. *Both* are in view.
Daniel first sees Antiochus IV (vv. 9-14) and then moves in
vision to the time of the end (vv. 23-27) and describes the
reign of the Antichrist, whom he calls the king of fierce
countenance.

But does not the fact that this king of fierce countenance
emerges during "the latter time of their kingdom" (v. 23),
suggest that the subject is still Antiochus IV and the last days
of the Greek Seleucid kingdom over which he reigned and
which came to a tentative end in Israel with the revolt of the
Maccabees and the death of Antiochus IV? This inference is
strong. However, it is negated by the fact that the king of
fierce countenance comes to his end in a dramatic conflict with
the Messiah. "He shall also stand up against the prince of
princes; but he shall be broken without hand" (v. 25). This
will occur at the second coming of Christ, toward the close of
the great tribulation period, when the career of the Antichrist
is climaxed in disaster. In contrast, Antiochus IV died a
natural death about 163 B.C., possibly from consumption,
while in Parthia where he had gone to put down a revolt.

Another indication that different persons are in view in
Daniel 8:9-14 and 8:23-7 is that a precise time limit is placed
upon the activities of Antiochus IV, as opposed to the activity

of the Antichrist. Though the Antichrist meets his end during the last days of the great tribulation period, the precise time is undetermined in this text. It comes only as he enters into conflict with the Messiah, the prince of princes. However, in contrast, verses 13-14 set forth the time of Antiochus' oppression of the land. "Then I heard a holy one speaking; and another holy one said unto that certain one who spake, How long shall be the vision concerning the continual burnt-offering, and the transgression that maketh desolate, to give both the sanctuary and the host to be trodden under foot? And he said unto me, Unto two thousand and three hundred evenings and mornings; then shall the sanctuary be cleansed" (Dan 8:13-14).

The fact that the 2300 evenings and mornings fit no known historical realities in the reign of Antiochus IV does not obviate the apparent meaning of this verse, namely that the abominations of Antiochus IV are given an exact time limit. 2300 days are almost seven years. No two significant events, 2300 days apart, can be found in the history of this era between 175 and 163 b.c., to form the boundary of this period. Even if the 2300 mornings and evenings are reduced to 1150 full days, this period of less than three years has no two outstanding events in Antiochus' history to mark off the beginning and end of its boundary. However, even though we cannot cite two precise historical events in the reign of Antiochus IV which would begin and end the enumerated days, the fact remains that the days of Antiochus IV are numbered. Beyond that precisely stated period he will be immobilized and will harm the host of God's people and desecrate the sanctuary no more. However, in contrast, the reign of the Antichrist has no such precisely stated termini—at least in these verses. He will come to an end, but when this will happen is not given in precise figures as in the destiny of Antiochus IV.

Therefore in Daniel 8:23-27 the king of fierce countenance,

who is the Antichrist, is described. This name seems to come from Deuteronomy 28:50 where it is used of the enemies of Israel, who give no quarter and will utterly devastate the nation. The king of fierce countenance, the Antichrist, is skilled at "understanding dark sentences" (v. 23). This Hebrew noun is used for Samson's riddle in Judges 14:12; and for the Queen of Sheba's hard questions (1 Kings 10:1). He can understand riddles, and the riddles that he understands are of a political and diplomatic nature. Verse 25 confirms this, for "through his policy he shall cause craft to prosper in his hand."

This is Machiavellianism of the highest order—for it was the sixteenth-century Florentine statesman who theorized that any political means, no matter how unscrupulous, is justified when a ruler employs it to establish a strong central government. This political theory the Antichrist will exploit to its fullest by his deceit and cunning craft. He will arise amid the world chaos caused by the catching away of the church; because when the church is raptured a large segment of the world's responsible leadership will be suddenly removed from the earth. One can readily understand the world-wide confusion that this will cause. In the midst of this chaotic political scene the Antichrist will arise, and with his shrewdness he will bring about world stability very rapidly because he will be able to size up the riddle of world events and bring order out of the chaos.

The condition of the world, rendered temporarily chaotic by the rapture, may explain why the United States is not found in Bible prophecy. Even though this nation is Christian in name only, America still has a larger percentage of born-again believers in its population than any other important country. When Jesus comes for his own, thousands of responsible leaders in government, industry, education, religion, the arts, and the professions will be removed. With these leaders taken to meet the Lord in the air, the structure of government, industry, education, the arts, and the professions will be so weakened that it will reduce the United States to an impotent and prostrated nation. This also explains why Russia, with its atheistic communist leadership, is virtually unaffected by the rapture and can offer a substantial threat to Israel during the tribulation period. Though all countries where Christians are in places of leadership will be affected by the rapture, it will affect no other country like it will affect the United States. Apparently she does not recover from this loss, for the United States plays no ascertainable role during the tribulation period. Therefore, the political center of the world during the reign of the Antichrist will shift back to that area within the boundaries of the old Roman empire in Europe. The Western Hemisphere will be only an adjunct. The locality where the final act of human history will be played out will be Western and Eastern Europe, along with the Middle East. Again the center of world political and imperial power will be Western Europe where it was located when God's prophetic time clock stopped in the first century. It is in this political arena that the king of fierce countenance will demonstrate his diplomatic genius and enable the countries there to recover from the shock of the rapture.

Just as the power of Antiochus IV "waxed exceedingly great" (Dan 8:9), so will the Antichrist "become mighty" (v. 24). The fact that his power *becomes* mighty (Leupold's translation) indicates that his beginnings will be small. This confirms the fact that he will arise at first as the head of the revived Roman empire and then, probably at midtribulation, he will become a virtual world dictator through his defeat of Russia in the Middle East (Eze 38-39). Though he "shall destroy wonderfully, and shall prosper and do his pleasure, and he shall destroy the mighty ones and the holy people" (v. 24), he does not accomplish this in his own strength. Behind him is the power of Satan (cf. 2 Th 2:9; Rev 13:2, 4).

Here then is the Antichrist pictured in Daniel 8 as a

Machiavellian king of fierce countenance who will rise to power in Western Europe by craft and cunning intrigue. Behind his craftiness and his artful deception is the cunning power of Satan. He will walk triumphantly through the blood of both the mighty men of the earth and also the saints of God, until he enters into conflict with the prince of princes, then "he shall be broken without hand" (v. 25), i.e., without the hand of man, but by the Messiah Himself (cf. Dan 2:44-45; 7:21-22, 26-27; 11:45).

The Prince That Shall Come

The second name that the book of Daniel applies to the Antichrist is "the prince that shall come" (Dan 9:26). This name is given to him in an indirect way, for the reference is actually to "the people of the prince that shall come," i.e., the Roman army.

The term *prince* appears twice in Daniel's prophecy of the seventy weeks (9:24-27). The identity of the prince is not the same in both references.

The first time the name appears in this prophecy it refers to the Messiah, "the anointed one, the prince." "Know therefore and discern, that from the going forth of the commandment to restore and to build Jerusalem unto the anointed one, the prince, shall be seven weeks, and threescore and two weeks: it shall be built again, with street and moat, even in troublous times" (Dan 9:25). He shall be cut off after sixty-nine weeks have run their course. It is generally understood that the term *weeks* in this prophecy does not refer to weeks of days, but to weeks of years. A week of years was just as familiar to the Jews as a week of days is to us, for the Jews not only had a week composed of six days which terminated in a Sabbath Day, they also had a week composed of six years which terminated in a sabbatical year.

The angel said to Daniel, "Seventy weeks [heptads] are decreed upon thy people" (9:24). The word *heptad* means a gathering of seven, just as our word *dozen* means a gathering of twelve. But seven what? Obviously they are sevens of some unit of time—either seconds, minutes, days, months, or years. If these were *heptads* composed of seven days each, then sixty-nine weeks, or 483 days would not provide time enough to accomplish what the prophecy says would happen during that period, namely, the rebuilding and subsequent destruction of the city. The inference, therefore, is clearly one of seventy weeks of years; for a total of 490 years. At the end of sixty-nine weeks of years, or 483 years, beginning with the decree to rebuild the walls of Jerusalem, the Messiah, the anointed one, will be cut off. Again there is general agreement among conservative Bible expositors that the *terminus a quo* of this prophecy—the decree in question which was to mark the beginning of the time—was issued in 445 B.C. by Artaxerxes, the Persian king (Neh 2:1-8). There were other decrees. One was issued in 538 B.C. by Cyrus, to rebuild the Lord's house (Ezra 1:1-4; 5:13-17). Another was issued by Darius in 517 B.C. (Ezra 6:1-12); however Darius' decree had reference to the rebuilding of the temple only. Only the decree of Artaxerxes had to do with the city and the walls (cf. Neh 2:13-15; 17; 6:15.) Without conceding the necessity of mathematical preciseness, the elapse of 483 years from 445 B.C. brings us to the first century and the time of Messiah's death on the cross. If we knew all the calendar variations that are involved in calculating the passage of time, no doubt the time lapse would be exact.*

Since scholars are still debating the exact year of both the birth and the death of the Messiah, we have no dogmatic conclusions about the precise calendar year in which Daniel's sixty-nine weeks of years terminated. We can only be sure that when the Messiah was cut off, the sixty-nine weeks (483

*For further study of the mathematical problems of this prophecy, the reader is referred to Sir Robert Anderson's *The Coming Prince,* (Grand Rapids: Kregel, 1954), and Alva J. McClain's *Daniel's Prophecies of the Seventy Weeks,* (Grand Rapids: Zondervan, 1962).

years) had run their course, and had reached their *terminus ad quem.*

But not only is the Messiah Prince referred to in this prophecy, but the Antichrist is also referred to as "prince." When the Messiah Prince is cut off after the sixty-nine weeks, then "the people of the *prince that shall come* shall destroy the city and the sanctuary; and the end thereof shall be with a flood, and even unto the end shall be war; desolations are determined" (Dan 9:26).

The order of events is this: first, the Messiah will be cut off at the end of sixty-nine weeks. The death of Jesus upon the cross occurred sometime in the fourth decade of the first century A.D. This terminated the sixty-nine weeks, or 483 years, dating from the decree to rebuild the walls of Jerusalem, issued in 445 B.C. At this point the prophetic time clock stopped, for Israel had rejected the Messiah and therefore would be set aside in the blindness of her unbelief (Ro 11:25). However, this setting aside of the nation is not permanent, for God has established an everlasting covenant with Israel (Gen 12:1-3). The Lord will yet deal with the nation Israel in Messianic redemption.

> For I would not, brethren, have you ignorant of this mystery, lest ye be wise in your own conceits, that a hardening in part hath befallen Israel, until the fulness of the Gentiles be come in; and so all Israel shall be saved: even as it is written, There shall come out of Zion the Deliverer; He shall turn away ungodliness from Jacob: And this is my covenant unto them. When I shall take away their sins (Ro 11:25-27).

However, between this Messianic redemption of Israel in the future, and the close of the sixty-nine weeks at the cross, the great parenthesis intervenes. This is the mystery age of the church which none of the Old Testament prophets saw, but which was revealed to the apostle Paul (Eph 3:1ff.), and which will run its course in history between Pentecost and the rapture. Not until the church, the body of Christ, is completed and taken out of the world at the rapture, will the time clock begin to tick again and the seventieth week, or seven years of tribulation, be fulfilled in Israel.

The second in the order of prophetic events, previewed in Daniel's prediction, is an event which will take place after Messiah is cut off, but before the establishment of the covenant mentioned in verse 27. This is an event that will occur during the great parenthesis, the age of the church, between the sixty-ninth and the seventieth week. This event is the destruction of the city by the people of the prince. It is a clear reference to the destruction of Jerusalem by the Roman army in A.D. 70.

As a result of Jewish unrest and overt hostility, due largely to Nero's mismanagement of Judean affairs, Vespasian invaded Judea in A.D. 67. However, it was his son Titus who actually took the city after 139 days of siege, in A.D. 70. He destroyed the city and the sanctuary, precisely as Daniel had predicted more than five hundred years before. Therefore, verse 26 was fulfilled in the first century A.D. The two events mentioned in verse 26 were separated by some forty years. The cutting off of the Messiah marked the end of the sixty-nine weeks. The destruction of the city and the sanctuary occurred *outside* the period decreed upon Israel, and some forty years *within* the period of the great parenthesis. It is interesting that Jesus sets these two events—the rejection of the Messiah and the destruction of Jerusalem—in cause-and-effect relationship.

> And when he drew nigh, he saw the city and wept over it, saying, If thou hadst known in this day, even thou, the things which belong unto peace! but now they are hid from thine eyes. For the days shall come upon thee, when thine enemies shall cast up a bank about thee, and compass thee round, and keep thee in on every side, and shall dash thee to

the ground, and thy children within thee; and they shall not leave in thee one stone upon another; because thou knewest not the time of thy visitation (Lk 19:41-44).

According to the calculations of Sir Robert Anderson, the 483 years of Daniel's sixty-nine weeks terminated with the Lord's triumphant entry into Jerusalem (Lk 19:37ff.).

The "people of the prince" therefore are identified as the Roman army which took the city in A.D. 70 and destroyed the temple. Jesus predicted the destruction of the temple also when he said in his great prophetic discourse that there "shall not be left here one stone upon another, that shall not be thrown down" (Mt 24:2). Today the western wall of the temple area faces a flat open space which separates it from the upper city. During the days of the second temple this flat space was a valley called the Tyropoeon Valley, or the "valley of the cheesemakers." For many years it has been assumed that across this valley, connecting the temple area with the upper city, ran two bridges. The place where one of these bridges is supposed to have connected with the temple area can be clearly seen today. It is called Robinson's Arch.† When Titus took Jerusalem in A.D. 70, he ordered that the rubble of the destroyed temple be pushed into the steep Tyropoeon Valley, thus raising the level of the valley so that some fourteen to nineteen layers of Herodian stonework were covered by the mounting debris. Archaeologists are working in this area today and have uncovered a level of charred earth con-

---

†The theory that the upper city and the temple area were connected by two bridges across the Tyropoeon Valley may now be open to serious question in the light of recent archaeological discovery. Writing in *The Jerusalem Post,* September 22, 1971, Dr. Avraham Biran, head of the Government Antiquities Department, says, "Preconceived notions—some 100 years old—have had to be abandoned. The model of a long bridge built on high arches connecting the Western Hill or Upper City with the Temple Mount is no longer true. Nor, indeed, does Josephus say that there was such a bridge. The description in Josephus of many steps leading from the Tyropoeon Valley up to the southwestern corner of the Temple is borne out by archaeology. The arch that bears Robinson's name supported the platform that led to the Royal Basilica on the Temple Mount."

taining a number of coins which were struck in the second year of the revolt, A.D. 67. This valley, which archaeologists are uncovering even now, and which is filled with the great Herodian masonry and other debris, is a mute testimony to the total destruction which Titus imposed upon the temple area and to the accuracy of the prediction of Daniel, and also of that which Jesus uttered on the Mount of Olives.

The prediction of Daniel that the people of the prince will destroy the city and the sanctuary makes even more credible the thesis of a revived Roman empire. Since it was the Roman army that fulfilled this prophecy in A.D. 70, it implies that the prince himself, the Antichrist, will arise out of a Roman empire context. Since it cannot be the ancient Roman empire, some form of that empire must be revived in the last days, out of which the prince, the Antichrist, will arise. How else could the ancient Roman army be also "the people of the prince that shall come"?

This name *prince that shall come* implies therefore that he will be a mighty conqueror like his Flavian predecessors, the Roman emperor Vespasian and his son Titus, who followed his father upon the throne in A.D. 79.

Notice a twice-repeated fact in Daniel 9:26-27—desolations are determined upon the city and the sanctuary. It is mentioned first in verse 26 in connection with the fall of Jerusalem in A.D. 70, when the people of the prince, the Roman army, came. But the idea is repeated in verse 27. This time the "abomination of desolation" (Mt 24:15) comes in the midst of the seventieth week. After the sixty-nine weeks have run their course, terminating with the cutting off of the Messiah, and after the age of the church has run its course, then the seventieth week, or last seven years, will begin. It is in the midst of this last seven-year period that the abomination of desolation comes and "wrath [shall] be poured out upon the desolate [city and sanctuary]" (v. 27). During this time it will not be the people of the prince, but the prince himself who will come upon the "wing of abominations."

When is this abomination of desolation imposed upon the city and the sanctuary? Jesus said it would be during a time that he called "great tribulation" (Mt 24:21, cf. v. 15). Daniel indicates that it will occur "in the midst of the week" (9:27). Jesus spoke both of a time of tribulation (Mt 24:9-14) and a time of great tribulation (Mt 24:15-28). Since Daniel divides the period under consideration into two halves, this would indicate that the seventieth-week period of tribulation is of seven years' duration and that it is further divided into two three-and-one-half-year divisions. The latter half is known as the great tribulation. It is during the last three-and-one-half years of the great tribulation that the abomination of desolation is revealed and terror wrought upon both the sanctuary and the city of Jerusalem.

But at what point in the prophetic period of the seventieth week does this take place? Daniel also indicates this. He says, "And he [the prince, the Antichrist] shall make a firm covenant with many for one week: and in the midst of the week he shall cause the sacrifice and the oblation to cease" (9:27). Since the subject of the prophecy is "thy people" (v. 24), the Jews, it is a clear inference that the "many" with whom the Antichrist makes a covenant is also Israel. This covenant will be broken and the abomination of desolation will be revealed three and one-half years into the final seven-year period. The countdown begins when the church is raptured. The first three and one-half years will be one of covenant relation between Israel and the Antichrist. At midtribulation period the covenant is broken. The last three and one-half years will be a time of great tribulation, a time of intense suffering for Israel, in which both the city and the sanctuary are made desolate by the abominations wrought by the Antichrist.

We now look at the seventieth week in the light of these

two divisions and their meaning for both the city and the sanctuary, as well as "thy people," Israel.

When the church is translated and all born-again believers are taken out of the world, the king of fierce countenance will immediately emerge as a political genius who will stabilize the world in the midst of the threatened chaos caused by the raptured church. A part of his political strategy will be a covenant made with the nation Israel. This will make Israel a protectorate of the revived Roman empire which is headed by the Antichrist. For three and one-half years the nation Israel will remain secure under this covenant with the Antichrist and the Roman empire. It is this period which the prophet Ezekiel describes when he speaks of Israel dwelling securely in unwalled cities (Eze 38:8, 11, 14). It is during this period that the Levitical priesthood and offerings will be resumed in the temple. This is indicated by the fact that the sacrifices cease when the covenant is broken at midtribulation. If they cease, they must have begun. Their beginning probably takes place when the temple is rebuilt. Jesus indicates that the temple would be functioning again during this time, though he spoke of it as "the holy place" (Mt 24:15). The apostle Paul tells us clearly that the temple is again in existence during the tribulation (2 Th 2:4). Therefore, the covenant which the Antichrist establishes with the nation Israel early in the seventieth week permits Israel to rebuild the temple and to reinstitute the sacrificial system.

However, if conditions are then as they are now, to take this sacred spot from the Muslims and give it back to Israel would be a matter of worldwide issue. The reconstruction of the temple will therefore be a political matter and one of international concern, because the temple area is now a Muslim holy place. The only part of the sacred temple precincts that Israel can really call her own now is the western wall at which the Jews gather to pray. This area is guarded by Israeli police and military men. But the rest of the area which is situated upon the summit of Mount Moriah is in the hands of the Arabs. This is where the first temple of Solomon and the second temple of Herod were located. Here is also located the only place upon earth where sacrifices can be offered. In fact, the Israeli rabbinate has declared the Temple Mount off limits to Jews who wish to pray there. On occasions the Betar youth movement, a right-wing movement composed of bearded young Orthodox Jews, will even now attempt to say prayers in the holy compound in order to try the edict of the Israeli rabbinate. When this happens, Israeli police quickly drag them away, for this is recognized Arab territory.

The Dome of the Rock and the El Aksa Mosque, two of Islam's most holy shrines, are located on the Temple mount. World opinion would not now permit the Jews to take over this sacred area, which has been held by Muslims, with but a few intervals, for fifteen hundred years. It is only with the sanction of the revived Roman empire that Israel can expropriate this sacred Muslim area for her own use, even though it is now an Israeli possession, and has been since the Six-Day War in June, 1967. But when the seventieth week begins, the Antichrist, who is more powerful than world opinion, or Muslim opposition, will permit the Jews to replace the Dome of the Rock with a third temple.

This temple will be built with great expedition during the first part of the tribulation period. In it the ancient Levitical priesthood and offering will resume their function again. It may be that they will even relocate the original furnishings of the holy place and the holy of holies, for history never recorded their destruction. In fact, there is strong tradition to indicate that they are still in existence, ready to be revealed in the end time when they will be used again. Perhaps the furnishings of the holy place are in Rome where they were taken after the Roman conquests of Judea. Though later captured by the Vandals in A.D. 544, the temple menorah, the table for shewbread, the garments of the priest, along with the silver trumpets which were sounded for morning and evening sacrifice, may have ended up in Constantinople when the Vandal Kingdom was overthrown. Even though the vessels of the first temple were taken to Babylon (cf. Jer 28:3), perhaps the ark of the covenant is hidden out on Mount Nebo where the book of 2 Maccabees (2:1-7) says that the prophet Jeremiah hid it. Or it may be hidden under the temple area, somewhere in the vast recesses of Solomon's quarries which run under the city, where another tradition says that the ark was hidden.

In addition, there is still another tradition about the preservation of the elaborate system of ceremony carried out in the second temple. When Jerusalem was under siege by the Roman army, none could leave the city under Zealot threat of death. Rabbi Jochanan ben Zakkai, sensing that the end of the city would spell the doom of Judaism, had himself conveyed out of the city in a coffin and into the camp of the Roman general Vespasian. Because this learned rabbi predicted that Vespasian would soon become the emperor of Rome, the future emperor granted Rabbi Jochanan permission to establish a small school of Jewish learning. The first *yeshiva*, or Jewish academy of learning, was established at the town of Jabneh. When the second temple fell, the rabbis set about to record in meticulous fashion all the temple ceremonies. At first they were transmitted verbally, then they were recorded in the Talmud. The preservation of these orders of service may yet be utilized as a guide in the services of the tribulation temple, along with the original furnishing of the first and second Temples, which may be found.

Even if the sacred vessels are not found, they can be reconstructed from existent records, both in Scripture, as well as in other Jewish literature, and from pictures of them that remain in stone. For example, we know exactly what the menorah from the second temple looked like. There is a picture of this sacred candlestand carved upon the Arch of

Titus in the Roman Forum. The Ark of the Covenant is supposed to be depicted on a stone from the synagogue in Capernaum. These and other archaeological resources could be used as guides by craftsmen who would recreate the furnishings of the tribulation temple.

Some Jewish tradition has it that the Sanhedrin will also be established before the advent of the Messiah. Since this ruling body is an inseparable part of ancient Judaism, it might very well appear during the tribulation period, along with the reconstituted temple and ceremonial system. The only problem is one of the special ordination which the Sanhedrin had. However, this problem was anticipated as far back as the sixteenth century by a Jewish scholar named Jacob Berab. Rabbi Jacob had fled Spain where he was born in 1474. Crossing North Africa he finally settled in Safed, which was the great center of Jewish learning in Palestine. There he died in 1546.

Berab and many other Jews who fled the persecutions in Spain believed that these days of suffering were the birth pangs of the coming Messiah. In those days many believed that the only way to bring order to the new community of exiles from Europe was to establish the ancient Sanhedrin, which had ceased with the fall of the second temple. The ancient Sanhedrin, many believed, went back in unbroken succession to the seventy elders assembled by Moses. In this succession each pupil had received ordination from his teacher who in turn had received ordination from his teacher—back to the time of Moses. In fact, even though the Sanhedrin had ceased to function after the Great Revolt, private ordination of teacher and pupil had continued until the fourth century A.D. Only then was the chain of ordination broken. But since it had been broken for centuries, how could it be reestablished? Jacob Berab, rabbi of Safed, proposed a way. He noted that Maimonides had suggested on the basis of Isaiah 1:26 that there surely must be a way to restore ordination.

Since the Messiah would not innovate anything when he arrived, the ordination of the Sanhedrin must be by human means. Therefore, Maimonides suggested that the scholars in Palestine agree to ordain one of their number in the ancient classical sense. (True ordination could only take place in Palestine.) This one could, in turn, ordain the rest of the body, and the ancient Sanhedrin would thereby be reestablished.

However, after Rabbi Jacob was ordained in order that he might ordain the rest, a dispute broke out between him and Rabbi Levi ibn Habib, in which the Jerusalem rabbi insisted that his Safed brethren had misunderstood Maimonides. In spite of Rabbi Levi's objections, the four who had been ordained in Safed ordained another generation, and they in turn ordained still another generation. But at this point the new ordination ceased and the new Sanhedrin died. But this Responsa, as the body of correspondence which concerns itself with the issue of Sanhedrin ordination is called, may yet be of value in setting up the Sanhedrin during the early part of the tribulation period.

The tribulation revival of the temple sacrifices and services will be short-lived, lasting only three and one-half years, until the mid-tribulation period. Daniel says, "In the midst of the week he shall cause the sacrifice and the oblation to cease" (9:27). What the Antichrist permitted to be started, he will abruptly stop. He will do so for the same reason that Antiochus IV Epiphanes had the sacred sacrifices stopped in his day, namely, in order to force an alien cult upon the Jews and to focus worship upon himself. The Antichrist will destroy the great world church for the same reason. He will permit no religious rivalry either in Israel or among the gentiles. It is then that the abomination of desolation will be set up in the temple. The altar of Yahweh will be replaced with the image of the beast (Mt 24:15; 2 Th 2:4-5; Rev 13:14-15). What Antiochus IV attempted to do in Israel in the long ago, the

Antichrist will achieve. Israel will be forced to worship the image of the beast. If they do not, they will die, just as they did in the days of Antiochus IV.

Many in Israel will yield to the cult of the beast, just as many in Israel yielded in the Hellenistic era to the edicts of Antiochus IV. But others will not yield, and they will suffer intensely during this time. "For then shall be great tribulation, such as hath not been from the beginning of the world until now, no, nor ever shall be. And except those days had been shortened, no flesh would have been saved: but for the elect's sake those days shall be shortened" (Mt 24:21-22). The elect of whom Jesus speaks here are those Jews who refuse to yield to the cult of the Beast and who remain true to their ancient faith. Jeremiah speaks of this same time as a time of Jacob's trouble. He also sees that it is this very time of tribulation that will prepare the faithful in Israel for the coming Messiah.

> For thus saith the LORD: we have heard a voice of trembling, of fear, and not of peace. Ask ye now, and see whether a man doth travail with child: wherefore do I see every man with his hands on his loins, as a woman in travail, and all faces are turned into paleness? Alas! for that day is great, so that none is like it: it is even the time of Jacob's trouble; but he shall be saved out of it. And it shall come to pass in that day, saith the LORD of hosts, that I will break his yoke from off thy neck, and will burst thy bonds; and strangers shall no more make him their bondman; but they shall serve the LORD their God, and David their king, whom I will raise up unto them. Therefore fear thou not, O Jacob my servant, saith the LORD; neither be dismayed, O Israel: for, lo, I will save thee from afar, and thy seed from the land of their captivity; and Jacob shall return, and shall be quiet and at ease, and none shall make him afraid. For I am with thee; saith the LORD, to save thee: for I will make a full end of all the nations whither I have scattered thee, but I will not make a full end of thee; but I will correct thee in measure,

and will in no wise leave thee unpunished (Jer 30:5-11, cf.
Dan 12:2).

THE KING WHO SHALL DO ACCORDING TO HIS WILL

The third name that is given to the Antichrist in the book
of Daniel is "the king [who] shall do according to his will"
(Dan 11:36). Once again we are faced with the same question
that was raised in Daniel 8. Is this king Antiochus IV or is
he the Antichrist?

Just as in Daniel 8, in chapter 11 both Antiochus IV
Epiphanes and the Antichrist are in view. Antiochus IV is
depicted in 11:21-35; and then the more remote figure of the
Antichrist is pictured from verse 36 through 12:4.

Daniel 10 through 12 forms a prophetic unit. Chapter 10
introduces the final vison of Daniel, which occurred in the
third year of Cyrus, King of Persia. This was near the seventieth year of Daniel's captivity in Babylon—dating from 605
B.C. Perhaps the first contingent of Jews had already returned
to Jerusalem. The Babylonian captivity had purged the Jews
of idolatry. They were returning to Judah as strict monotheists, never again to yield to the temptation to worship idols.
Since this was the case, a number of questions must have
occurred to Daniel and his fellow exiles. Was the golden age
about to dawn in Israel? Would she enter into a new era of
Messianic blessing and righteousness in her strict devotion to
Yahweh? Had the exile sufficiently purged the idolatrous
tendencies of Israel so that the time of Messianic redemption
was now upon her? Questions such as these are answered in
Daniel's final vision. This vision was given to Daniel by the
angel who says, "I am come to make thee understand what
shall befall thy people in the latter days; for the vision is yet
for many days" (10:14). The vision then sweeps the history
of the nation Israel from this third year of Cyrus (10:1)
through the period of Persian dominion (11:2), Greek dominion (11:3), the period of conflict between the Ptolemies

of Egypt and the Seleucids of Syria (11:4-20), up to the rise
and reign of Antiochus IV Epiphanes (11:21-35). The vision
then concludes with a picture of the reign of the Antichrist
(11:36-12:4). Though the exile was drawing to an end in
Daniel's day, and though Israel would again return to the
land, the day of Messianic glory will not come yet. Israel was
to suffer many things through the many years that lay ahead,
for this vision runs the course of Israel's history until the time
of the end.

When the vision was concluded, Daniel saw two men on
either side of the river,

> "And one said to the man clothed in linen, who was above
> the waters of the river, How long shall it be to the end of
> these wonders? And I heard the man clothed in linen, who
> was above the waters of the river, when he held up his right
> hand and his left hand unto heaven, and sware by him that
> liveth for ever that it shall be for a time, times, and a half;
> and when they have made an end of breaking in pieces the
> power of the holy people, all these things shall be finished"
> (12:6-7).

Not understanding when this climactic event, the final breaking of Israel, the holy people, will take place, Daniel asks,
"O my Lord, what shall be the issue [latter end, marg.] of
these things." The man responds, "Go thy way, Daniel; for
the words are shut up and sealed till the time of the end"
(12:9). So Daniel sees that there is yet in store for Israel
suffering that will run its course until the time of the end.
In addition, the end is marked by the breaking of the holy
people—Israel—within a specified period. The period is designated, "a time, times, and a half." This is the three and
one-half years of the great tribulation which will bring to a
climax God's purging of his holy people Israel.

Therefore, Daniel sees that future history still holds a great
deal of suffering for the nation Israel. The exile only re-

lieved Israel of her idolatry. The course of history must yet purge her of rebellion and ready her to accept the coming Messiah. This will transpire during the long course of history that leads down to the time of the end. But only after the great tribulation period has prepared her will Israel come to the final age of Messianic glory. This is why the prophet Jeremiah says, "Behold, the tempest of the LORD, even his wrath, is gone forth, a sweeping tempest: it shall burst upon the head of the wicked. The fierce anger of the LORD shall not return, until he have executed, and till he have performed the intents of his heart: in the latter days ye shall understand it" (Jer 30:23-24).

There is no passage in the prophetic Word exactly like Daniel 11 in which future history and the movement of nations back and forth across the map of the Coele-Syria is presented in such precise detail. Daniel wrote these words more than two hundred years before the empire of Alexander the Great broke up and Israel became the pawn of Egypt and Syria. Yet history has shown these prophetic details to be precise and accurate, so precise in fact that liberal scholars have declared these passages must have been written only after the events had actually taken place, by some unknown author during the Maccabean period, using the name of Daniel.

Is Daniel 11 a product of the second century B.C., written by some unknown author in the Maccabean period using the name of Daniel, and therefore *history written as prophecy?* Or is it the product of the sixth century B.C. Babylonian-exile period, and therefore *prophecy written as history?* Since all true prophecy is history written in advance, we choose to believe that the prophetic details of Daniel 11 were given under the inspiration of the Holy Spirit in the sixth century B.C. Daniel was writing history, but writing it centuries before it actually happened.

It is interesting to note that when Alexander the Great

came to Jerusalem in 332 B.C., he was met by the high priest out upon Mount Scopus (Talmud, *Yoma* 69). Alexander recognized the high priest as one whom he had seen before in a dream he had while still in Macedonia. He therefore spared Jerusalem the plunder and torment she had often endured in previous centuries. Because of this merciful treatment of the Jews in Jerusalem, Alexander was taken into the temple and shown the prophecy of Daniel which gave him renewed assurance of victory over the Persians. The priests showed Alexander that he was the subject of some of Daniel's predictions. Josephus records the event:

> And when the book of Daniel was shewed him [probably 7:6; 8:3-8, 20-22; 11:3] wherein Daniel declared that one of the Greeks should destroy the empire of the Persians, he supposed that himself was the person intended; and as he was glad, he dismissed the multitude for the present, but the next day he called them to him, and bade them ask what favours they pleased of him; whereupon the high priest desired that they might enjoy the laws of their forefathers, and might pay no tribute on the seventh year. He granted all they desired. (*Ant.* 11. 8., 5.)

So accurate was Daniel that Alexander could read his scroll and recognize contemporary events in Daniel's words, written over two hundred years before. Unless Josephus just made up the story, it is puzzling how the priests could show Alexander this prophecy if the book of Daniel was not written until the time of the Maccabees, over 150 years after Alexander the Great lived and died, as many modern critics maintain.

After picturing the coming dominion of Persia, Greece, the Ptolemies of Egypt, and the Seleucids of Syria over Israel (11:2-20), Daniel then predicts in great prophetic detail the last malevolent Seleucid ruler to have absolute reign in Judah, Antiochus IV (11:21-35).

First the rise of Antiochus IV is previewed in 11:21-24.

> And in his place shall stand up a contemptible person, to
> whom they had not given the honor of the kingdom: but he
> shall come in time of security, and shall obtain the kingdom
> by flatteries. And the overwhelming forces shall be over-
> whelmed from before him, and shall be broken; yea, also
> the prince of the covenant. And after the league made with
> him he shall work deceitfully; for he shall come up, and
> shall become strong, with a small people. In time of security
> shall he come even upon the fattest places of the province;
> and he shall do that which his fathers have not done, nor
> his fathers' fathers; he shall scatter among them prey, and
> spoil, and substance: yea, he shall devise his devices against
> the strongholds, even for a time.

Antiochus IV is called "the contemptible person, to whom
they had not given the honor of the kingdom" (v. 21). The
kingdom was not Antiochus' for the legitimate heir, Deme-
trius, was at this time a hostage in Rome. Antiochus secured
the throne by political intrigue when his brother Seleucus IV
was murdered by Heliodorus. Heliodorus probably intended
putting the infant son of Seleucus IV, also named Antiochus,
upon the throne in order that Heliodorus himself might reign
as regent. But Antiochus IV, who was in Athens when the
news came of his brother's death, moved to seize the government. He was aided by Eumenes, king of Pergamum, who
came to his assistance with an army. When Antiochus IV
marched into Antioch the people declared him king, 176 B.C.
Opposition dissolved before him. Spiritual opposition, such
as was manifest in Onias III, the legitimate high priest, was
overcome. As the "prince of the covenant," Onias III is murdered (vv. 22-23). Antiochus IV will secure his kingdom,
Daniel says, by doing what his fathers would never have
dreamed of doing. He will distribute his spoils among his
subjects (v. 24a), and in addition he will direct his hostilities
against the strongholds of Egypt (v. 24b).

Antiochus' conquests of Egypt are now described in 11:25-27:

> And he shall stir up his power and his courage against the king of the south with a great army; and the king of the south shall war in battle with an exceeding great and mighty army; but he shall not stand; for they shall devise devices against him. Yea, they that eat of his dainties shall destroy him, and his army shall overflow; and many shall fall down slain. And as for both these kings, their hearts shall be to do mischief, and they shall speak lies at one table: but it shall not prosper; for yet the end shall be at the time appointed.

His first invasion of Egypt occurred after the Egyptian army had crossed its own border to threaten the Syrian empire of Antiochus in 171-170 B.C. The Syrians met them and defeated the Egyptians before they could cross the desert. Antiochus crossed into Egypt and moved up to Memphis. Jerome, substantiated by 1 Maccabees 1:16, says that Antiochus IV was formally crowned king of Egypt. Daniel describes this defeat of Ptolemy IV, the king of the south (Egypt), in verses 25-27.

In the summer of 170, Antiochus IV, having subdued Egypt, returned home by way of Jerusalem where he robbed the temple of much gold and put many Judaeans to death (1 Mac 1:20-24; 1 Mac 5:1ff). "Therefore there was great mourning in Israel, in every place where they were" (1 Mac 1:25). "Then shall he return into his land with great substance; and his heart shall be against the holy covenant; and he shall do his pleasure, and return to his own land" (Dan 11:28). Rome was now threatening the entire Mediterranean basin as a result of her victory in Macedonia. Antiochus IV must move to annex Egypt in order to forestall Rome's spreading power. The Roman Senate viewed the proposed annexation of Egypt by Antiochus as a threat to Rome's best interests. Consul Popilius Laenas delivered the mandate to

Antiochus IV from the Senate, demanding that he leave Egypt, which he reluctantly agreed to do.

It was 168 B.C. when Antiochus IV begrudgingly left Egypt and then vented his frustrated fury upon the Jews, as he returned to Syria through Judah. Daniel 11:29-30 describes this: "At the time appointed he shall return, and come into the south; but it shall not be in the latter time as it was in the former. For ships of Kittim shall come against him; therefore he shall be grieved, and shall return, and have indignation against the holy covenant, and shall do his pleasure: he shall even return, and have regard unto them that forsake the holy covenant."

Again Antiochus IV entered Jerusalem. This time thousands in Judah were slaughtered. Many more were taken captive and were sold into slavery. Antiochus IV came to the temple, and with the help of the apostate high priest, Menelaus, he stripped the temple of its remaining treasures, and then ordered that Judah be Hellenized. He left Apollonius, a Mysian officer, to enforce his Hellenizing edicts upon the Jews. The Jews were forbidden to practice their ancient religion. Anyone who observed the Sabbath was guilty of treason and subject to capital punishment. Circumcision was forbidden. Daily temple sacrifices were abolished. A heathen altar was established in the temple and swine offered upon it. All of which was in fulfillment of Daniel 11:31: "And forces shall stand on his part, and they shall profane the sanctuary, even the fortress, and shall take away the continual burnt-offering, and they shall set up the abomination that maketh desolate." Many Jews yielded to the prohibitions of Antiochus: "And such as do wickedly against the covenant shall he pervert by flatteries" (v. 32a). Others did not: "But the people that know their God shall be strong and do exploits" (v. 32b). First Maccabees 1:52-64 describes these terrible days when some of the Jews apostatized while others remained true to their historic faith, just as they will do during the tribulation period.

> Then many of the people were gathered unto them, to wit, every one that forsook the law; and so they committed evils in the land; And drove the Israelites into secret places, even wheresoever they could flee for succour. Now the fifteenth day of the month Casleu, in the hundred forty and fifth year, they set up the abomination of desolation upon the altar, and builded idol altars throughout the cities of Juda on every side; and burnt incense at the doors of their houses, and in the streets. And when they have rent in pieces the books of the law which they found, they burnt them with fire. And wheresoever was found with any the book of the testament, or if any consented to the law, the king's commandment was, that they should put him to death. Thus did they by their authority unto the Israelites every month, to as many as were found in the cities. Now the five and twentieth day of the month they did sacrifice upon the idol altar, which was upon the altar of God. At which time according to the commandment they put to death certain women, that had caused their children to be circumcised. And they hanged the infants about their necks, and rifled their houses, and slew them that had circumcised them. Howbeit many in Israel were fully resolved and confirmed in themselves not to eat any unclean thing. Wherefore they chose rather to die, that they might not be defiled with meats, and that they might not profane the holy covenant: so then they died. And there was very great wrath upon Israel (1 Mac 1:52-64) .

The unrestrained slaughter of the Jews by Antiochus IV is predicted in Daniel 11:33: "And they that are wise among the people shall instruct many; yet they shall fall by the sword and by spoil, many days." This is substantiated by such passages as 1 Maccabees 2:23; 3:41; 5:13; 2 Maccabees 6:11. Finally, "a little help" will come for the suffering Jews as a result of the revolt of the Maccabees: "Now when they shall fall, they shall be helped with a little help; but many shall join themselves unto them with flatteries. And some of them that are wise shall fall, to refine them, and to purify, and to make them white, even to the time of the end; because it is yet for the time appointed" (11:34-35).

Daniel describes the Maccabean revolt in terms of Israel being "helped with a little help" (v. 34). Three years to the day after Antiochus IV had erected the abomination of desolation in the temple, the temple had been recaptured and re-dedicated, December, 165 B.C. With the restoration of the temple the Hasidim were satisfied. They dropped out of the revolt. However, the sons of Mattathias, the revolutionary priest of Modin, now pressed for national independence. John Hyrcanus I, grandson of Mattathias of Modin, had his government recognized by the Syrians. Though the Seleucid authority in Palestine did not end until the death of Antiochus Sidetes in 129 B.C., never again would Israel be plagued with a Seleucid ruler like Antiochus IV. However, the degree of religious and political independence that was gained during the reign of the Hasmonean kings was short-lived and of "little help" on the great scale of Jewish history.

In 63 B.C. the Roman army under Pompey marched into the Maccabean Kingdom of Judah and conquered it and re-named it Judea. From then on, through three Jewish revolts against Rome, Judea suffered under their Roman overlords. The first revolt of the Jews was put down in A.D. 70 when Titus destroyed the city of Jerusalem. The second occurred in the second decade of the second century A.D.; however, it was really a revolt that occurred outside the land—in Egypt, Antioch, Cyrene, and Cyprus. It took Trajan three years to quell this rebellion of the Jews. Finally, in A.D. 132, Simon ben Cozeba, or Bar Kokhba, arose as a military Messiah and led a revolt against Rome during the reign of the emperor Hadrian. Those Jews who were not able to escape into Parthia were killed or sold into slavery. Jerusalem was forbidden to the Jews; and with this, the Roman phase of Jewish history came to an end in A.D. 135 during the reign of Hadrian. Thus the "little help" of verse 34 reflects the minimum independence, achieved through the Maccabean revolt, and the subsequent reign of the Hasmoneans between 165 B.C. and 63 B.C., barely a century of semiindependence until Israel was again under the imperial power of Rome.

The career of Antiochus IV came to an end during the time of the Maccabean revolt, but not in connection with it, for his death occurred in Parthia about 163 B.C., where he had gone to put down another uprising among his subjects. For this reason Antiochus IV Epiphanes ceases to be the subject of Daniel's prophecy after 11:35, where his death naturally occurred in the chronology of these verses.

Though Daniel was prophesying events from two to four hundred years in the future in the preceding verses, his vision now sweeps into the far distant future and he describes the Antichrist as "the king who shall do according to his will" (11:36-39). Already twenty-five hundred years have passed and this person whom Daniel saw has not yet come upon the scene of world events. In Daniel 11:36-39 the characteristics of this king are set forth. His conflicts are presented in verses 40-45. These conflicts will be discussed later in relation to the end of the career of the Antichrist.

Since the passage Daniel 11:2-35 has been literally fulfilled in past history, there is no reason why we should not look for a literal fulfillment of the remaining portion of Daniel's prophecy in future history. Dr. Solomon Zeitlin, professor of rabbinic law and lore at Dropsie College, has written a monumental two-volume history of the second commonwealth, called *The Rise and Fall of the Judaean State*. Though he would not contend for the verbal inspiration of the Old Testament Hebrew Scripture, nor for the sixth century B.C. authorship of the book of Daniel, it is a delight to read his account of the Ptolemaic and Seleucid era in Judah and note how clearly the events of Daniel 11 follow the history of this period. Because of the precise historical accuracy of Daniel 11, the third century A.D. pagan philosopher Porphyry attacked the book of Daniel as a forgery. He saw that the actual correspondence between the facts of history and the prophecy of Daniel 11 were so precise that he believed they could not have been written in the sixth century B.C., several hundred years before they actually happened. Accordingly, he took the position of many modern critics, namely, that Daniel was written after the events transpired. Jerome wrote his *Commentary on Daniel* to refute Porphyry. Thus the controversy between Jerome, who stood for the integrity of Scripture; and Porphyry, who was the prototype of modern critical rejection of Daniel as predictive prophecy, has continued until now. The fact that every verse in Daniel 11, up to verse 35, has been literally fulfilled, lends credence to the expectation of the literal fulfillment of the remaining prophecies about the king who will do according to his will, found in Daniel 11:36—12:4.

Though most liberal expositors tend to identify the king who shall do according to his own will as Antiochus IV Epiphanes, and verses 36 and following as a continuation of the description of Antiochus IV which began with verse 21, they also concede that these verses have no such precise historical fulfillment as do the preceding verses. In other words, they concede a break between verse 35 and 36, if not in subject, then certainly in fulfillment. Jerome, writing in the fourth century A.D., said,

> The Jews believe that this passage has reference to the Antichrist, alleging that after the small help‡ of Julian [Julian the Apostate, Roman emperor from A.D. 361-363] a king is going to rise up who shall do according to his own will and shall lift himself up against all that is called god, and shall

‡The "little help" of Daniel 11:34 I have interpreted as the Maccabean revolt.

speak arrogant words against the God of gods. He shall act in such a way as to sit in the Temple of God and shall make himself out to be God, and his will shall be prospered until the wrath of God is fulfilled, for in him the consummation will take place.[1]

Adds Jerome, "We too understand this to refer to the Antichrist." The king who will do according to his own will, or pleasure, we recognize to be the Antichrist whom Daniel also presents as the little horn in chapter 7, the king of fierce countenance in chapter 8, and the prince in chapter 9. The time of his advent upon the scene of world history is the same as that presented in the vision of the great image in chapter 2 and the vision of the ten-horned beast in chapter 7. He will come upon the scene of world events just prior to the second coming of Christ. In fact, the prophetic word is consistent in its indication that he will reign as Beast for just three and one-half years before the second coming.

The Antichrist is characterized in two ways in Daniel 11:36-39. First, he is characterized by what he does not worship. He is presented in the light of his self-willed rejection of all the traditional views of deity. In this he will blaspheme the Lord, "speaking horrible things against the God of gods," (Leupold's translation) (v. 36). In addition, he shall not "regard the gods of his fathers" (v. 37). This does not necessarily infer that the Antichrist is a Jew, for the word used here is Elohim—the general Semitic term for deity—and not Yahweh—the covenant God of Israel. "His fathers" indicates the whole of mankind rather than merely the Jews. Therefore, all that the sum total of human culture has taught man about God—and human culture tends to confirm the fact of deity rather than deny it—apart from the specific revelation of God in Scripture and in Jesus Christ, will be rejected by the Antichrist. Where he rejects at this point is the God of natural theology.

But what about the God of supernatural theology, the God

that is revealed in Scripture and in the Lord Jesus Christ? This revelation of God he also will reject. This is indicated in the statement, "Neither shall he regard . . . the desire of women" (v. 37) . This does not refer to some abnormal rejection of the female sex. Rather "the desire of women" has a Messianic flavor. Every Hebrew woman desired to be the mother of the Messiah, and to be the one in whom Genesis 3:15 found fulfillment. Therefore, the "desire of women" is objective. It is a Person. It refers to the Lord Jesus Christ. The Antichrist will not only reject the God of natural theology—the God whom nature has revealed, and the God whom the collective culture of all mankind has either consciously or unconsciously affirmed—but he will also reject the God of revealed theology—the Lord Jesus Christ. He will not be an atheist, nor even an agnostic. He is not in doubt about the existence of God. His will be a blatant rejection of the God he knows to exist. Daniel says that he will not regard any god. He knows what Deity is. But he has a contempt for Deity that far exceeds in its malignancy any disbelief about the mere existence of that which is divine. Why does he do this? In order that he might "magnify himself above every god" (v. 36, cf. 37b) . He is motivated by the same egomania that caused Antiochus IV to claim that he was *theos epiphanes,* "God manifest!" Antiochus IV did not reject the fact of god. He was a true Hellenist and believed in the Greek pantheon, but he included himself among that pantheon and proclaimed that he too was god. The Antichrist will do the same thing, except that he will not include himself among the divine Trinity, but he will realize that he is a vital part of the diabolical trinity which is composed of Satan, the Antichrist, and the false prophet. Hence, his is a blasphemous rejection of the traditional view of the supremacy of God.

In the second place, the Antichrist is characterized by what he does worship. He worships the "god of fortress" (v. 38) . This is the same as the "foreign god," mentioned in the next verse. His sole confidence is in military might. This is his god. He will dedicate all his fiscal resources in the pursuit of military power. He will also invest with glorious recognition all those who will support him in this endeavor. He will even divide the land of Israel for a price (v. 39). Joel 3:2 may be a reference to this very thing. "I will gather all nations, and will bring them down into the valley of Jehoshaphat; and I will execute judgment upon them there for my people and for my heritage Israel, whom they have scattered among the nations; and they have parted my land."

The prophet says that the battle of Armageddon will be a judgment against the nations who have scattered Israel and who have divided the sacred land for a price. The division of the land probably occurs during the tribulation period when the Antichrist sells territory in Israel in order to finance his great military machine. However, the sacred land of Israel is inviolable, and the Antichrist cannot desecrate it with impunity. The judgment of Armageddon, which probably climaxes in the Valley of Jehoshaphat, as we shall later see, is a stipulated judgment of God against the nations in general, and the Antichrist in particular, for his division of the land.

Daniel 11:40-45 presents the conflicts of the Antichrist and the final destruction which his kingdom will suffer in the very land which he violated. We shall return to these verses later as we discuss the conflicts of the Antichrist.

3

Antiochus IV: A Type of the Antichrist

DURING THE FIRST YEAR of the reign of Belshazzar, king of Babylon, Daniel the prophet had a dream, the substance of which is recorded in Daniel 7:1-28. He sees four beasts emerging from the great sea. These beasts represent the four great world empires whose succession constitutes the times of the gentiles. They are Babylon, 7:4; Medo-Persia, 7:5; Greece, 7:6; and Rome, 7:7.

THE TWO HORNS OF DANIEL SEVEN AND EIGHT

As Daniel contemplates the fourth beast which represents ancient Rome, he describes it is "terrible and powerful, and strong exceedingly; and it had great iron teeth; it devoured and brake in pieces, and stamped the residue with its feet; and it was diverse from all the beasts that were before it." He also notes that the beast has ten horns. Out of these ten horns "there came up among them another horn, a little one, before which three of the first horns were plucked up by the roots; and, behold, in this horn were eyes like the eyes of a man, and a mouth speaking great things" (Dan 7:8). Without taking note of the age of the church which separates the ancient Roman empire from the revived Roman empire of the last days, Daniel views the Antichrist arising out of the ten-nation confederation that constitutes this revived form of the Roman empire during the tribulation period. This little horn which has the eyes of a man and which speaks great things is the Antichrist. This is clear from the fact that he will make war with the saints and "prevailed against them; *until* the ancient of days came [that is, until the second coming of Christ], and judgment was given to the saints of the Most High, and the time came that the saints possessed the kingdom" (Dan 8:21-22).

Daniel sees a different little horn in chapter 8. "And out of one of them came forth a little horn, which waxed exceedingly great, toward the south, and toward the east, and toward the glorious land" (Dan 8:9).

If the little horn of Daniel 7:8 is the Antichrist, then what is the identity of the little horn of Daniel 8:9? Does this little horn also represent the Antichrist? An answer of yes or no must be qualified. Only typically can the little horn of Daniel 8:9 be construed as the Antichrist. Actually, the little horn of Daniel 8:9 represents a person whose coming was yet future in Daniel's day, but who has already crossed the stage of history as far as we are concerned. The little horn of Daniel 8 is the sinister ruler of the house of Seleucus, Antiochus IV Epiphanes, who reigned in Syria between 175 and 163 B.C. This identity is made clear in Daniel 8:19 and following. The identification of this little horn with Antiochus IV is also clarified by comparing the text of Daniel with the history of the Greek world in the second, third, and fourth centuries B.C. In addition, note that the little horn arose out of *one* of the four notable horns (8:8-9). The *one* of the four notable horns was the horn that represented Alexander's General Seleucus. For he, along with Ptolemy, Cassander, and Lysimachus, inherited Alexander's empire when he died. Antiochus IV arose several generations later out of the horn which represents the Seleucid dynasty.

ANTIOCHUS IV EPIPHANES: THE LITTLE HORN OF DANIEL EIGHT

In Daniel 8 the prophet sees this little horn emerge, just as he did in chapter 7. But this time the animals with which the horn is associated are different in number, as well as in kind, from those which he previously saw in chapter 7. The ram and the he-goat which he now sees, represent not the entire scope of the times of the gentiles, as the vision in the previous chapter did, but only the Persian and Greek segment of it.

The first of these animals which Daniel sees is a ram with two horns (Dan 8:3). This ram and its two horns represent the Medo-Persian empire (Dan 8:20). The higher of the two horns speaks of the supremacy of Persia in comparision to its Median component. In the days of its power (539-334 B.C.) the Persian empire spread it dominion in all directions: "Pushing westward, and northward, and southward; and no beasts could stand before him" (Dan 8:4). However, as Daniel watches, "a he-goat came from the west over the face of the whole earth, and touched not the ground: and the goat had a notable horn between his eyes" (Dan 8:5). The he-goat is Greece and the notable horn between his eyes is Alexander the Great (Dan 8:21), who conquered the Persians in the fourth century B.C. In 334 B.C., with an army of thirty-five thousand, Alexander appeared in the northwest corner of Asia Minor. The Persian king, Darius III, did not take his threat seriously. Alexander defeated the Persians at the river Granicus, and thereby abolished Persian rule over the Greek cities of the western coast. In 333 B.C. Alexander met the Persian king himself at the Cilician Gates of Syria. Alexander won a second victory over Darius' armies at the battle of Issus. Alexander also took the family of Darius captive at Issus. The Persian king by this time began to realize the threat that Alexander posed. Darius, therefore, tried to negotiate with him on at least two occasions. He offered Alexander territory, a large sum of money, and his own daughter in marriage. But Alexander had now determined a course of world conquest. In 332 B.C. he moved down the coast of Palestine to Egypt, after taking Tyre and Gaza in two hard sieges. In

331 B.C., having mastered Egypt, Alexander retraced his steps through Syria and turned east across the Tigris and Euphrates rivers where he won another decisive victory over the armies of Darius. He then occupied the Persian king's capitals at Persepolis and Susa.

It is this whole conquest that is pictured in Daniel 8:6-7. "And he (Alexander) came to the ram that had two horns (Darius), which I saw standing before the river, and ran upon him in the fury of his power. And I saw him (Alexander) come close unto the ram, and he was moved with anger against him (Darius), and smote the ram, and brake his two horns (Medo-Persia); and there was no power in the ram to stand before him; but he cast him down to the ground, and trampled upon him; and there was no one that could deliver the ram out of his hand." However, having pushed his empire as far as India, "when he was strong, the great horn was broken" (Dan 8:8). Alexander died in Babylon in the year 323 B.C. at the age of thirty-three.

Though it was only a little more than a decade between the time Alexander crossed the Dardanelles, until his death in Babylon, his conquests changed the course of western history. Alexander, who in his youth had been tutored by the great Aristotle himself, left a legacy of Hellenistic culture which would conquer the ancient world. Only the Jews would resist it. When Hellenism finally clashed with Judaism in Palestine, it would become the instrument employed by Antiochus IV Epiphanes in his attempt to stamp out Judaism. This clash was yet many years off. However, Alexander's conquests set the stage for the final conflict between Judaism and Hellenism that was to occur in Palestine a century and a half after Alexander died.

As Daniel's vision continues, he sees four horns coming up out of the place where the great horn (Alexander) was broken. "And the he-goat magnified himself exceedingly: and when he was strong, the great horn was broken; and instead of it there came up four notable horns toward the four winds of heaven" (Dan 8:8). These four horns represent the four generals who finally took over the empire of Alexander after his death. Though there was a power struggle among Alexander's generals following his death, by the year 301 B.C., Cassander was recognized as king in Macedonia, Lysimachus had received Asia Minor, Ptolemy was in control of Egypt, and Seleucus had Syria. These are the four notable horns of Daniel 8:8. It was the last two of these horns, Ptolemy and Seleucus, who would play the dominant role in Judean affairs for the next century and a half.

The Ptolemaic dynasty is the common name of the fifteen Macedonian kings who ruled in Egypt after the breakup of Alexander's Greek empire, 323 until 30 B.C. Ptolemy Soter was in control of Egypt when Alexander died. He converted this military command into a kingdom over which he and his descendants reigned for almost three hundred years. During the third century B.C. the territory of the Ptolemies included Palestine, but Antiochus III conquered it and converted it into a Syrian buffer state (198 B.C.). The last Ptolemaic king was the son of Cleopatra and Julius Caesar named Caesarion. He was murdered in 30 B.C. under orders from Octavian. The house of Ptolemy appears as the king of the south in Daniel 11:6-35, where the numerous conflicts between the Ptolemies and Seleucids are pictured. The Ptolemaic dynasty is best remembered by us for Ptolemy II (Philadelphus, 285-247 B.C.) who ordered a translation of the Hebrew Old Testament into Greek for the library at Alexandria. Tradition says that it took seventy-two Jewish scholars just seventy-two days to complete the translation which we call the Septuagint. This was the text of the Old Testament which the Apostles commonly used and which is usually quoted in our New Testament.

The Seleucid dynasty is the name given to the reigning kings of Syria between 312 and 64 B.C. The first Seleucus was a cavalry officer in the army of Alexander the Great. He was one of the *diadochi* (successors) who successfully parted the empire after the great conqueror's death. The House of Seleucids was composed of Seleucus I (312-280 B.C.); Antiochus I (280-262/1 B.C.); Antiochus II (261-247 B.C.); Seleucus II (247-226 B.C.); Seleucus III (226-223 B.C.); Antiochus III the Great (223-187 B.C.); Seleucus IV (187-175 B.C.); and Antiochus IV Epiphanes (175-163 B.C.). Other kings in the Seleucid line continued to reign after this, until finally the weak and unsettled Syrian kingdom was taken over in 64 B.C. by Pompey, who made it into a Roman province.

Though it is an oversimplification, generally speaking, the Ptolemaic dynasty dominated the Jews during most of the third century B.C., while the Seleucids were in control during the years immediately preceding the Maccabean revolt. The last of these Seleucids to have any significant rule in Judah was Antiochus IV Epiphanes, the great-great-great-grandson of the first Seleucus. It is Antiochus IV who is the little horn of Daniel 8:9-14. After the Maccabean revolt the somewhat diminshed authority of the Seleucids continued in Judah until the death of Antiochus VII in 129 B.C. Then there was such constant internal conflict within the House of Seleucus that they had no time to be concerned with Judean affairs. John Hyrcanus was thereby free to rule as a king in Israel, 134-104 B.C. In fact, Professor Snaith says that he actually took the title of king some years before his death.[1] However, many scholars believe that it was John Hyrcanus' son, Aristobolus I, who was actually the first in the Hasmonean line to use the title of king.[2]

"And out of one of them came forth a little horn, which waxed exceedingly great" (Dan 8:9). Between verses 8 and 9, Daniel skips over more than a century of history. He moves from the early division of Alexander's empire among the four notable horns at the end of the fourth century B.C., to the time when the little horn, Antiochus IV, arose in the House of Seleucus to govern Syria. In another place, Daniel does describe this century or so which is omitted here in chapter 8 (Dan 11:5-20). However, between Daniel 8:8 and 9, the prophet moves directly from the time of Alexander's immediate successors to the time of Antiochus IV.

The writer of 1 Maccabees puts it this way, "So Alexander reigned twelve years, and then died. And his servants bare rule every one in his place. After his death they all put crowns upon themselves; so did their sons after them many years: and evils were multiplied in the earth. And there came out of them a wicked root, Antiochus surnamed Epiphanes, son of Antiochus the king, who had been an hostage at Rome, and he reigned in the hundred and thirty and seventh year of the kingdom of the Greeks" (1 Mac 1:7-10).

Between Nehemiah, which is the last historical book in the Old Testament, and the time of the Greek king of Syria, Antiochus IV, two hundred and seventy years pass. There is no Jewish literature to shed light on this era, nor is there any record of successive political events in Israel. A door is opened upon Israel only momentarily as she is brought into contact with some imposing power such as Persia, Greece, or the empires of the Ptolemies and the Seleucids. Though the relationship between Antiochus IV and the Jews had momentous effects upon human affairs, both in history and in prophecy, as far as Antiochus is concerned, his contact with Judah was of little moment. It was important only as it determined the border between Ptolemaic Egypt and Seleucid Syria, for he who dominated Palestine had a buffer state for protection and was in control of important trade routes. The Syrian empire had once stretched from the borders of Egypt around the Fertile Crescent to the Persian Gulf. In some areas it touched the Caspian Sea and the Black Sea. It was bounded on the west by the Aegean Sea and included much of Asia Minor. However, since the days of Antiochus III, the Romans had been reducing the size of the Syrian empire.

Nevertheless, the Syrian empire was still vast in the days of Antiochus IV.

In the midst of this empire Judah was only a dot on the map. After the exile, Nehemiah was left with a little community of Jews gathered about the temple of the Lord in Jerusalem. This same community of Jews could be found there two and one-half centuries later when Antiochus IV came to power. The high priest was the chief local ruler in Judah in those days. Though the area around Jerusalem was inhabited and tilled by Jews, we must realize that this area was no more than some ten or fifteen miles in any direction, and that is all. It was certainly not the imposing country of Jesus' day, nor of our day.

Antiochus IV Epiphanes is important to us for he is history's foremost type of the Antichrist. By race a Macedonian, he was by culture and education a Greek. Hence he was a foreigner in the eyes of the Syrians, as well as the Jews, over whom he reigned. Antiochus was the fourth of thirteen Seleucid kings to bear the name *Antiochus,* a Greek word which means "withstander."

Antiochus IV Epiphanes (ca. 212-ca. 163 B.C.) was the third son of Antiochus III the great. He had lived in Rome, where he spent his early years as a hostage. After his father died, his brother Seleucus IV Philopater ruled from 187 to 175 B.C. When his brother was assassinated, Antiochus had to seize the throne from a usurper, Heliodorus. Antiochus IV reigned from 175 B.C. until his death in 163 B.C.

In 170 B.C. Ptolemaic Egypt attempted to reconquer Seleucid Palestine. In turning back this invasion of his buffer state, Antiochus IV, the Seleucid king, followed the fleeing Egyptians into their own country. Conquering them, he set up a protectorate over Ptolemy VI which immediately failed when Antiochus IV withdrew from Egypt. This necessitated a second Egyptian campaign in 168 B.C. However, this time the Roman Senate ordered him out of Egypt. Antiochus IV underwent a humiliating public encounter with the Roman envoy Gaius Popilius Laenas at Alexandria. He had asked the Roman representative for time to consider the Senate's edict. Popilius Laenas drew a circle around Antiochus IV and told him to "decide on the spot and not go out of that ring until he had given an answer to the Senate whether he would have peace or war with Rome." Antiochus IV obeyed the Senate and withdrew.

After his first invasion of Egypt, while returning home to his capital in Antioch, Antiochus IV visited Jerusalem and "entered proudly into the sanctuary" (1 Mac 1:21) and carried off many of its treasures. When he left Jerusalem which he had devastated, "there was great mourning in Israel in every place where they were" (1 Mac 1:25ff). But this was only the beginning. This time, when Antiochus IV returned through Judah, from his second invasion of Egypt, he was to vent his frustrations upon the hapless Jews themselves. Thousands of Jews were killed and many more were taken slaves.

As a result of the rebuff by Rome in which Egypt was denied to him, Antiochus IV needed Judah more than ever as a buffer against the south. In order to insure a solid front against the Romans' threat to his empire, Antiochus IV also needed a people welded together in a common unity. The chosen instrument for this goal was the Greek culture of Hellenism. This is why, according to 1 Maccabees 1:41ff, Antiochus IV sought throughout his whole kingdom to impose a common culture and religion on his subjects. Tacitus says, "King Antiochus endeavored to abolish Judaian superstition and to introduce Greek civilization" (*History* 5:8). In his determination to unify his empire by imposing a common Hellenistic culture on everyone, Antiochus IV realized that he must stamp out Judaism. The practice of Judaism was therefore forbidden. Anyone caught observing the Sabbath or circumcising a child would be killed. The Hebrew

Scriptures were ordered destroyed. The temple was turned into a Greek house of worship, and swine were offered in sacrifice on its sacred altars. Otto Markholm, who has done an outstanding monograph on Antiochus IV, says,

> As the history of the Jews in antiquity shows, the Greeks, and also the Romans, always had great difficulty in grasping the realities of the Jewish way of life with its monotheistic religion, its strict adherence to the laws of the torah, and worst of all, its absolute seclusion from the surrounding world. To the enlightened Greeks of the Hellenistic period this attitude implied a narrowness of mind which bordered on misanthropy and seemed tacitly to challenge the superiority of the Hellenistic culture, of which all Greeks were firmly convinced. The inability to understand often resulted in contempt and enmity. In this respect Antiochus IV was presumably neither worse nor better than the majority of the Greeks who entered into contact with the Jews. But in his case, his position as the secular overlord of the Jewish people made his lack of understanding disastrous.[3]

This attempt to Hellenize the country by force was one of the darkest hours in the history of Israel. It will only be rivaled by the great tribulation period when the Antichrist, the antitype of Antiochus IV Epiphanes, will again attempt to stamp out Judaism. The climax of this sad era came in 166 B.C. when some of Antiochus' officers attempted to enforce pagan worship upon the inhabitants of the little village of Modin which was located between Jerusalem and Joppa. An aged priest named Mattathias refused to offer the sacrifice. He inspired the villagers to turn upon Antiochus' soldiers. Thus began a revolt, led by Mattathias and his sons, that would finally bring religious freedom, and ultimately a short-lived political independence to the Jews. The Maccabean revolt brought an end to the persecutions of Antiochus IV. A few years later, Antiochus IV himself died, 163 B.C., while on an expedition in the east.

ANTIOCHUS IV EPIPHANES—DANIEL'S PICTURE OF THE COMING ANTICHRIST

Twice Daniel describes the reign of Antiochus IV: Daniel 8:9-14, and again in 11:21-45. But each time he moves beyond the reign of Antiochus IV and pictures the coming reign of the Antichrist. Just as Isaiah begins with a description of the king of Babylon and lapses into a description of Satan (Is 14:1-20), and just as Ezekiel begins with a description of the king of Tyre from which he moves on into a description of Satan (Eze 28:1-19), so Daniel employs the same literary method to present the Antichrist. In each case he begins with Antiochus IV, but his vision soon moves to the end of the age where his picture of Antiochus IV merges with a picture of the Antichrist. This is consistent with the method of the Hebrew prophets, however, for they often move into the prophetic future by describing some contemporary event. This is not to say that Daniel is conscious of the fact that he is seeing two different persons who are separated from each other by many hundreds of years—already more than two millennia. Daniel is only recording his vision and the interpretation of this vision which was given to him (Dan 8:15-17). However, in the light of the fuller revelation of God in the prophetic word, we now recognize that Daniel is actually presenting the person of the Antichrist by first presenting the person of Antiochus IV.

Jerome, in his fourth century A.D. commentary on the book of Daniel, said that most of the early church fathers "hold that that which occurred under Antiochus was only by way of a type which shall be fulfilled under Antichrist."[4]

Antiochus IV Epiphanes was a type of the future Antichrist in two significant ways: first, in his persecution of the Jews; and second, in his proud attempt to exalt himself to a position of deity. However, this does not exhaust the relationship between Antiochus IV and the Antichrist. There are many more parallels, as well as contrasts, between these two figures.

When known historical facts about the person and the reign of Antiochus IV are compared with the revelation of the Antichrist in the prophetic Word, many more similarities become clear.

PERSECUTOR OF THE JEWS

Antiochus IV Epiphanes is a type of the Antichrist in his severe persecution of the Jews. Both of these men cast Israel into great tribulation.

When Antiochus IV returned from his second invasion of Egypt in 168 B.C., he heard that a revolt had broken out against him in Jerusalem. The revolt was most likely due to the circulation of a false rumor that Antiochus IV had been killed in Egypt. Antiochus IV was still smarting under the humiliating encounter with the Roman representative, Gaius Populius Laenas, who had ordered him out of Egypt. This sort of humiliation could do severe damage to the ego of a god!

The conflict in Jerusalem was between the followers of Jason, a deposed high priest, and Menelaus, whom Antiochus IV himself had placed in the office of high priest. Therefore, Antiochus IV considered the rebellion of the Judeans as a rebellion against himself. When he entered the city he had thousands of Jews slaughtered. He took many more captive and sold them into slavery. He authorized Apollonius to enforce his edicts of Hellenization upon the Jews. Sabbath observance was forbidden. It became unlawful to read the Torah. Anyone circumcising a child was to be killed. Though many Jews yielded to the edicts of Antiochus IV and denied their heritage under threat of death, many more did not. It was they who suffered and died rather than deny their ancient faith.

Stories in Josephus and 2 Maccabees portray the cruelty perpetuated upon the Judeans by this mad tyrant, Antiochus IV, whom the Jews called "the devourer, the unjust one in purple, the cruel, the rejector of the light." A great group of faithful Jews were caught in a cave observing the Sabbath. The entrance was sealed and fires set to suffocate them. Two mothers had circumcised their infants. They were paraded about the city with the infants tied to their breasts and finally thrown over the wall. Eleazar, an aged scribe, was put to death for refusing to eat swine's flesh. A mother was forced to watch as her seven sons were tortured to death. She followed them to the grave as she too refused to conform to the edicts of Antiochus IV. These are but an indication of the horrors perpetuated upon the Jews by Antiochus IV, who murdered with abandon.

The task of the authorities, who were consigned to hunt down and mercilessly kill Jewish fugitives who had refused to obey the decrees of Antiochus IV, was considerably eased by the fact that the Jews would not fight on the Sabbath. The persecutors were quick to take advatage of the fact that the Jews would not defend themselves on the Sabbath, but that they chose rather to die than to violate the law. On the Sabbath day, while strictly obeying the Torah, hordes of Jews were butchered like cattle as they offered no resistance (1 Mac 2:29-30; 2 Mac 6:11).

The malevolence of Antiochus IV is unique, for he was the first person in history to persecute a people exclusively for their religious faith. "Religious persecution was previously unknown in the history of civilization," says Solomon Zeitlin.[5] The polytheism which characterizes all pagan religions encouraged tolerance. Always before, a conquered people was required to accept the god of the conqueror—but this was of little consequence, for the victorious god was just added to the list of other gods already worshiped. Only monotheists like the Jews could not assimilate foreign gods into their worship. The issue was clear, for *Yahweh,* the God of Israel, could not abide in the same temple with Zeus. Therefore, the Jews faced death rather than yield to the edicts of Antiochus IV. "How familiar it all seems to us, who look back along such a dreadful vista of religious persecutions," says Professor Bevan in his *Jerusalem Under the High Priests.*[6] "But it was a new thing then. Israel had never gone through such a crisis before. And when we reckon up our debt to Israel, we must remember that it is this crisis which opens the roll of the martyrs."[7] With this thesis Professor Arnold Toynbee agrees, for he finds no record of religious persecution before the Maccabean period. But just as Israel suffered the *first* religious persecution in history, so Israel will suffer the *last* persecution in history. While Antiochus IV fomented the first religious persecution of the Jews, the Antichrist will perpetuate the last one during the great tribulation period.

Jesus described the horror of this coming persecution that Israel will suffer under the Antichrist. "For then shall be great tribulation, such as hath not been from the beginning of the world until now, no, nor ever shall be. And except those days had been shortened, no flesh would have been saved: but for the elect's sake those days shall be shortened" (Mt 24:21-22). It is called "the time of Jacob's trouble" in Jeremiah 30:7; and Daniel says that it will be "a time of trouble, such as never was since there was a nation" (Dan 12:1).

There is another interesting fact about these two eras of persecution, the first under Antiochus IV, and the last under the Antichrist. Both are seen as that which providentially purges the Jews and readies them for a new experience with God. Though we do not consider the Apocrypha inspired, listen to what the writer of 2 Maccabees says in the prologue to his stories of the martyrdom of Eleazar and the Seven Brothers under Antiochus IV.

> Now I beseech those that read this book, that they be not discouraged for these calamities, but that they judge those punishments not to be for destruction, but for a chastening of our nation. For it is a token of his great goodness, when wicked doers are not suffered any long time, but forthwith punished. For not as with other nations, whom the Lord

> patiently forebeareth to punish, till they be come to the
> fulness of their sins, so dealeth he with us, lest that, being
> come to the height of sin, afterwards he should take venge-
> ance of us. And therefore he never withdraweth his mercy
> from us: and though he punish with adversity, yet doth he
> never forsake his people (2 Mac 6:12-16).

Now listen to what the prophets say about Israel's suffering
during the great tribulation period under the Antichrist.
"And it shall come to pass, that in all the land, saith the LORD,
two parts therein shall be cut off and die; but the third shall
be left therein. And I will bring the third part into the fire,
and will refine them as silver is refined, and will try them as
gold is tried: they shall call on my name, and I will hear
them: I will say, It is my people; and they shall say, the LORD
is my God" (Zec 13:8-9). "For a small moment have I for-
saken thee: but with great mercies will I gather thee. In
overflowing wrath I hid my face from thee for a moment;
but with everlasting lovingkindness will I have mercy on thee,
saith the LORD thy Redeemer" (Is 54:7-8).

DEMANDER OF WORSHIP

During the first few years of his reign, the Syrian ruler was
known simply as King Antiochus. But around 169 B.C. Antiochus added the title *Theos Epiphanes* to his name, which
means "God manifest." This is the second significant way in
which Antiochus IV Epiphanes was a type of the Antichrist.
The evidence is strong that Antiochus IV not only encouraged
the worship of Zeus, but he encouraged the worship of himself
also. On many of the coins that survive from that day can be
seen the figure of Zeus whose features closely resemble those
of Antiochus IV Epiphanes. One which can be seen in the
British Museum, a silver tetradrachma, has the head of
Antiochus IV as if he were Zeus, crowned with laurel. Its
inscription reads: "Of King Antiochus, God Manifest, Vic-
tory-bearer." Therefore, beyond the abstract claim to deity,

Antiochus IV probably identified himself with the supreme god Zeus.

It was his identification with the supreme Greek god Zeus that gave Antiochus IV the pretext for looting temples in every part of his Syrian domain. At Hieropolis, where the temple deity was feminine, he claimed the temple treasury as his wife's dowry. But in Jerusalem he seized the temple treasury in the name of Zeus whom he identified with himself.

> And after that Antiochus had smitten Egypt, he returned again in the hundred forty and third year, and went up against Israel and Jerusalem with a great multitude, and entered proudly into the sanctuary, and took away the golden altar, and the candlestick of light, and all the vessels thereof, and the table of the shewbread, and the pouring vessels, and the vials, and the censers of gold, and the veil, and the crowns, and the golden ornaments that were before the temple, all which he pulled off. He took also the silver and the gold, and the precious vessels: also he took the hidden treasures which he found. And when he had taken all away, he went into his own land, having made a great massacre, and spoken very proudly (1 Mac 1:20-24).

However, this was only the beginning of the sacrilege of Antiochus IV.

He not only looted the temple on his first return from Egypt, but he later profaned it by turning it into a Greek house of worship. Josephus says, "And when the king had built an idol altar upon God's altar, he slew swine upon it, and so offered a sacrifice neither according to the law, nor the Jewish religious worship in that country. He also compelled them to forsake the worship which they paid their own God, and to adore those whom he took to be gods; and made them build temples and raise idol altars, in every city and village, and offer swine upon them every day."[8]

Both the temple in Jerusalem and the Samaritan temple on

Mount Gerizim were renamed. "Not long after this the king sent an old man of Athens to compel the Jews to depart from the laws of their fathers, and not to live after the laws of God: and to pollute also the temple in Jerusalem, and to call it the temple of Jupiter Olympius; and that in Gerizim, of Jupiter the Defender of Strangers" (2 Mac 6:1-2).

The temple in Jerusalem was dedicated not only to Zeus, but also to Antiochus IV himself, as we have noted. After Antiochus IV had issued his decree, forbidding the observance of the law, and the offering of sacrifices in the temple, about five months later on "the fifteenth day of the month Casleu, in the hundred forty and fifth year, they set up the abomination of desolation upon the altar" (1 Mac 1:54). This was about the middle of December in the year 168 B.C. It was the midnight hour for the Jews.

When the temple was finally recovered and cleansed a few years later, the Jews established a perpetual feast to commemorate its cleansing and its deliverance from the abomination of desolation. This is the Jewish feast of Hanukkah. Even today it is observed during the month of December and has been since the days of the Maccabean victory and the reclamation of the temple. Hanukkah is derived from a Hebrew word which means dedication. The feast is also called the Feast of Dedication and the Festival of Lights. The latter name for the celebration is used because of a tradition that when the temple was recaptured by Judas Maccabaeus no undefiled oil could be found for the temple lights. One consecrated container of oil for the lights was found, with enough oil for only one day. However, by a miracle, the oil lasted for eight days. For centuries the Jews celebrated this miracle by burning lights outside their homes. But during the Middle Ages this practice became dangerous and they started burning them indoors. This started the custom of putting the candles in the widows of Jewish homes when the

Feast of Hanukkah is celebrated. Hanukkah is often spelled *Chanukah* because of the difficulty of transliterating the word from Hebrew into English.

Three times the abomination of desolation is referred to in Daniel. Twice the reference is to the abomination which will be placed in the temple by the Antichrist, 9:27 and 12:11. The third reference is to the pollution of the temple by Antiochus IV. "And forces shall stand on his part, and they shall profane the sanctuary, even the fortress, and shall take away the continual burnt-offering, and they shall set up the abomination that maketh desolate" (Dan 11:31). We do not know exactly what the abomination of desolation was which Antiochus IV erected in the sacred precincts of the temple. The term is "one of abhorrence for a pagan symbol," says Professor Zeitlin, as he cites a comparison in 1 Kings 11:7. Many expositors believe the abomination was the pagan altar built on the stone platform which in the second temple was the place of sacrifice, and upon this altar swine were offered. Others believe that it was an image, perhaps of Zeus, but whose likeness was that of Antiochus IV Epiphanes also.

Jesus referred to this passage in Daniel when He announced that the abomination of desolation was yet to come, for Antiochus' abomination of desolation was only a type: "When therefore ye see the abomination of desolation, which was spoken of through Daniel the prophet, standing in the holy place" (Mt 24:15). Though the abomination had a typical fulfillment in Antiochus IV, its greater fulfillment will come when the image of the Antichrist is set up in the temple during the great tribulation period. In passing, we might observe that Jesus regarded Daniel as a prophet. He speaks of Daniel as one who really was forecasting the future, rather than merely as a literary artist who wrote contemporary history under the guise of prophecy.

There are three similarities between the desecration of the temple under Antiochus IV and the desecration of the temple under the Antichrist. These similarities are also seen in the self-deification of Antiochus IV and the self-deification of the Antichrist during the tribulation period.

1. The Antichrist will bring an end to the sacrifices. Just as Antiochus IV forbade the sacrifices in Zerubbabel's temple (1 Mac 1:45; Dan 11:31), so will the Antichrist cause sacrifices to end in the tribulation temple. "In the midst of the week he shall cause the sacrifice and the oblation to cease" (Dan 9:27b). This suggests that during the first half of the tribulation, when the Jews are living peacefully under the terms of the covenant made with the Antichrist (Dan 9:27a), the temple will have been rebuilt in Jerusalem and the ancient sacrifices begun again. The fact that the temple will be rebuilt during the tribulation period is also substantiated by the words of Jesus in Matthew 24:15; as well as those of Paul in 2 Thessalonians 2:4. The termination of the sacrifices occurs just before the abomination of desolation is set up (Dan 12:11). This verse in Daniel tells us that the continual burnt offering ceases a thousand two hundred and ninety days before the end. This means that the sacrifice will be stopped by the Antichrist at midtribulation period. The reason why the Antichrist stops the sacrifices is the same reason why Antiochus IV had them stopped in his day, in order to divert worship to himself.

The numbers in Daniel 12:11-12 present a small problem. Usually the three and one-half years of the great tribulation period are designated by 1260 days, or forty-two months. Biblical months are of thirty-days' duration. Thus, from midtribulation to the second coming of Christ is three and one-half-years, or forty-two months, or 1260 days. But Daniel speaks of 1290 days, which would leave thirty days unaccounted for. In the next verse he speaks of 1335 days, which would leave seventy-five days unaccounted for. Our interpretation is this: From the time that the Antichrist breaks the covenant with Israel, at midtribulation until the second coming of Christ is 1260 days, or the generally accepted time of three and one-half years. However, before the millennial reign of Christ is established, and after the second coming of Christ ends the great tribulation period, there are certain prophetic events which must take place. These are the resurrection of the Old Testament saints along with the tribulation saints, the final regathering and regeneration of Israel, and the judgment of the nations. There must be time between the end of the great tribulation and the beginning of the millennium for these three events to transpire. Apparently the remaining thirty days in Daniel 12:11 and the remaining seventy-five days in verse 12, have reference to this interim between the end of the tribulation and the beginning of the millennium.

2. The Antichrist's image is placed in the temple just as an image was placed there in the days of Antiochus IV (Dan 9:27; 12:11; Mt 24:15; 2 Th 2:4). We are not certain what the abomination of desolation was which Antiochus IV placed in the temple. It was probably an image of Zeus made to resemble Antiochus himself. However, the abomination of desolation placed in the temple in the time of the Antichrist will certainly be an image of the Beast made by "them that dwell upon the earth" (Rev 13:14). The "earth dwellers" in the book of Revelation are those people who are the followers of the Antichrist. This image is then animated by the false prophet. "And it was given unto him to give breath to it, even to the image of the beast, that the image of the beast should both speak, and cause that as many as should not worship the image of the beast should be killed" (Rev 13:15). Since the false prophet is to the Antichrist what the Holy Spirit is to Jesus Christ, it is the false prophet that breathes something akin to life into the image. The image speaks. This is one of the signs performed by the false prophet that directs worship to the Beast.

3. The Antichrist magnifies himself as God. Daniel 8:25

says, "he shall magnify himself in his heart." In 11:36 Daniel further amplifies this by saying, "he shall exalt himself, and magnify himself above every god, and shall speak marvelous things against the God of gods." Paul says that the Antichrist will "exalt himself against all that is called God or that is worshipped; so that he sitteth in the temple of God, setting himself forth as God" (2 Th 2:4).

There is no question that Antiochus IV Epiphanes thought of himself as a god. There was probably a touch of madness about the man that caused him so to think. In fact, the Jews in derision nicknamed him Antiochus "Epimanes" which means "mad," instead of Antiochus Epiphanes which means "God mainifest" (Polybius, 26:1; Livy 41:20). In his dramatic poem *Judas Maccabaeus,* Henry Wadsworth Longfellow describes a conversation between the Hellenistic high priest Jason and Antiochus.

Antiochus says, "Now tell me, Jason, what these Hebrews call me when they converse together at their games."

Jason replies, "Antiochus Epiphanes, my Lord; Antiochus the Illustrious."

"Oh, not that" replies Antiochus, "that is the public cry; I mean the name they give me when they talk among themselves, and think that no one listens; what is that?"

Jason answers, "Antiochus Epimanes, my Lord."

The king says, "Antiochus the Mad! Ay, that is it. And who hath said it? Who hath set in motion that sorry jest?"

Longfellow develops his poem as Jason places the blame for this "sorry jest" upon the seven brothers whose martyrdom is described in 2 Maccabees 7. However, the madness of Antiochus IV is not fiction, but fact. Antiochus IV died at Tabae in Persis in the winter of 164-163 B.C. The Encyclopaedia Britannica says that he died of consumption. There are two accounts of his death in 2 Maccabees. One (1:13-17) says that he was stoned to death, the other (9:7) says that he fell from a chariot. However, Polybius says that he was super-

naturally deranged. Almost everyone is impressed with the
fact that in Antiochus IV there was a vein of madness that ran
the course of his life.

Though Antiochus' delusive belief that he was god can be
attributed to madness, the Antichrist's insistence that he is
god can be attributed only to Satan (cf. Rev 13:4). In fact,
the Antichrist will be the second person of a diabolical trinity that emerges during the great tribulation. In this trinity
of evil, Satan is to be compared to God the Father, the Antichrist is analogous to Jesus the Son, and the false prophet is
the counterpart of the Holy Spirit. As god, the Antichrist
will demand the worship of all the earth dwellers. He will
tolerate no rival deities. In the second century B.C. many in
Israel yielded to the assumed divine authority of Antiochus
IV. "Yea, many also of the Israelites consented to his religion,
and sacrificed unto idols, and profaned the sabbath" (1 Mac
1:43). Just so, many in Israel will also worship the Antichrist.
Zechariah presents this fact under the figure of one whom the
prophet calls "a foolish shepherd" and a "worthless shepherd"
(11:15, 17). Israel rejected the one whom the Lord sent to
shepherd them and sold him for thirty pieces of silver (Zec
11:13). In his place they chose the false shepherd "who will
not visit those that are cut off, neither will seek those that are
scattered, nor heal that which is broken, nor feed that which is
sound; but he will eat the flesh of the fat sheep, and will tear
their hoofs in pieces" (Zec 11:16).

It is interesting how authoritative the word of the Antichrist is. His speech is his most potent characteristic. "And
there was given to him a mouth speaking great things and
blasphemies" (Rev 13:5). Daniel also pictures him as having
"a mouth speaking great things" (7:8; cf. Dan 7:20, 25;
11:36). When Mattathias of Modin summoned the people
to rebellion against Antiochus IV and to fight in the defense
of their ancient faith, it was to the Law that he made his
appeal. "Whosoever is zealous for the Torah, and maintain-

eth the covenant, let him come forth after me," cried the old priest (1 Mac 2:27). Because the Law was the outward symbol of the faith of the Jews, it was therefore to be the object of Antiochus' fury. It is for this reason that his soldiers "rent in pieces the books of the law which they found, [and] burnt them with fire. And whosoever was found with any book of the testament, or if any consented to the law, the king's commandment was, that they should put him to death" (1 Mac 1:56-57). But just as the word of the Lord was suppressed in ancient Israel, so it will be suppressed and replaced by the word of the Antichrist in tribulation Israel. It is the Antichrist's inspiring word that will be heard and that will carry authority for the unbelieving Jew in that day, just as ancient Israel heard and revered the divine word of the Torah.

Hence the Antichrist has cast his shadow before him upon the stage of history in the person of Antiochus IV Epiphanes. But as horrible as were the persecutions, and as terrible as was the blasphemy of Antiochus IV; he was only a type and a shadow of the Antichrist. Israel is yet to experience her worst persecution during the great tribulation period, and is yet to experience the most blasphemous attempts of all time to force the Jews to abandon their ancient faith and worship the image of the beast.

4

Similarities Between Antiochus IV and the Antichrist

DANIEL WAS CARRIED CAPTIVE into Babylon probably in 605 B.C. Other waves of captives were to follow. Ezekiel, for example, came to Babylon in 597 B.C. as a result of a second invasion of Judah by Nebuchadnezzar. Therefore, Ezekiel and Daniel were contemporaries in their prophetic ministry. However, we must realize that many scholars do not agree that the prophecy of Daniel is a product of the exile. The first person to challenge this view was the Neoplatonist Porphyry who, writing in the third century A.D., said that Daniel was written in the Maccabean period, about 167 B.C. Many modern scholars believe that an unknown writer in the second century B.C. recorded past and present historical events under the guise of apocalyptic prophecy and attributed it to the sixth century Daniel, and that there was no fraudulent attempt on the part of the writer. Rather, this was merely a literary method employed by the writer to encourage the Jews of his day who were suffering persecution under Antiochus IV. (In like manner, many believe that the book of the Revelation is an apocalyptic encouragement written for Christians of the first century who were suffering under the persecution of the Roman emperor Domitian.)

The thesis of this hypothetical writer who calls himself Daniel, say these scholars, is to show that just as the Babylonian world tried to blot out any evidence of Yahweh, the God of Israel, but failed, so Antiochus IV will fail. Note the victory of the young men who refused the king's meat, and the victory of the three Hebrews in the fiery furnace, and the victory of Daniel in the lion's den. All show the power of God to keep his own in the face of persecution. Those who take this position also interpret the fourth division of Nebuchadnezzar's image (the legs and feet partly of iron and partly of clay) as the Seleucid kingdom under Antiochus IV, instead of the Roman empire. In this way the writer of Daniel is supposed to be encouraging his contemporary readers to believe that as the stone cut without hands destroyed the fourth empire, so God will destroy the empire of the Seleucid Antiochus IV. The reason why many believe that the veiled reference in the fourth part of the image is to Antiochus IV is because all previous empires were actually named in Daniel—Babylon, Medo-Persia, and Greece (Dan 2:37; 8:20-21)—but not the fourth, the Seleucid empire. The writer would naturally leave it unnamed if the Seleucids were currently in power. His readers would know to whom the fourth empire referred, but not the authorities, if they should happen to read the scroll.

However, with no a priori assumptions about the limitations of the prophetic Word, we proceed on the premise that Daniel is prophesying in the sixth century B.C. and that writing during the exile he records the most amazing and accurate record of future events, both near and far, that can be found in all the Bible. Daniel sees the rise of the Medo-Persian empire which actually occurred before he died. But if we pick an arbitrary point of reference during the lifetime of Daniel, say 550 B.C., when the prophet saw the rise of Alexander the Great and his conquest of the Persian empire, he was looking 216 years into the future. Daniel also saw the death of Alexander and the subsequent division of his empire, 250 years distant. The career of Antiochus IV, which Daniel sees in such great detail, was 375 years in the future. The world dominion of the Roman empire was more than 500 years in the future when Daniel wrote. The revived Roman empire, along with the rise of the Antichrist, which Daniel also saw, is already separated by a distance of more than 2500 years from Daniel's time.

Assuming that the book of Daniel was written for a greater prophetic purpose than that of encouragement for the suffering Jews during the Maccabean period, we have warrant for interpreting the career of Antiochus IV Epiphanes as typical and prophetic of the Antichrist.

The First Similarity

The first of these similarities which we note is that both Antiochus IV Epiphanes and the Antichrist try to impose an alien system of belief and conduct upon the Jews. For just as Antiochus IV attempted to impose Hellenism upon the Jews of his day, the Antichrist will try to impose the cult of the beast upon the Jews of his day.

Alexander the Great (356-323 B.C.), in his conquest of the Near Eastern world, had set the stage for the final assault of Antiochus IV and his attempt to force Hellenistic culture upon the Jews. Greek culture had been known in western Asia before the time of Alexander, for archaeologists have now found indications that Greek mercenaries were trading in Egypt, Syria, and Palestine by the seventh century B.C. However, it was the policy of the great conqueror to attempt to mold Greeks and Asiatics as one in a common culture. Alexander not only invaded a country with swords and spears, but with something even more potent—a body of ideas. These ideas represent the mental activity of the people who inhabited the southern part of the Balkan peninsula. They called themselves Hellenes. Thus, we call this body of ideas which gave direction to the Greek way of life, Hellenistic culture. Their way of thinking about the world was unique. It had been growing in the Greek city-states for the last few centuries before Alexander. It expressed itself in the language, the literature, and the political structure of the Greeks. So profound was Hellenism that the rational, as well as the political philosophy of mankind dates itself either before or after the advent of Hellenism. Apart from Jesus Christ, Hellenism is the greatest influence that Western civilization has ever experienced. We are still working out the germinal ideas and ideals that Hellenism planted in the western world two millennia and more ago.

Alexander's strategy for Hellenizing his empire was twofold. First, he established Macedonian colonies and new Greek cities all over his empire, populating them with Greek soldiers. This caused the spread of *koine*, or common Greek, as the lingua franca of the empire and in turn facilitated the spread of Hellenism. Second, Alexander encouraged mixed marriages between Greeks and Asiatics. By this strategy, Alexander had planned a worldwide empire based upon a common language, custom, and culture. Though the realization of this dream began in his lifetime, it was Alexander's successors who actually saw Greek culture conquer the world. In Coele-Syria* it was Antiochus IV Epiphanes who attempted to finalize the process, for he too was impressed with the fact that his empire could not stand against a rising Roman power unless it was unified. It was Hellenism that could produce this unity.

Though Greek culture and traditional Judaism did not

---

*Coele-Syria is a Greek name which means "hollow Syria." It was given to that area which lay between the Lebanon and Anti-Lebanon Mountains. However, it was also used to cover the entire territory of the Seleucids which extended from Egypt in the south to the Euphrates in the east. Many names are applied to the Holy Land at different periods of Jewish history. The land was Canaan before the Hebrew conquest. Then it became Israel. After the death of Solomon it became Samaria in the north and Judah in the south. After the exile the name Judah remained. During the Greek period it was also known as Coele-Syria. When the Romans conquered the country it became Judea. After the revolt of Bar Kokhba the Romans called it Palestine (after the Philistines) in contempt for the Jews. Today the name of the new Jewish state is Israel.

clash head-on until the reign of Antiochus IV Epiphanes, its
wiles were influencing the youth in Judah in the years prior
to his reign. In the early part of the second century B.C.
Judah was an island in the midst of a sea of Hellenism. To
the southwest lay Egypt, a most powerful advocate of the
Greek way of life. Due south was Idumea whose painted
tombs even today show ample evidence of Greek cultural influence. North of Judah was Samaria with a garrison of Macedonian troops, and on the west Greek cities dotted the sea-
coast from Philistia to Phoenicia. In Jerusalem itself the
Greek way of life pressed its influence, especially upon the
young. Circumcision was a source of great embarrassment to
Jewish youths who engaged naked in athletic events. Some
even had themselves surgically uncircumcised to avoid derision. Games, horse races, and the theatre were popular with
Jewish youths, who even dressed like the Greeks.

The gymnasium was as much a part of the essence of the
Greek state as were the political assemblies. It was here that
the fundamental tendency of the Greek mind was expressed—
its striving for beauty of form. The gymnasium influenced
the Greek youth as he grew to manhood also because it was
the social center where the youth found companionship and
inspiration to follow the cultural patterns of the Hellenistic
system. Styles of dress were also set there, expressed in the
broad brim hat, the *chlamys* draped about the shoulders, and
the high-laced boots. Many Jewish youths were seen walking
the streets of Jerusalem dressed in this way, during the reign
of Antiochus IV.

Next after the gymnasium, the stadium and the hippodrome were the outward signs of Greek culture. Athletic
games and horse races were held here. Entertainment of a
higher sort found expression in the drama. A theatre hol-
lowed out of a hillside was the place where the masterpieces
of the Athenian dramatists were produced—the plays of Soph-
ocles, Euripides, and Aeschylus, for example—which were

seen then and are still being produced today. At an even higher level than that of the gymnasium, the hippodrome, or the theatre, a more enduring part of Hellenism, cast its spell over the individual. This was the influence of the Greek philosopher, the Greek artist, and the Greek man of letters.

However, this pagan philosophy of life which Alexander had introduced in the East and which Antiochus IV now attempted to force upon the Jews was a real threat to the spiritual values by which the Jews for centuries had determined their own way of life. Around 180 B.C., Joshua ben Sira wrote *Ecclesiasticus* in order to instill in the youth of his day, who were being threatened by Hellenism, the fear of the Lord which he believed was essential to the survival of Hebrew wisdom. His book is a part of the *Apocrypha*.

Even before the accession of Antiochus IV to the Seleucid throne, undercurrents of opposition to Hellenism were being felt in Syria-dominated Judah. "The pious ones" (Hasidim), with their passionate zeal for the law, were dedicated to the defense of the historic faith of the Jewish people. A conflict was inevitable between the Jewish aristocrats who were protagonists of Hellenism, and these champions of the law, for this new culture not only affected the youth in Judea, but influenced the aristocracy in Jerusalem to espouse the Greek way of life in order to retain their wealth, power, and prestige. The full force of Hasidic opposition was felt during the Maccabean revolt, when the policy of religious toleration exercised by the Ptolemies of Egypt, and the earlier Seleucid rulers, was reversed in an attempt to stamp out Judaism. Then the conflict became more than ideological—the Greek way of life versus the Hebrew way of life—it became a life-and-death struggle.

Though many Jews struggled against it, we must not misunderstand its otherwise universal appeal. With the exception of the resistance that Antiochus IV found among some of the Jews, "all the heathen [nations] agreed according to the word of the king" (1 Mac 1:42). There is no trace of opposition to Hellenism generally among the Asiatics. Antiochus did not have to force this way of life upon the vast majority of his people in Coele-Syria. In fact, its appeal was so dynamic that envoys from various communities were seen about the court petitioning that they might be allowed, through the king's authority, to set up a gymnasium, and form a body of *epheboi*, and to register the inhabitants of their city as Antiochenes (cf. 2 Mac 4:9). Only the Jews resisted and therefore only the Jews had to be forced to yield to this way of life. But why this isolated pocket of resistance in Judah to a Hellenism which would weld together the empire of Antiochus IV? It was due solely to the Jews' religion. To Antiochus, then, the answer was simple: stamp out the Jews' religion and replace it with Greek religion. It had been done elsewhere. Do it to the Jews. This seemed simple enough. Thus Antiochus started upon his course of removing all traces of Judaism. It is this same Judaism that will become a similar barrier to the unity of the empire of the Antichrist. Therefore, the Antichrist will also attempt to do in the tribulation what Antiochus IV attempted to do in the past.

The first step Antiochus IV took was to bring a strong military contingent to occupy Jerusalem. Menelaus, the Hellenistic high priest, probably directed Apollonius and his Mysian mercenaries in the massacre of all known opposition. A new fortress of great strength was built upon Mount Zion and the city was secured. Then followed the attempt to extinguish Jewish religion. The temple services were halted. An altar to Zeus was placed in the sanctuary on which swine were offered. The high priest, Menelaus, took part in the institution of these services. Other pagan rites were introduced such as the monthly observance of the king's birthday, and the Dionysiac festival in which the inhabitants of Jerusalem went in procession through the streets with their heads crowned with ivy. Sacred prostitution may also have been introduced.

However, to purge the city was much easier than to subdue the countryside, for it was in the little country village of Modin that the revolt began which would finally defeat the Hellenizing attempts of Antiochus IV.

Now the similarity is apparent. Just as Antiochus IV attempted to impose an alien way of life, Hellenism, upon the Jews, using force and threat of death, so will the Antichrist attempt to force the cult of the beast upon the Jews during the great tribulation period. And just as in the days of Antiochus, so it will be during the great tribulation period, that many Jews will reject their religious heritage and will follow the cult of the beast. Others will not, however, and will suffer the same fate as Eleazar and the seven brothers (2 Mac 6:18—7:42) ; for the Antichrist, as Daniel 7:21 states, made "war with the saints, and prevailed against them."

Here is Daniel's picture of the attempts of the Antichrist to force an alien way of life upon tribulation Israel. "And he shall speak words against the Most High, and shall wear out the saints of the Most High; and he shall think to change the times and the law; and they shall be given into his hand until a time and times and half a time [three and one-half years]" (Dan 7:25). The Antichrist will disregard those fundamental arrangements of life that time has shown to be right, and will substitute in their place things that are alien. This has been done before. For example, during the French Revolution a ten-day workweek was imposed upon society. It did not work, for apart from the revelation of God, experience has demonstrated that a six-day workweek, followed by a day of rest, is fundamental to the very nature of man. It is this sort of time-proven balance that the Antichrist will attempt to upset and replace with his own designs upon religion and society. Though he will attempt to do this, he will no more succeeed than Antiochus IV did in his attempt to impose an alien way of life upon the Jews. Daniel says that he will "think" to change the times and the laws. The verb means "intend." He will wear out the saints of God with these intentions, but they are destined to failure. Daniel gives the Antichrist three and one-half years to strive for this goal before judgment sets in against him (Dan 7:25b-26).

THE SECOND SIMILARITY

The second similarity between Antiochus IV Epiphanes and the Antichrist is that each has a religious leader who aids in his attempt to impose an alien way of life upon the Jews. The prototype of the false prophet, the religious leader who aids the Antichrist, is the high priest Menelaus, who aided Antiochus IV in his Hellenizing program.

In 1896 two incomplete copies of a document which is now called the Damascus Document or the Zadokite Document, and which dated from the Middle Ages, were found in an old Cairo synagogue. Parts of this same document were also discovered among the Dead Sea Scrolls. It speaks of an age of wrath which was to fall upon the Jews 390 years following the fall of Jerusalem in 587 B.C. The year of wrath would then be 196 B.C. To this date may be added another twenty years in which we are told that the remnant of Israel was "like blind men groping for the way." The prediction reads like this:

> So, in the Era of Anger, the era of the three hundred and ninety years, when He delivered them into the hand of Nebuchadnezzar, king of Babylon, He took care of them and brought to blossom alike out of the priesthood and out of the laity that root which had been planted of old, allowing it once more to possess the land and to grow fat in the richness of its soil. Then they realized their iniquity and knew that they had been at fault. For twenty years, however, they remained like blind men groping their way, until at last God took note of their deeds, how that were seeking Him sincerely, and He raised up for them one who would teach the Law correctly [this term is usually rendered,

"Teacher of Righteousness"] to guide them in the way of His heart and to demonstrate to future ages what He does to a generation that incurs His anger, that is, to the congregation of those that betray Him and turn aside from His way.[1]

The time noted, 390 years plus twenty years more, would bring us to the approximate time when Antiochus IV came to the throne of Coele-Syria, when God is to raise up a leader, a religious figure who is called the "teacher of righteousness." Some scholars believe that the "teacher of righteousness" is Onias III, the last of the Zadokite line of high priests, who was murdered at the instigation of Menelaus, in 171 B.C. However, two more figures appear in this document. One is called the "man of scorn," and the other is called the "wicked priest." Many scholars believe that the "man of scorn" who appears in this tract as an enemy of the Essenes, is Antiochus IV; and that the "wicked priest" is Menelaus. But whatever the identity of these figures might be, it is interesting that the concept of an evil ruler who has a religious leader to further his cause, is found here in the Dead Sea Scrolls. Just as Henry VIII had an Archbishop Cranmer to further his nefarious schemes, we know that this idea also found fulfillment in the reign of Antiochus IV who had his Menelaus. It will also be repeated during the reign of the Antichrist in the great tribulation.

When Antiochus IV came to the throne of Syria, Onias III, the legitimate high priest, was in Antioch. In his absence from Jerusalem, Antiochus appointed the brother of Onias to the high priestly office. This brother, Jason, promised to pay a higher tribute to Syria than Onias had paid. This was reason enough for Antiochus to replace Onias III with Jason. The new high priest threw himself into the Hellenizing movement. His involvement is demonstrated by his change of name. His real name was the Hebrew Joshua. But he had it changed to the Greek Jason. When he became high priest in

175-174 B.C., he had a gymnasium built in Jerusalem, soon to be thronged by priests following the Hellenistic ideals of body, culture and beauty.

However, the real type of the false prophet does not seem to be Jason but his successor, Menelaus. Jason was at least a member of the priestly family, but his successor was not of the seed of Aaron. Menelaus was a Benjamite. When Menelaus deposed Jason he also had the legitimate high priest, Onias III, killed. (It is interesting to note the schizoid tendency of Antiochus IV, who, when he heard the news of the death of Onias III, wept bitterly,[2] though he had killed thousands of Jews himself.) Menelaus had already desecrated the temple when, on one occasion, he led Antiochus IV into the Holy Place and allowed him to remove some of the golden vessels. Menelaus also pursued Hellenization of the Jews with a zeal even unknown to Jason. However, he was not merely interested in imposing this alien culture upon the Jews, but he was determined to bring all Jews into allegiance to Antiochus IV, who thought himself to be god, and to Greek culture as their only way of life. Professor Zeitlin says, "The Temple itself was consecrated to Zeus Olympus. Menelaus was no longer the high priest of the Temple of the God of Israel, but a priest subordinate to Antiochus Epiphanes."[3]

The Antichrist also has his Menelaus. He is the beast out of the earth who appears in Revelation 13:11-18.

> And I saw another beast coming up out of the earth; and he had two horns like unto a lamb, and he spake as a dragon. And he exerciseth all the authority of the first beast in his sight. And he maketh the earth and them that dwell therein to worship the first beast, whose death-stroke was healed. And he doeth great signs, that he should even make fire to come down out of heaven upon the earth in the sight of men. And he deceiveth them that dwell on the earth by reason of the signs which it was given him to do in the sight of the beast; saying to them that dwell on the earth, that they

should make an image to the beast who hath the stroke of the sword and lived. And it was given unto him to give breath to it, even to the image of the beast, that the image of the beast should both speak, and cause that as many as should not worship the image of the beast should be killed. And he causeth all, the small and the great, and the rich and the poor, and the free and the bond, that there be given them a mark on their right hand, or upon their forehead; and that no man should be able to buy or to sell, save he that hath the mark, even the name of the beast or the number of his name. Here is wisdom. He that hath understanding, let him count the number of the beast; for it is the number of a man: and his number is Six hundred and sixty and six.

Jesus announced in his prophetic discourse on the Mount of Olives, recorded in Matthew 24, that there would appear false prophets as well as false Messiahs. It is important to note that the idea of a false Christ and a false prophet appear together only in Matthew 24:24; though false Christs are mentioned in 24:5; and false prophets are mentioned in 24:11. Why? In his prophetic discourse Jesus deals with four successive eras of Israel's future history: a time of *travail* (24:4-8); a time of *tribulation* (24:9-14); a time of *great tribulation* (24:15-28); and a time *after the tribulation* (24:29-34). These four periods mark the time of suffering that Israel is to endure before the Jews come to know the Lord Jesus Christ as their true Messiah when he comes a second time to earth.†
The time of travail will be marked, among other things, by the appearance of false Christs (24:5). However, note that false prophets are not mentioned here. This is the time of Israel's suffering just before the fall of Jerusalem in A.D. 70. Many false Christs appeared in that forty-year span after the death of Jesus and before Titus came to destroy the city. Four of them are mentioned in the book of Acts. The age of the

†For a further development of this subject, see the author's exposition of Matthew 24 in *Jesus' Prophetic Sermon,* (Chicago: Moody, 1972).

church intervenes between verses 8 and 9 of Matthew 24. As is characteristic of the Old Testament prophets, Jesus takes no note of the age of the church here, for his subject is the nation Israel.

Next Jesus mentions an era in which false prophets—but apparently no false Christs—will appear (24:9-14). This is the time of tribulation which will occur during the first three and one-half years of Daniel's seventieth week and just after the rapture. Though the nation Israel will be back in the land in unbelief during this period, and will be at peace under the protective covenant of the head of the ten-nation confederation, some believing Jews will be greatly persecuted during this time.

During this first half of the tribulation period, false prophets will appear—but apparently not false Christs. However, during the last part of Daniel's seventieth week, which is the great tribulation period, both false Christs and false prophets, in combination, will appear (24:15-29). Notice that for the first time Jesus speaks of both together. "For there shall arise false Christs, *and* false prophets, and shall show great signs and wonders; so as to lead astray, if possible, even the elect" (Mt 24:24). The reference is to the Antichrist, the beast out of the sea (Rev 13:1-10); and the false prophet, the beast out of the land (Rev 13:11-18). Though the Antichrist will have already appeared on the world scene as the head of the revived Roman empire, and as Israel's benefactor during the first half of the tribulation period, he now will turn upon Israel to persecute all the Jews into submission to himself as god. At this time, during the great tribulation, the false prophet will come upon the stage of history also to enforce the edicts of the Antichrist, and to direct worship to his person, just as Menelaus did for Antiochus IV Epiphanes long ago.

Many expositors do not see two different persons in the two beasts of Revelation 13. Dr. Ironside, for example, suggests that the first beast is the world system of evil, and the second is the personality of evil. Dr. DeHaan says that both beasts are descriptions of a single person—the Antichrist. However, since the false prophet is mentioned three times by name in the book of Revelation (16:13; 19:20; 20:10), each time in association with the Antichrist, there is ample warrant to identify the beast of Revelation 13:11ff as a distinct person, the false prophet. John says, "And I saw another beast coming up out of the earth" (Rev 13:11). The word translated "another" in verse 11 is the same word that Jesus used in John 14:16 when he spoke of the coming of the Holy Spirit. The word means not "another of a different kind," but "another of the same kind." Therefore, just as the Holy Spirit is a distinct Person, but the same as Jesus in essence, so the false prophet is a distinct person, but of the same essence as the Antichrist, for both are motivated by Satan who has completely taken over their personalities. This idea is substantiated by the fact that both emerge from below onto the stage of human history. The Antichrist is out of the sea (Rev 13:1), while the false prophet comes up out of the earth (Rev 13:11). While it is true that the sea may stand for the gentile nations, and the land for the nation Israel, the symbol also conveys the idea that their origin is the same, a sublevel of humanity. This does not mean that the Antichrist will not be human, for he will be. But just as Jesus was human yet fully controlled by God, so the Antichrist will be a human yet fully controlled by Satan. Just as the origin of the divine trinity is from above (Jn 3:31), so the origin of the diabolical trinity is from beneath (cf. Rev 11:7).

As noted before, the false prophet is to the Antichrist what the Holy Spirit is to Jesus Christ. The contrasts between the two, namely, between the false prophet and the Holy Spirit, are too numerous not to be conclusive. For example, the Holy Spirit is the third person of the divine trinity (Mt 28:19), while the false prophet is the third person of a diabolical trinity (Rev 16:13). The Holy Spirit is to be seen as directly opposite to the "unclean" spirit (Rev 16:13). The Holy Spirit anointed Jesus at the beginning of his three-and-one-half-years' ministry (Lk 3:22); just so, the false prophet joins himself to the Antichrist at the beginning of the last three and one-half years of his career. The advent of the Holy Spirit was accompanied by fire; so fire authenticates the coming of the false prophet (Rev 13:13). The Holy Spirit is the giver of life (Jn 6:63); the false prophet is the giver of death (Rev 13:15). The Holy Spirit seals (Eph 4:30); the false prophet marks (Rev 13:16). The Holy Spirit empowered the Lord Jesus Christ (Acts 10:38); the false prophet will empower the Antichrist (Rev 13:14). The Holy Spirit does not speak of himself, but only in connection with Christ (Jn 16:13f); just so, the false prophet speaks, not of himself, but in connection with the Antichrist (Rev 13:12). The Holy Spirit leads to the worship of Jesus (Jn 4:23f; Phil 3:3); so the false prophet leads to the worship of the Antichrist (Rev 13:12). The Holy Spirit is the Spirit of truth (Jn 16:13); the false prophet is the spirit of deception (Rev 13:14). The ultimate penalty for the rejection of the Holy Spirit is spiritual death, so the ultimate penalty for rejecting the witness of the false prophet is physical death (Rev 13:15).

THE THIRD SIMILARITY

The third similarity between Antiochus IV Epiphanes and the Antichrist is to be found in their relationship to the Roman empire. There is no doubt that Antiochus IV had healthy respect for Roman society and for Roman political life, and especially for Roman military power. This is the only way to explain his action when he immediately backed away from the conquest of Egypt at the word of the Roman Senate. There is no doubt that Roman policy and power greatly influenced Antiochus—as it will greatly influence the Antichrist in the future.

The battle of Magnesia, 190 B.C., brought an end to the hostilities between Rome and Antiochus III the Great, father of Antiochus IV Epiphanes. The terms of peace were severe. Antiochus III was to give up his possessions in Europe and in Asia Minor, except Cilicia. He was to pay Roman war expenses, estimated at fifteen thousand talents of silver. Hannibal of Carthage, whom Antiochus III had befriended, was to be surrendered to Rome. In addition. as token of his willingness to abide by the terms of the treaty, the Syrian king was to hand over twenty hostages, among whom was Antiochus IV, the king's son.

Antiochus IV was in his twenties when he arrived in Rome —having been born around 212 B.C. He went to Rome in the spring of 189 B.C., and spent the next twelve years of his life there. As an imperial political hostage he was given a house provided by public funds. Later Antiochus IV expressed appreciation to the Roman Senate for his cordial treatment while living in Rome (Livy 42. 6.9.). There is no doubt that he was greatly influenced by what he saw and learned there, for at this time Rome was becoming more and more the focus of the political life of much of the Graeco-Roman world. We know that Antiochus IV, when he came to power, copied the Roman army's organization, discipline, and practice. He was greatly impressed with the Roman democratic procedures also. This is indicated by the fact he would try to impress the people of Antioch in a very dramatic and sensational way with these political theories. (cf. Polybius 26; Livy 61. 20.1). It is a matter of history that Antiochus IV would put on a Roman toga and go among the citizens of Antioch asking them to vote for him for various offices in city government. And having been duly elected, he would sit and listen and make disposition of disputes among the citizens. This has been interpreted by many as an indication of his erratic behavior and evidence of his madness. However, Markholm believes that this indicates his interest in teaching Roman democratic procedures to his own subjects.

It was Rome also that impressed him with a strong sense of the need of political unity. When he came to the throne he found his kingdom in disunity. This he determined to remedy. The means that he used were not Roman but Greek, for he believed that Hellenism would be the chief unifying factor. However, the awareness that only a strong unified empire could withstand pressures from both within and without, and that that unity, though cultural in essence was to be imposed by imperial military power, was Roman theory. Therefore, much in the later life of Antiochus IV indicates that while spending his formative years in Rome, he had been duly impressed with the republic which was rapidly becoming an imperial power.

The Antichrist will be greatly influenced by the Roman empire in his day, for he will reign as a new Roman caesar, the leader of the revived Roman empire which will arise around the Mediterranean basin, within the geographical confines of the ancient Roman empire.

To the Romans the world was a circle of land—*orbis terrarum*—bounding the Mediterranean Sea. The Romans called it "Our Sea"—*Mare Nostrum*. The name may have been arrogant, but it was accurate, for from the time of Claudius every inch of the Mediterranean coastline was in Roman hands. From north to south the ancient Roman empire stretched for two thousand miles. From west to east its extent was nearly three thousand miles. Rome's frontiers ran for ten thousand miles. In modern terms it encompassed Spain, Portugal, France, the Lowlands, Britain, Switzerland, South Germany, Austria, Hungary, the whole of the Balkans, Romania, Turkey, Syria, Lebanon, Jordan, Israel, Egypt, and North Africa. The early empire of the Antichrist will cover much, if not all, of this same area, for it will be a revival of the ancient Roman empire.

Publius Cornelius Scipio (185-129 B.C.), grandson of the great Roman general Scipio Africanus, was given the task by the Roman Senate of wiping the city of Carthage off the map. As the city fell, the commander watched the destruction impassively. But then he turned to his friend, the Greek Polybius, and said, "It is all so beautiful, and yet I have a foreboding that the same fate may fall on my own country." And so it did a few centuries later. However, whereas Carthage was plowed and sown with salt, and a curse pronounced over it, never again to rise, fallen Rome will rise again. Nothing of Punic culture survived. The Romans utterly destroyed the Carthaginian libraries. Little survives of their temples, their palaces, or their marble statues. A few inscriptions, some ostraca, and what references to Carthaginian customs survive in Greek histories, are all that archaeologists have to work with in order to learn what they can about this ancient foe of Rome. But how different the fate of the Roman empire. Fallen, it will arise again in the last days under the Antichrist, the final Roman Caesar of Revelation 17:10-11.

The capacity of Rome to revive has already been noted in history. The ancient Roman empire is supposed to have died long ago. Its western division was lost to invading hordes from Europe. This happened in the fifth century A.D. The eastern division existed longer, but it too passed from time into the pages of history. However, the spirit of Rome, dead for a thousand years, arose again during the Renaissance. As the Middle Ages drew to a close, the ideas that were Roman lived again in the new intellectual and cultural movement that swept across central and southern Europe, and was essentially a rebirth of classical ideas. The influence of Rome was felt again everywhere in Europe. Anything this dynamic can rise once more. And that is exactly what the prophetic Scriptures indicate. The Roman empire will revive again in a ten-nation confederation during the tribulation period, after the translation of the church.

The Antichrist will arise out of a federation of ten nations which will be confined geographically within the bounds of the ancient Roman empire. The Emperor Trajan, whom the Middle Ages regarded as the perfect emperor, reigned from A.D. 98 until A.D. 117 and pushed the geographical limits of the Roman empire to its farthest extent. Only the savage tribes of northern Europe and of central Africa, along with the mysterious nations of the Orient, lived beyond the borders of the empire. The *Pax Romana*, the Roman peace, extended from northern Britain, where Hadrian's wall was to mark the border, to the vast Sahara Desert. It ran from the borders of Portugal to the east as far as Persia, where Trajan looked upon the Gulf, as Alexander the Great had done centuries before. For two hundred years after the time of Augustus, people within the pale of this circle were to live out their lives sheltered by the protective power of Imperial Rome.

The revived Roman empire of the tribulation period will again be located within this ancient circle. But what gives warrant for such an assumption? Nowhere in Scripture is the term *revived Roman empire* to be found, but the idea is strongly implied. Inference is drawn from the fact that the form of the fourth world empire, which Daniel sees in chapter two and in chapter seven, is in existence at the second coming of Christ.

> And in the days of those kings shall the God of heaven set up a kingdom which shall never be destroyed, nor shall the sovereignty thereof be left to another people; but it shall break in pieces and consume all these kingdoms, and it shall stand for ever. Forasmuch as thou sawest that a stone was cut out of the mountain without hands, and that it brake in pieces the iron, the brass, the clay, the silver, and the gold; the great God hath made known to the king what shall come to pass hereafter: and the dream is certain, and the interpretation thereof sure (Dan 2:44-45).

After this I saw in the night-visions, and, behold, a fourth beast, terrible and powerful, and strong exceedingly; and it had great iron teeth; it devoured and brake in pieces, and stamped the residue with its feet: and it was diverse from all the beasts that were before it; and it had ten horns. I considered the horns, and, behold, there came up among them another horn, a little one, before which three of the first horns were plucked up by the roots: and, behold, in this horn were eyes like the eyes of a man, and a mouth speaking great things. I beheld till thrones were placed, and one that was ancient of days did sit: his raiment was white as snow, and the hair of his head like pure wool; his throne was fiery flames, and the wheels thereof burning fire. A fiery stream issued and came forth from before him: thousands of thousands ministered unto him, and ten thousand times ten thousand stood before him: the judgment was set, and the books were opened, (Dan 7:7-10).

In both of these visions there are four great world empires that pass before Daniel. We have noted that they are Babylon, Medo-Persia, Greece, and then Rome. However, it is the last one that is intact when the second coming of Christ occurs. This can only mean one of two things. Possibly the spirit of Rome lives on in history. It was revived during the Renaissance and will persist until the second coming of Christ. Or it means that the ancient Roman empire itself will be revived in the last days and is to be on the world scene at the second coming of Christ. We take the latter view.

It is important to note that the age of the church intervenes between the first and second coming of Christ. This Paul calls a "mystery," for the existence of the church is not seen by the Old Testament prophets (Eph 3:1-6). During the age of the church, God's prophetic time clock has stopped. The church age is the great parenthesis that exists between the sixty-ninth and seventieth week of Daniel's time prophecy in 9:24ff. When God ceased to deal with Israel nationally, in the first century, due to her rejection of the Messiah, Israel was under the dominion of the ancient Roman empire. Two thousand years have already passed while Israel is disbursed among the nations and is exiled in unbelief. However, Israel is being regathered today, and soon, when the church is caught out of the world at the rapture, God will again deal with Israel nationally during the tribulation period. But the interesting fact is that Israel will not only be in the land again—just as the Jews were when God ceased to deal with them nationally, two thousand years ago—but they will be back again under the dominion of the Roman empire, just as they were two thousand years ago when God ceased to deal with them.

A second inference that postulates a revived Roman empire in the last days is that the Antichrist arises out of the Roman empire. But more, he arises out of a ten-nation confederation that constitutes this revived form of the empire. In Daniel 7 the prophet views four successive empires. The first three—Babylon, Medo-Persia, and Greece—are set forth under the figures of a lion, a bear, and a leopard (Dan 7:3-6). The fourth beast, which is unidentified, verse 7, Daniel says is "terrible and powerful, and strong exceedingly; and it had great iron teeth; it devoured and brake in pieces, and stamped the residue with its feet: and it was diverse from all the beasts that were before it." This is the ancient Roman empire. It has been so identified almost universally until the modern critical method set the book of Daniel in the Maccabean period and influenced some modern scholars to identify the fourth beast with Greece, or more precisely, with the Seleucids. However, we take the view that the fourth beast is not only the ancient Roman empire, but that Daniel is also viewing its revived form in the last days. He does not note the age of the church which separates the two expressions of the *ancient* and *revived* Roman empire, for no Old Testament prophet is aware of the mystery of the church age.

This fourth beast has ten horns. The ten horns seem to

characterize the composition of the revived Roman empire, for it is out of them that the Antichrist arises. Therefore, we place the unmentioned age of the church just before the words "and it had ten horns," at the end of Daniel 7:7. Out of the ten horns arises another—which supersedes the preceding ten horns. This speaks of the Antichrist's rise to power from among the ten kings which constitute the ten-nation confederation. The method of his conquest is set forth in Daniel 7:20 as the prophet explains that three horns fell in connection with the rise of the little horn, the Antichrist. Apparently there is some resistance among the various confederated nations. The Antichrist must conquer three of them, and then the rest of them capitulate to his control. The rider upon the four horses in Revelation 6:1-8 depicts this same era, for, though the horses are different, the rider is the same. He is the Antichrist who rises at the beginning of the tribulation period as the head of the revived Roman empire. Later, probably at midtribulation, as a result of the events pictured in Daniel 11:40-43 and in Ezekiel 38 and 39, the Antichrist will become a world dictator. But at the beginning of the tribulation period his rise to power is within the geographical limits of the ancient Roman empire, represented by the ten horns, or ten kings. These he either subdues, in the case of the three (Dan 7:24), or with whom he confederates (Rev 17:12).

The third inference which substantiates the belief that the Roman empire will revive again is the fact that the fourth empire, over which the Antichrist reigns in its final form, continues until the second coming of Christ (cf. Dan 2:44; 7:21-22). Obviously, ancient Rome did not so persist. Hence, there will be a revival of the empire just before the Lord returns.

The Antichrist will appear in the last days to express for the last time that theme which had worked itself out in Roman history from the very first. The theme is the appearance of a dictator-savior who appears in order to reclaim Rome from the threat of complete destruction. The first of those dictator-saviors who appeared in Roman history was Marcus Furius Camillus, while the last one will be the Antichrist.

In the year 390 B.C. the Romans were at their lowest ebb. The city had been ravaged by Gauls who were herdsmen and who had drifted westward from the plains of central Europe and for a century had been pouring down the valley of the Danube into France and Spain. In 390 B.C. the Gauls had met the Roman army eleven miles north of the city. The battle was soon over, and the Romans, having been decisively beaten, fled in confusion. Three days later the Gauls marched into the city, and when they left, Rome was a smoking ruin. Plutarch says that they withdrew only after they received a ransom to do so. Rome all but perished, only to revive again, largely through the efforts of the first dictator-savior, General Marcus Furius Camillus.

In the new American Heritage history, entitled *Ancient Rome,* Robert Payne says, "Camillus belongs to a type that recurs frequently in Roman legend and history. He appears at a time when Rome is given over to anarchy and the edifice is crumbling; he restores order by his commanding presence and the energy of his personality; in alliance with the aristocracy and the military leaders, he presents himself as the saviour of his country; and having stamped Rome with his own image, he spends his last days in a melancholy quarrel with the people. The theme of the dictator as saviour was to be repeated not only under the republic, but during the empire."[4]

The Antichrist will be the last of this series of dictator-saviors who will appear to unite the ten-nation confederation, within the geographical bounds of the ancient Roman empire, into the final and revived form of the Roman empire.

When the Antichrist emerges as a new caesar at the head of

the revived Roman empire, he will face the same problem that Antiochus IV faced. Daniel says that the empire which the Antichrist will head will be like a mixture of iron and clay.

> And whereas thou sawest the feet and toes, part of potters' clay, and part of iron, it shall be a divided kingdom; but there shall be in it of the strength of the iron, forasmuch as thou sawest the iron mixed with miry clay. And as the toes of the feet were part of iron, and part of clay, so the kingdom shall be partly strong, and partly broken. And whereas thou sawest the iron mixed with miry clay, they shall mingle themselves with the seed of men; but they shall not cleave one to another, even as iron doth not mingle with clay (Dan 2:41-43).

It will be an empire as strong as iron, but with the constant potential of falling apart. The Antichrist will have to spend the first part of his reign in welding together his empire—just as Antiochus IV did. And just as Antiochus used the force of ideas embodied in Hellenism to accomplish this unity, the Antichrist will also use the force of ideas to accomplish the unification of the people in his domain. The Hellenistic ideas that Antiochus used had a strong religious element in them. The Antichrist will also use religion to weld together his empire. During the first three and one-half years, the forces of cohesive religion will center in Judaism and in the apostate church. But during the great tribulation period, the religious maelstrom will have the Antichrist himself at its center.

At first the Antichrist will permit the Jews to practice their ancient religion. This seems to be his policy until midtribulation period (cf. Dan 9:27). He will also permit the apostate world church to continue its worship. But this too he will terminate at midtribulation (cf. Rev 17:1ff). When he stops the worship of both Jews and gentiles at midtribulation, he will then divert the religious inclinations of these two groups to himself, just as Antiochus IV tried to stamp out Judaism and divert the worship of the Jews to himself. By the cohesive power of their religious devotion to himself, the Antichrist can hold together his empire of iron and clay as he moves on to worldwide dominion during the great tribulation period. Of course, Antiochus IV never succeeded in unifying his empire through Hellenism because the Jews never completely submitted to it. However, the Antichrist will succeed in his attempts to force the worship of himself upon a large part of the world population because of the seductive power of the false prophet who will accomplish for the Antichrist what Menelaus was not able to accomplish for Antiochus IV (cf. Rev 13:4, 12).

THE FOURTH SIMILARITY

The fourth similarity between Antiochus IV Epiphanes and the Antichrist is that they both suffered opposition from a faithful remnant. Antiochus IV was opposed by a pious remnant called the Hasidim, while the Antichrist will be opposed by the 144,000. It was the faithful remnant in Antiochus' day that kept him from completely conquering the Jews, and it will be the 144,000 who preach the gospel, and who will keep the Antichrist from complete success in his day.

The only reason why Palestinian Judaism did not come to an end during the terrible days of persecution under Antiochus IV was due to this group of people known as the Hasidim. The name means "pious ones." It was the Hasidim who took a firm stand against Hellenism. Their one concern was to put a fence about the Law and to attend to its preservation as one would tend a precious flower bed. Though they joined with Mattathias in open revolt, they left the conflict when it became clear that Judas, Mattathias' son, had national independence, as well as religious independence, in view. The Hasidim's passionate devotion to the Law of God was so intense that they literally kept alive the faith of the fathers during those dark days. The aim of the Hasidim was to imbue the whole nation with their zeal for the Law in order to prepare the people for the coming day of salvation. Theirs was a new movement of repentance, much like that of John the Baptist, and of course much like that of the 144,000 during the tribulation. The writer of 1 Maccabees says of them:

> Then came unto him a company of Assideans [Hasidim], who were mighty men of Israel, even all such as were voluntarily devoted unto the law. Also all they that fled for persecution joined themselves unto them, and were a stay unto them. So they joined forces, and smote sinful men in their anger, and wicked men in their wrath: but the rest fled to the heathen for succour. Then Mattathias and his friends went round about, and pulled down the altars: and what children soever they found within the coast of Israel uncircumcised, those they circumcised valiantly. They pursued also after the proud men, and the work prospered in their hand. So they recovered the law out of the hand of the Gentiles, and out of the hand of the kings, neither suffered they the sinner to triumph (1 Mac 2:42-48).

Many believe that Psalm 79:2 refers to the Hasidim who were slain by Antiochus IV because they would not surrender their faith. "The bodies of thy servants have been given to be meat unto the fowls of heaven, the flesh of thy Hasidim unto the beasts of the earth. They have shed their blood like water around Jerusalem, and there was none to bury them" (translation of The Jewish Publication Society, cf. also I.C.C.). The Hasidim were strict legalists who, if left alone to study and observe the law, did not care whether the nation was independent or a subject people. But the fact is that they were not left alone. When Antiochus IV denied them and all other Jews the right to observe the law, he stirred up a hornet's nest. They then became a strong force of resistance to the Hellenizing program of Antiochus IV. The Hasidim, who later developed into the sect of the Pharisees, kept alive a personal devotion to the law of God when all the institutions of Israel had been swept away in the edicts of Antiochus IV. It was one thing to suppress the institutions of Israel such as the temple worship, circumcision, Sabbath observance, along with copies of the Torah; but quite another thing to crush the spirit of devotion in the Hasidim. This Antiochus IV was never be able to do because of their zeal for their ancient faith.

The spirit of the Hasidim will emerge again at the end of the age during the reign of the Antichrist. However, this time it will not be a zeal for the Torah, but for the gospel. Jesus said, "And this gospel of the kingdom shall be preached in the whole world for a testimony unto all the nations; and then shall the end come" (Mt 24:14). Those who will preach the gospel of the kingdom, in the Hasidic spirit of opposition to the Antichrist will be the 144,000 (Rev 7:1ff). These are Jews who will be converted early in the tribulation period. They will be committed to the gospel of the kingdom just as the rest of unbelieving Israel will be committed to the restored temple services. It is their witness that will keep the Antichrist from gaining complete religious dominion over all mankind, just as the witness of the Hasidim kept Antiochus IV from gaining complete religious dominion in his day.

Since the Antichrist is unable to martyr any of the 144,000 (Rev 14:1), they will preach the gospel of the kingdom during the entire tribulation period. Their message will be that which John the Baptist preached in his day: Repent (Mt 3:2), and behold the Lamb (Jn 1:29). Many will be won to Christ as a result of their testimony during the tribulation period. The Antichrist will martyr many of their converts (Rev 7:14), though he will be unable to touch the 144,000 themselves. It is their witness that will block the complete spiritual dominion of the Antichrist as his time finally runs out and the great tribulation ends.

The Fifth Similarity

A fifth similarity cannot be pressed too far, though it is interesting. Both Antiochus IV Epiphanes and the Antichrist are reported dead, but appear alive again. This does not suggest that Antiochus IV experienced a resurrection, for he was actually not dead when the rumor of his death was circulating. However, the fact that he was reported dead, and then appears alive to reap vengeance upon the Jews is significant, especially since the same thing seems to occur during the career of the Antichrist.

It happened this way. When Antiochus IV invaded Egypt for the second time and was rebuffed by the Roman legate, somehow the rumor spread all over Coele-Syria that Antiochus IV had been killed in Egypt (2 Mac 5:5). Jason, who had been replaced in the office of high priest by Menelaus, accepted the rumor as fact, and attacked the city of Jerusalem and drove Menelaus into the citadel for refuge. Civil war broke out in Jerusalem between the followers of Jason and the followers of Menelaus. Jason did not get enough support, however, to retain control of the city. When news reached Antiochus IV who was marching his army up the coast in retreat from Egypt, he considered the revolt as one against himself and stormed the city. In reprisal, he not only slaughtered thousands of Jews, but accompanied by Menelaus, Antiochus also entered the temple and stripped it of all its treasures. Thus Antiochus IV, reported dead, appeared alive to pour out his wrath upon the Jews.

Three times in Revelation 13 it is said that the beast, who is the Antichrist, had a death wound that was healed: "And I saw one of his heads as though it had been smitten unto death; and his death-stroke was healed: and the whole earth wondered after the beast" (v. 3); "And he maketh the earth and them that dwell therein to worship the first beast, whose death-stroke was healed" (v. 12); "they should make an image to the beast who hath the stroke of the sword and lived" (v. 14). Some have suggested that the death stroke was suffered by the Antichrist at midtribulation period, possibly as a result of the conflict with the enemy from the uttermost parts of the north (Eze 38:6, 15; 39:2). It is from this death stroke that he arises again and assumes his new position as the beast out of the sea. All the world wonders at this course of events, for he who was the head of the revived Roman empire, and who was killed in battle, has returned to life and now becomes the world dictator and fierce persecutor of the Jews.

Other Bible scholars interpret the resurrected beast as a historic figure who, having died in past centuries, has returned to life. The most popular candidates are Antiochus IV Epiphanes, who was the first ruler to persecute the Jews, and Nero, who was the first Roman emperor to persecute the church. Judas is a strong contender also. No conclusion will be drawn at this time about the death stroke suffered by the Antichrist. Later an interpretation will be presented. But for now, it is the fact of the Antichrist's apparent death and resurrection, in contrast to what happened to Antiochus IV, that we are noting.

THE SIXTH SIMILARITY

The last similarity we note is that the Jews were saved from the tyranny of Antiochus IV Epiphanes by the advent of a great deliverer. That great deliverer who came upon the scene in the second century B.C. was Judas Maccabaeus. Just so, the tyranny of the Antichrist will draw to a close when the great Deliverer comes upon the scene of world events, at the close of the tribulation period. This, of course, is the second coming of Christ.

In the apocalyptic book of Enoch, the era which we call the times of the gentiles is presented under the figure of a succession of animals. Israel is a race of white sheep. Her oppressors are presented under the figure of lions, boars, eagles, and other animals. Though God has delivered up his people to the gentiles, they are watched over by a number of angels. These angels, typified as seventy shepherds, guard Israel from the time of the Babylonian exile until the end time of final redemption. These sheep (Israel) give birth to lambs (Hasidim) who attempt to revive Israel. "Behold, lambs were borne by these white sheep and they began to open their eyes and to see, and to cry to the sheep. But the sheep did not cry to them and did not hear what they said to them, but were exceedingly deaf, and their eyes were exceedingly and forcibly blinded" (*Enoch* 90:6-7). "But the ravens [Seleucid Antiochus IV] flew upon those lambs and took one of those lambs [Onias III] and dashed the sheep in pieces and devoured them." Then as the writer watches, he sees a deliverer emerge. "And I saw till a great horn of one of the sheep branched forth, and the eyes were opened, and it cried to the sheep, and the ram saw it and all ran to it. . . . And those ravens fought and battled with it and sought to destroy his horn, but they had no power over it." Professor Charles believes that this work was written during the early days of the Maccabean revolt and that the horned sheep is Judas Maccabaeus, whom the Hasidim saw as a God-given deliverer.[5]

It happened like this. The Hasidim's spirit of resistance to Antiochus IV needed only a leader. This leader soon emerged from the obscure country village of Modin. The emissaries of Antiochus IV had erected pagan altars in every village of Judah (1 Mac 1:51). One day they came to Modin and requested the aged priest Mattathias to offer a sacrifice upon the pagan altar to set a good example for the others. He refused. Another Jew agreed to offer the sacrifice. Mattathias slew him, and then he and his sons fell upon the soldiers of Antiochus IV and slew them. With his five sons he fled to the hills in order to escape the vengeance of the king. Others joined him until a sizeable guerrilla force was able to operate in Judah in opposition to the forces of the Syrian king.

From their mountain strongholds, Mattathias and his followers raided the villages of Judah, killing soldiers and taking venegeance upon Hellenizing Jews. Soon after the revolt began, Mattathias died. Judas, the third son of Mattathias, was chosen as the military leader of the resistance. He was nicknamed *Maccabee* which means "the hammer."

At first Antiochus IV underestimated the force of the resistance. He sent inferior generals against them until one after another the armies of Antiochus IV were beaten back. Faced with another revolt in Parthia, Antiochus IV could not throw the full strength of his army into the Jewish conflict. He chose to lead his forces in Parthia and left Lysias in command to put down the uprising among the Jews. The Maccabean resisters won a decisive battle at Emmaus in which the Syrian army was all but annihilated. This victory not only provided the rebels with much needed supplies, but it also opened the door to Jerusalem. Judas and his army then moved on Jerusalem. Menelaus and his sympathizers fled. The rebels took the city, all except the fortress which was known as the Akra. With much rejoicing, they then moved into the temple area and pulled down all the pagan altars upon which swine had been offered.

The abomination of desolation having been removed, the temple was cleansed and rededicated to the Lord. The date was December, 165 B.C. Beginning with the twenty-fifth day of Kislev, they began the Festival of Lights. Hanukkah to this day recalls the reclamation of the temple by Judas Maccabaeus, who is remembered as Israel's great deliverer. Though the struggle for independence was to continue, never again would Antiochus IV be able to desecrate the temple and murder Jews.

So shall the tyranny of the Antichrist end by the coming of the Deliverer. Paul says, "And so all Israel shall be saved: even as it is written, There shall come out of Zion the Deliverer; He shall turn away ungodliness from Jacob" (Ro

11:26). It is the coming of this Deliverer, the Lord Jesus Christ, which John describes in Revelation:

> And I saw the heaven opened: and behold, a white horse, and he that sat thereon called Faithful and True; and in righteousness he doth judge and make war. And his eyes are a flame of fire, and upon his head are many diadems; and he hath a name written which no one knoweth but he himself. And he is arrayed in a garment sprinkled with blood: and his name is called The Word of God. And the armies which are in heaven followed him upon white horses, clothed in fine linen, white and pure. And out of his mouth proceedeth a sharp sword, that with it he should smite the nations: and he shall rule them with a rod of iron: and he treadeth the winepress of the fierceness of the wrath of God, the Almighty. And he hath on his garment and on his thigh a name written, King of Kings, and Lord of Lords . . . And I saw the beast, and the kings of the earth, and their armies, gathered together to make war against him that sat upon the horse, and against his army. And the beast was taken, and with him the false prophet that wrought the signs of his sight, wherewith he deceived them that had received the mark of the beast and them that worshipped his image: they two were cast alive into the lake of fire that burneth with brimstone (Rev 19:11-16, 19-20).

5

The Spiritual Distinctives of the Antichrist

IT HAS BEEN almost universally assumed that the Antichrist will become to many in Israel a false Messiah. While it is true that he will set himself in the temple and demand worship (2 Th 2:4), it is not at all clear that he poses as Israel's Messiah when he does this. But, just as many have assumed that the Antichrist is to be a persecutor of the church, when there is no warrant for this assumption; so many have assumed that the Antichrist will be accepted by apostate Israel as a false Messiah. There is no real evidence that this is the case either.

This assumption concerning Israel's acceptance of the Antichrist as a false Messiah, is derived from two sources. First, this theory is based upon an interpretation of John 5:43 which assumes an antithesis between Jesus, the true Messiah, and the one who comes in his own name, supposedly the Antichrist, whom Israel will accept. "I am come in my Father's name," said Jesus in this passage, "and ye received me not: if another shall come in his own name, him ye will receive." We have noted that in his great prophetic discourse Jesus warned that false Messiahs and prophets would appear during the course of Israel's future history. False Christs would appear in numbers during the time of Israel's travail (Mt 24:4-8, cf. v. 5); i.e., during the forty years that remained to Israel between the cross and the coming of the Romans who destroyed the city in A.D. 70. Again false prophets appear in plural numbers during the first half of the tribulation period (Mt 24:9-14) ; and once more, both false prophets and false Christs will appear during the great tribulation period (Mt 24:15-28). However, the fact of plurality indicates that no one person is in view. In each era Jesus indicated that there will be a rash of false prophets and false Messiahs. In fact, the greatest rash of them will occur during the great tribulation period, contemporaneous with the revelation of the Antichrist. "Then if any man shall say unto you, Lo, here is the Christ, or, Here; believe it not. For there shall arise false Christs, and false prophets, and shall show great signs and wonders ; so as to lead astray, if possible, even the elect" (Mt 24:23-24). The people of Israel could accept any one of these as Messiah. They have many options which will be offered to them during both the first half of the tribulation, and during the great tribulation period itself.

One of those options will not be the Antichrist. For he will appear first as a benevolent dictator and political benefactor of Israel, and then as the persecutor of Israel—but not as a Messianic deliverer. This is not to say that he will not be worshiped, for he will. He will be worshiped by apostate Jews who long ago gave up their hope of supernatural Messianic redemption and became agnostics like many Reform Jews even today. However, the Antichrist will not be worshiped as Messiah, but as god.

The second reason why many have assumed that the Antichrist will be a false Messiah, and will be accepted as such by many in Israel, is because they have followed Irenaeus in his theory that the Antichrist will be a Jew out of the tribe of Dan. Irenaeus based this conclusion on a reference to the tribe of Dan in Jeremiah 8:16, which says, "The snorting of his horses is heard from Dan: at the sound of the neighing of his strong ones the whole land trembleth; for they are come, and have devoured the land and all that is in it; the city and those that dwell therein."

There is no doubt that Jeremiah predicted a sinister threat to come from the territory of Dan. However, the threat is the Babylonian invasion; and the tribe of Dan is only mentioned because it was originally located on Israel's northern border, which was also the path of the coming invaders in the sixth century when Jeremiah prophesied. In addition, Irenaeus coupled with this passage from the prophet the observation that the tribe of Dan was omitted in the listing of the twelve tribes of Israel in Revelation 7:5-8, inferring that this tribe was left out because Dan produced the Antichrist. However, it should be noted that Ephraim is also left out of the list. Nevertheless, Irenaeus concluded from this evidence that the Antichrist would be a Jew and would originate from the tribe of Dan.

However, to say that the Antichrist will neither be a Jew nor received as Messiah, is not to say that he will have no spiritual distinctives. He will. But the spiritual worship that he will demand is more in the nature of a pagan god than that of a Hebrew Messiah. The same thing was true of Antiochus IV Epiphanes. His dominion in Israel had spiritual overtones. But he did not relate to Israel as a Messianic deliverer. Rather, he came in the guise of a pagan god demanding worship and submission, for he conceived of himself as a part of the Greek Pantheon. The Antichrist will do the same. He will force Israel, along with the rest of mankind, to worship him during the great tribulation period. But he will appeal spiritually to all men in the same way, as a pagan god—just as Antiochus IV did—and not merely to Israel as a Messianic deliverer.

In fact the Messianic deliverer is anticipated *because* of the Antichrist and not in concert with him. In the Old Testament the Messianic hope in Israel is associated with the belief that before the Messiah comes there will be a time of unparalleled oppression, along with a widespread apostasy, and a falling away; all of which finds expression in connection with a sinister figure who will appear upon the stage of history—the Antichrist or Anti-Messiah. So horrible did the common conception of the pre-Messianic sufferings become that some of the Talmudic rabbis even prayed that the Messiah might not appear in their day (*Sanhedrin* 98b). This idea is incorporated in Daniel's use of Antiochus IV Epiphanes as a type of the Antichrist.

In Daniel the theme is fivefold. First, there will come an intense persecution. This will cause many to fall away, as the Hellenizing Jews did. Some, however, like the Hasidim, will remain faithful to Yahweh, the covenant God of Israel. The sinister figure is set forth in the person of the Greek little horn, Antiochus IV. Finally, a great deliverer is anticipated. In the second century B.C. the great deliverer is found in the Hasmonean family; and in particular, in Judas Maccabaeus, the hammer. This same general theme is repeated in the New Testament picture of the Antichrist. As he is presented by Jesus (Mt 24:9ff), by the apostle Paul (2 Th 2:1ff), and finally by John in the book of the Revelation, his career follows the same basic pattern as is presented in the Old Testament. However, in the New Testament many more details are added in the progressive revelation of Scripture. This pattern suggests that the Antichrist will not only be a warrior-king, but that he will also be a spiritual figure who will demand worship as god.

Many, both in Judaism and among the saints of the tribulation, will shrink from this spiritual demagoguery. Others, however, will be captivated by him, as in the days of Antiochus IV when the Hasidim resisted him, while the Hellenists among the Jews revered and served him. They did so, not because they believed Antiochus IV to be the Messiah, but because they accepted him as a god, whose new religion—Hellenistic culture—they deemed more appealing than their old Yahweh worship. Therefore, the Jews in the great tribulation period who submit to the Antichrist, do so, not because they are duped into believing that he is their long-awaited Messiah. Rather, theirs is a calculated rejection of the faith of their fathers. They accept an entirely new religion, the cult of the beast. This will be just as radical a shift in religious behavior for the Jews in that day as it was for the Jews in the second century B.C. who gave up Judaism, and turning to Hellenism, had themselves surgically uncircumcised as a mark of their rejection of the old faith. The mark of the beast will mean the same in the great tribulation period.

THE ABOMINATION OF DESOLATION

Jesus said that during the great tribulation period there will appear in the temple the abomination of desolation. "When therefore ye see the abomination of desolation, which was spoken of through Daniel the prophet, standing in the holy place (let him that readeth understand), then let them that are in Judaea flee unto the mountains" (Mt 24:15-16).

Though we are not sure just what the abomination was which Antiochus IV first placed in Zerubbabel's temple, we can be sure what the abomination is which will be placed in the rebuilt tribulation temple. Paul says that it is the Antichrist who sits in the temple (2 Th 2:4). However, we need not restrict Paul's words to the physical presence of the Antichrist himself. Rather, in the light of Revelation 13, it is an image of the Antichrist that is erected there and commands the worship of the people. Therefore, Jesus' reference to the abomination of desolation is fully illuminated by what John says in the Revelation.

> And he deceiveth them that dwell on the earth by reason of the signs which it was given him to do in the sight of the beast; saying to them that dwell on the earth, that they should make an image to the beast who hath the stroke of the sword and lived. And it was given unto him to give breath to it, even to the image of the beast, that the image of the beast should both speak, and cause that as many as

should not worship the image of the beast should be killed (Rev 13:14-15).

Perhaps the image is made to commemorate the return of the Antichrist from death. This is hinted at in verse 14, for the image is designated "to the beast who hath the stroke of the sword and lived." The fact that the Antichrist has experienced something like death and resurrection is hinted at more than once in this chapter (vv. 3, 12). Many believe that the Antichrist, during the first half of the tribulation period, as head of the revived Roman empire, is killed in battle—perhaps in the battle with Russia at midtribulation. He is then returned to life and advances upon the entire world destined to become a world dictator. Just as Jesus' resurrection from the dead gave him a new authority, so the resurrection of the Antichrist will give him a new authority, both as world dictator and as god.* Therefore, the earth people make this image to commemorate the return to life of the beast. The false prophet then animates the image (Rev 13:15), for "it was given unto him to give breath [spirit] to it, even to the image of the beast."

Those who agree to worship the beast receive the mark (vs. 16-17). This enables them to buy and sell. Those who do not receive the mark and persist in their old faith and practices are killed, just as they were in the days of Antiochus IV.

THE MARK OF THE BEAST

"Here is wisdom. He that hath understanding, let him count the number of the beast; for it is the number of a man: and his number is Six hundred and sixty and six" (Rev 13:18). It is the mark of the beast that enables those who have capitulated to the cult of the beast to buy and sell. However, the mark of the beast has spiritual significance. The

---

*We will interpret the meaning of the death stroke and the conjectured resurrection of the Antichrist when we discuss the title "Son of Perdition."

commercial privileges are only secondary. What is the meaning of this cryptic name: "666"?

All of John's readers recognized this method of calculating
a name by use of numbers. This method was known to the
Jews as *gematria*. The Greeks also practiced it, but not as
seriously as did the Jews. This transition from number to
letter, or from letter to number, was possible because most ancient languages did not have independent symbols which stand
for numbers, as we do. Rather, the letters of the alphabet were
used to designate numbers also. Roman numerals are a good
example of this. Hence, it was a simple matter to convert a
number into a name, or a name into a number. The rabbis
used this device in order to abstract meaning from an otherwise unintelligible passage of Scripture. In the Sibylline Oracles (1.324ff) the numerical value of "Jesus" is given as 888.
(The I.C.C., *in. loc,* gives the table: Iota = 10, Eta = 8, Sigma = 200, Omicron = 70, Upsilon = 400, and Sigma = 200.)
Then there is the often cited graffiti which Adolph Deissmann
mentions as having been found on the walls of Pompeii: "I
love the girl whose name is 545 [phi mu epsilon]."

Matthew may have been using *gematria* in his genealogy of
Jesus (Mt 1:1-17). In verse 17 he says, "So all the generations
from Abraham unto David are fourteen generations; and
from David unto the carrying away to Babylon fourteen generations; and from the carrying away to Babylon unto the
Christ fourteen generations." If this is taken literally then
there are some insurmountable problems in Matthew's calculations. However, we must realize that Matthew is using
the genealogy as a cryptogram. By the use of fourteen he sets
out an acrostic for David, which in turn, is a code reference to
Jesus. The name David in Hebrew has the numerical value of
14 (DVD = 4 + 6 + 4). Therefore, each section of his
genealogy which leads up to Jesus speaks of David in cryptic
form. If we appreciate Matthew's use of gematria here, then
the problem of harmonizing his genealogy with Luke's is re-

solved. They are not intended to be harmonized, for Matthew picks out just those ancestors of Jesus which will fit into his symbolic use of the genealogy.

However, the problem in Revelation 13:18 does not lie in turning a name into a number. That is simple. The real problem lies in turning the number back into a name. The reason why it is difficult is this. Though a name can have but one number, a number can stand for many different names; just as a column of figures has only one correct answer, but that answer may also fit many different sets of figures. It is for this reason that the 666 given in Revelation 13:18 has been subject to a variety of different interpretations—many of which have enough substance to make them plausible.

Irenaeus was the first person, so far as we know, who attempted to turn this number into a name. He found that 666 in Greek added up either to the name *Eunthas,* or to the name *Teitan.* But who could this be? The names are meaningless. This has caused most expositors to proceed in another way.

Assuming that the Revelation has some noted person in view, one whom its readers recognize, and whom the writer wished to positively identify, and thus confirm as the beast; most expositors pick a name and then attempt to reconcile it to the numerical value of 666. This is a legitimate procedure because without some *a priori* assumption as to who is meant, an impossible number of alternatives would have to be considered. Therefore, this cryptic puzzle is not intended to *identify* some totally unknown person. Rather, it is intended to *confirm* some already suspected person as the beast. The most popular subject of this cryptogram has been the Roman emperor Nero who was the first to persecute the church. Though he was dead by the time the book of the Revelation was written, there was a popular myth that declared he would return either from the dead or from exile, to become the beast. There was only one little problem in this identification. The Greek *Neron,* when turned into numbers, added up to

1005, and not 666. But when the Greek *Neron Kaisar* is trans-
literated into Hebrew it does produce the numerical equivalent of 666. The lesser number was possible in Hebrew for
the Hebrew had no vowels.

Other suggestions have been made which employ a different approach. Some believe that 666 is a double symbol,
because it can be made to produce another symbol which in
turn must be interpreted. For example, it is the six Roman
numerals which add up to 666: I (1) + V (5) + X (10)
+ L (50) + C (100) + D (500) = 666. Perhaps the implication of this symbol is that the Antichrist will be a Roman.
Since "beast" in the evil sense appears thirty-six times in the
book of Revelation, and since all the Roman numerals from
one to thirty-six add up to 666, this too might suggest that the
Antichrist is a Roman.

Although there are many, many more proposed solutions
to this puzzle, these will suffice to indicate what can be done
with the number 666.

Though it might very well be possible during the tribulation period, when a new caesar is at the head of a revived
Roman empire and has conquered virtually all of the world,
to reduce his name to the numerical value of 666; this will
not necessarily identify him as Antichrist. It will serve to confirm him as Antichrist to those who are aware of what the
book of Revelation teaches.

However, there is another truth hidden in this cryptic number, for it identifies not only a name, but also the character
of the Antichrist. This may be seen in two ways. In the received Greek text, 666 is composed of three Greek letters:
chi, xi, and sigma. The first and the last of these letters, chi
and sigma, also begin and end the word for Christ in Greek.
But the middle Greek letter, xi, resembles a crooked serpent.
This may be a symbolic presentation of the serpent character
of the Antichrist. In the second place, this idea is more clearly
indicated by the generally understood symbol of the numbers

themselves. Six is generally accepted as the number for *man*. It persistently falls short of the perfect number seven. Six is repeated three times. Three is generally accepted as a divine number, the number for God. Hence 666 indicates *a man who will make himself god*. Who that man is, the church will never know, for he cannot be revealed until the Lord catches away the church before the tribulation begins. But whoever he might be, his intent is clear. He will be a man who will make himself god. Antiochus IV Theos Epiphanes did this. The Caesars did this. So will the Antichrist. In fact, he will be the fulfillment of that which Antiochus IV was a prototype, and will arise as a new divine caesar of the Roman empire. He will embody in himself both of the blasphemous assumptions of the Seleucid ruler, Antiochus IV, as well as the Roman caesars. As they were men who made themselves out as god, so will the Antichrist. This concept is embodied in the cryptic number 666.

THE MAN OF SIN

In 2 Thessalonians 2, Paul refers to the Antichrist in three different ways. Though these are not proper names in context, they have virtually become such in the development of Christian thinking after Paul wrote these words. He refers to the Antichrist as the man of sin, and the son of perdition in verse 3, and as the lawless one in verse 7.

Paul discusses the coming of the Antichrist, whom he calls the man of sin, in order to relieve the Thessalonians of their anxiety about their possible exclusion from the rapture. Paul had declared in his first epistle to the Thessalonians that the church will escape the tribulation period which is coming upon the world through the rapture which will precede wrath. He had said, "For God appointed us not unto wrath, but unto the obtaining of salvation through our Lord Jesus Christ" (1 Th 5:9). The wrath of God against all sin generally may be in view here. However, in light of the context, the wrath which he spoke of in this verse is that which will be poured out upon the earth during the tribulation period (5:1ff). God has made a divine appointment for the church. That appointment is the rapture, by which the Lord will take the church out of the world before the tribulation period begins. However, the Thessalonians were suffering great persecution even then. They were naturally concerned about their lot in the light of Paul's previous teaching, especially since he had taught that the church would escape the tribulation. Had they somehow missed the rapture? Were they now in the tribulation period? Paul replies, "Now we beseech you, brethren, touching the coming† of our Lord Jesus Christ, and our gathering together unto him; to the end that ye be not quickly shaken from your mind, nor yet be troubled, either by spirit, or by word, or by epistle as from us, as that the day of the Lord is just at hand; let no man beguile you in any wise: for it will not be, except the falling away come first, and the man of sin be revealed" (2 Th 2: 1-3).

Though they were suffering persecution, the great falling away, which will mark the closing days of this age, had not occurred. Hence the rapture had not yet taken place. In addition, Paul also suggests that after the church is taken out, then the man of sin will be revealed. However, the revelation of the man of sin cannot occur until the church is gone. Therefore there are two things that should prove to the Thessalonians that the rapture has not yet taken place. First, the great falling away, which will immediately *precede* the rapture, has not happened; and second, the revelation of the man of sin, which will immediately *succeed* the rapture, has not occurred. Both should indicate to the Thessalonians that they have not missed the rapture. The appearance of the man of sin immediately after the rapture is the culmination of the

---

†This is the rapture. The second coming, which occurs after the tribulation period, is in view in verse 8.

great falling away that will occur immediately before the Lord Jesus returns for his own. The spirit of apostasy, which will be manifest in widespread fashion just before the rapture, will become intensified and personified in the Antichrist, *just after* the rapture. Therefore the only indication that the church will ever have that the advent of the Antichrist upon the stage of world history is imminent will be the great apostasy which occurs in the closing days of the church age. But even then, the church will be snatched away before the man of sin is actually revealed.

What then is the meaning of the name, man of sin? It must be explained in light of the context in which it is found. Since it is found nowhere else in Scripture, the context here will define it. In this section of his epistle, Paul is laboring to show the Thessalonian believers that the meeting with the Lord Jesus Christ in the air—the rapture of the church—has not yet taken place. We have already noted the two things that Paul indicates must happen before one can be sure that the tribulation period has begun, namely, the great apostasy and the revelation of the man of sin. These two things are related in Paul's thinking, even though they occur on either side of the rapture—the apostasy occurring in the church age, and the revelation of the man of sin occurring in the tribulation period. The coming of Jesus for the church separates the two. However, on the great plane of world events the two are not separated, for the world is not affected by the rapture, only by its results. The rapture is a secret event. As a thief in the night, the Lord Jesus will catch away his bride, the church. In a moment, in the twinkling of an eye, the church will disappear from the earth. This will be without fanfare. The world will know it has happened only when it awakens to the fact that suddenly all born-again believers have disappeared. However, from the world's standpoint the apostasy and the revelation of the man of sin are not separated. One simply merges into the other. The apostasy is climaxed in the man of sin. And that is Paul's point in using this name for the Antichrist. He will be the arch representative of the great apostasy. All the apostatizing tendencies that have been manifest during the closing months, or years, of the church age will now be personified in the man of sin. It is for this reason that so often the prophetic word notes the blasphemy of the Antichrist. "And there was given to him a mouth speaking great things and blasphemies; . . . And he opened his mouth for blasphemies against God, to blaspheme his name, and his tabernacle, even them that dwell in heaven" (Rev 13:5-6; cf. Dan 7:8, 11, 20, 25; 11:36-37).

THE SON OF PERDITION

There are only two passages in the Word of God in which this term, "Son of Perdition," is used. Paul uses it in 2 Thessalonians 2:3; with reference to the Antichrist. It is interesting that Jesus used the same term with reference to Judas Iscariot. "While I was with them, I kept them in thy name which thou hast given me: and I guarded them, and not one of them perished, but the son of perdition; that the scripture might be fulfilled" (Jn 17:12). Because Jesus also said, "Did not I choose you the twelve, and one of you is a devil? Now he spake of Judas" (Jn 6:70), many believe that Judas will be the Antichrist. Judas is the only man of whom it is said that Satan entered him (Lk 22:3). Other persons were possessed with demons, but only Judas is said to have been Satan-possessed.

Some have considered these three passages, coupled with our text, as sufficient evidence to identify Judas as the coming Antichrist. This position was held by the beloved Bible teacher, Dr. M. R. DeHaan.

It has also been observed that "Judas fell away, that he might go to his own place" (Ac 1:25). The Antichrist is described as "the beast that cometh up out of the abyss" (Rev 7:11). Therefore, some have inferred that Judas' "own place" is a very special place, the abyss, where Satan has kept him since the first century, ready to be revealed in the last days. If this were the case, it would explain, to some extent, why the Antichrist is viewed in Revelation 13:3, 12, 14 as one who recovered from a death stroke. But, at the same time, it would not explain why the death stroke was with a sword (Rev 13:14), when Judas Iscariot hanged himself (Mt 27:5). However, as interesting as this thesis is, it would mean that the Antichrist would be a Jew, and this is an improbable concession in the light of previous discussion. And since Judas certainly died (Ac 1:18) it would invest Satan with the power of resurrection, which is an impossible concession to make.

How then is the Antichrist the son of perdition? We propose the following theory. Some light may be cast upon this whole area of the death stroke of the Antichrist by looking at what happened to the apostle Paul. He was stoned in Lystra, and the citizens "dragged him out of the city, supposing that he was dead" (Ac 14:19). While in an unconscious state, Paul "was caught up into Paradise, and heard unspeakable words, which it is not lawful for a man to utter" (2 Co 12:4). Paul had received, as it were, a death stroke. At the same time he was thought to be dead, his spirit was caught up into the third heaven and there received a profound revelation from God. This same thing, in reverse, will happen to the Antichrist. The Antichrist, sometime during his career as caesar, will receive a death stroke. He will be no more dead than was the apostle Paul. But just as the citizens of Lystra thought Paul was dead, so the Antichrist will be thought dead.

It might be argued that the same Greek word for "having been slain" is used with reference to the death of Christ in Revelation 5:12 that is used of the beast in Revelation 13:3. While it is obvious that Jesus actually experienced death, it does not necessarily follow that the use of this word demands that the beast will also experience death, rather than just a simulated death. Many of John's contemporaries did not think that the Beast had actually died, for many of them applied this text to *Nero Redivivus* according to the great apocalyptic authority, Canon R. H. Charles.[1] The essence of the Nero Redivivus theory is that Nero did not actually experience death but escaped from Rome and took refuge in the East. Professor Charles says, "When Nero with the help of a freedman committed suicide and was cremated (Seut. *Nero* 49), so great was the public joy that the people thronged the streets in holiday attire. All, however, did not share in the belief of Nero's death. Thus Tacitus (*Hist.* 2.8) writes that there were many who pretended and believed that he was still alive and would return speedily to destroy his enemies."[2] This myth of the return of Nero is reflected in *The Sibylline Oracles,* verses 143-148; as well as in the fact that three different and successive impostors arose and claimed to be Nero returned from the East. One emerged in A.D. 69; a second came around A.D. 80; and a third in A.D. 88. Even the Talmud may reflect this belief that Nero was not dead but would return to take vengeance upon Rome, for it declared (*Yoma* 10a) that Rome would be destroyed by the Persians. To be sure, the legend of the return of Nero later reflected the assumption that Nero must arise from the dead. However, this tenet of the myth was added only after sufficient time had elapsed to preclude his remaining alive—due to old age. But in its earliest form, the belief was that Nero had not died, but had escaped into the East. This is important for it indicates that the terminology does not demand an actual death, for it was not so viewed by the advocates of the *Nero Redivivus* theory. This assumption is the basis of Professor Charles' exegesis of Revelation 13.

While the Antichrist's body lies in a state of suspended animation, or simulated death, his spirit will be taken into the abyss by Satan. Just as Satan took Jesus up into a high mountain and showed him all the kingdoms of the world, and offered them to him, if he would fall down and worship him; so Satan will take the Antichrist into the depths of the abyss and show him all the kingdoms of the world. Jesus viewed all the kingdoms of the world from above, which was a divine perspective. The Antichrist will be shown all the kingdoms of the world from a different vantage point—from beneath, which is the demonic perspective. Jesus refused to bow down to Satan. The Antichrist will not refuse, but will worship him. He will then come forth from the abyss (Rev 11:7), his death stroke healed, as it were, to conquer the world spiritually in the great tribulation, as he has already conquered it politically during the first three and one-half years of his tribulation reign. This is why Revelation 13:2 says that "the dragon gave him his power, and his throne, and great authority." It is in the light of this experience that the Anti-Christ is called the son of perdition (2 Th 2:3).

This term has been variously translated. *The Twentieth Century New Testament* says, "that Lost Soul." Williams translates it, "the one who is doomed to destruction." Knox renders it, "the champion of wickedness . . . destined to inherit perdition." *The New English Bible* calls him "the man doomed to perdition," while Taylor in *Living Letters* translates, "the son of hell." All suggest the complete capitulation of this human personality to Satanic dominion. The Antichrist, therefore, is not a supernatural being, like a fallen angel. Neither is he an historic figure, such as Antiochus IV Epiphanes, Nero, or Judas Iscariot, resurrected and returned to earth. Rather, he is a human personality who willfully gives himself to the complete dominion of Satan, and whom Satan transforms into the sinister world master and god he is destined to become.

THE LAWLESS ONE

It is not difficult to see, in the light of what has been previously said, why the Antichrist is viewed as one completely devoid of any allegiance to the law of God. Jesus came to do the will of the Father. The Antichrist is completely given over to the will of Satan. Satan tried, on the mount of temptation, to get Jesus to fulfill this office. He refused. But in in the time of the end Satan will find a human personality who will be completely abandoned to his control. Just as God did not claim the allegiance of mankind, except through his Son, the Lord Jesus Christ; so Satan will not directly claim the allegiance of mankind during the tribulation, but through the Antichrist.

Paul indicates why in the lawless one there will be a complete fulfillment of Satanic designs upon mankind, which Satan has never been able to fully realize before. "For the mystery of lawlessness doth already work: only there is one that restraineth now, until he be taken out of the way. And then shall be revealed the lawless one, whom the Lord Jesus shall slay with the breath of his mouth, and bring to nought by the manifestation of his coming, even he, whose coming is according to the working of Satan with all power and signs and lying wonders, and with all deceit of unrighteousness for them that perish" (2 Th 2:7-10a).

Up to now, and continuing through all the church age, Satan's complete take-over of any given individual is hindered by the Holy Spirit. But when the church, which the Holy Spirit indwells, is taken out of the world, the Holy Spirit will terminate His indwelling ministry also. No longer will he inhabit individual believers upon earth during the tribulation period. His indwelling is a unique ministry of the Spirit to the church, exercised between Pentecost and the rapture, which will not be repeated during the tribulation. While the Holy Spirit will be active during the tribulation period, as he was in the Old Testament, he will not continue his unique ministry of indwelling, which the church has experienced. But in this age of the church, which began at Pentecost and will be terminated at the rapture, the Holy

Spirit is present in the world in a distinctive way. This does not mean that the Holy Spirit indwells the unsaved individual. Not at all. He indwells only the believer after the new birth has taken place. However, the Holy Spirit does also exercise a distinctive work with reference to the lost world which will also cease at the rapture. This is his ministry of conviction which he carries on in association with his indwelling ministry. Note carefully the words of Jesus about this. "I will send him [the Holy Spirit] unto you. And he, when he is come [unto you], will convict the world in respect of sin, and of righteousness, and of judgment" (Jn 16:7b-8).

The Spirit may convict sinners during the tribulation. But this unique way of conviction—through the use of human personality—will cease at the rapture. During the tribulation he may very well fall upon people as he did in the Old Testament and therefore render a convicting ministry from without, but not from within from person to person as he does now. Though Satan is a world ruler of this darkness (Eph 6:12) and the "prince of this world" (Jn 14:30), his complete dominion is restricted by one whom Paul calls the "one that restraineth" (2 Th 2:7), that is, by the Holy Spirit.

However, after the rapture. when the church and the Holy Spirit are taken out of the world, Satan will be free to dominate completely, without hindrance, any individual who wills to be so dominated. This he does in the Antichrist who will be completely devoid of any law save that of Satan's will. Hence he is the lawless one. As Jesus was given the Holy Spirit without measure (Jn 3:34), so the Antichrist will have Satan without measure. Satan's presence in the Antichrist will be complete and unrestricted by any inhibiting force.

THE ANTICHRIST

Though the term *Antichrist* is the generally accepted theological designation for this world dictator who will appear in the tribulation period, this name is used by only one writer in the New Testament, the apostle John. It apears in 1 John 2:18, 22; 4:3 and in 2 John 7. And John uses it in a unique way, for he has in view the contemporary spirit of the Antichrist, more than the person of the Antichrist, who will appear in the last days.

Tertullian was of the first of the patristic writers to pick up this idea from John and to suggest that any current heretic or rebel against Christ is Antichrist. He also taught that this rebellious spirit would be personified in the Antichrist who will appear in the end of time. Cyprian and Origen followed this idea. Origen declared that the principle of the Antichrist has had or will continue to have, many proponents during the course of history; but from among these many Antichrists, there will come one whose type and forerunner the others have been. Therefore, the Antichrist, as he emerges in patristic literature, has both this contemporary aspect as well as the eschatological dimensions. Not only will the Antichrist appear at the end of time, but his spirit is now embodied in all the enemies of Christ.

It is the contemporary dimension of the Antichrist that is set forth in John's writings. Daniel hints at this idea when he uses Antiochus IV as an historical example, indicating in this that the spirit of Antichrist was already present in Antiochus IV. It is for this reason also that Daniel could move in his discussion of Antiochus IV to the Antichrist without even indicating the transition. Paul also hints at this same idea when he says that "the mystery of lawlessness doth already work" (2 Th 2:7), even before the revelation of the lawless one. But it is John who most clearly enunciates this contemporary theme in his theology of the Antichrist.

Paul's arch enemies were the Judaizers. In the early days of the gospel movement, while it was still under Jewish influence, the Judaizers were a real threat to the liberty, and hence to the universal appeal, and therefore to the spread of the gospel. But when the gospel moved away from a Jewish environment, into the Greek world, another threat emerged—gnosticism. Paul had witnessed the early rise of this heresy also and had written the Colossians to warn them against it, as he had written to the Galatians to warn them against the Judaizers. However, gnosticism did not move through the church like a plague until late in the first century, after Paul was dead. It was John who took up the pen against it. He felt the full force of this heresy. Through the flourishing church of Asia Minor gnosticism spread like a rank and noxious weed. It was the most deadly corruption that the church has ever known. Gnosticism (from a Greek word, *gnosis*, which means "knowledge") maintained that salvation was through a secret knowledge of divine things which was not communicated to ordinary Christians, but to those initiated in the mystery of this secret knowledge.

John combats this heresy with one of the cardinal doctrines of the Christian faith which the gnostics denied, namely, that Jesus Christ was God manifest in the flesh. It is these gnostic deniers of Jesus Christ whom John indicts as having the lying, deceiving spirit of Antichrist. "For many deceivers are gone forth into the world, even they that confess not that Jesus Christ cometh in the flesh. This is the deceiver and the anti-christ" (2 Jn 7). "Who is the liar but he that denieth that Jesus is the Christ? This is the anti-christ, even he that denieth the Father and the Son" (1 Jn 2:22; cf. v. 18). It is the spirit of Antichrist that, during all the course of history, will deny that Jesus of Nazareth is actually God manifest in sinless flesh. The gnostics said that Jesus was a phantom, and not actually God come to earth in human form. Therefore, any religious system, no matter what its name, that denies the incarnation, is moved by the spirit of Antichrist.

This spirit of Antichrist which denies the incarnation will continue to appear in the course of history until it is finally climaxed and is personified in the archdenier of the incarnate Christ, the Antichrist himself. But why is the incarnation the issue? Because the incarnate Christ—God manifest in human flesh—is the direct opposite of what the Antichrist will be—Satan manifest in human flesh. Though the lost world is now confronted with this decision of choosing either Christ or Satan, during the tribulation it will be confronted with this ultimate antithesis. Either yield allegiance to God manifest in the flesh—Jesus Christ; or yield allegiance to Satan manifest in the flesh—the Antichrist. Mankind has always been presented with these alternatives; it is faced with this issue even now. Many delay a decision for Christ today. However, in the tribulation each must make manifest his allegiance in a positive way by either accepting or rejecting the mark of the beast. Therefore, during the tribulation period, that which is now essentially a spiritual decision, will become dramatically personified, as the tribulation citizen is confronted with the issue of acceptance or rejection of the Antichrist. To reject the incarnate Christ today is fraught with spiritual consequences. However, the rejection of Antichrist, incarnate Satan, during the tribulation period will be fraught with literal physical consequences, as well as spiritual. The consequences of this rejection appear in Revelation 13:16-17: "And he causeth all, the small and the great, and the rich and the poor, and the free and the bond, that there be given them a mark on their right hand, or upon their forehead; and that no man should be able to buy or to sell, save he that hath the mark, even the name of the beast or the number of his name."

THE BEAST

The last name Scripture applies to the Antichrist is the beast. In Revelation 13:1 John sees a beast coming up out of the sea. He also sees another beast which is mentioned in verse 11. They are not the same. The first beast is the Antichrist. The second is the false prophet. This first beast has seven heads and ten horns, and upon these horns are ten diadems. The ten horns may represent the ten-nation confederation which comprises the revived Roman empire. The seven heads may represent the seven kings that yielded to the little horn after he had first subdued three of them (Dan 7:20, 24). Upon the heads are the names of blasphemy.

At first the beast is viewed as a political figure. This is suggested by the animals that are mentioned in connection with him. He is like a leopard, with the feet of a bear, and the mouth of a lion. All three of these animals are mentioned in Daniel 7, where the lion represented Babylon, the bear represented Medo-Persia, and the leopard represented Greece (7:3-6). These are the first three forms of gentile world power. The fourth, the Roman empire, is not presented here in John's vision because the beast himself is a part of that fourth kingdom, for he is the head of the revived Roman empire.

As the representative of the final form of gentile world power, the beast has power, a throne, and great authority. This is given to him by Satan (v. 2). However, the beast is destined to be more than a political figure. "And they worshipped the dragon because he gave his authority unto the beast; and they worshipped the beast, saying Who is like unto the beast?" (Rev 13:4). What happened to this world conqueror to cause him also to be worshiped? Between John's vision of the beast as a political figure (v. 2) and his view of the beast who claims worship as a god (v. 4), there is a statement about the beast's death stroke (v. 3). John says, "And I saw one of his heads as though it had been smitten unto death; and his death-stroke was healed: and the whole earth wondered after the beast."

Here is a strange event in his career which changes the role of the Antichrist from a world conqueror into that of a spiritual figure who is to be worshiped as god. It is this great abyss experience of which we spoke in our discussion of the son of perdition, which produces this dramatic change in his career. This experience seems to occur at midtribulation period, for the beast has forty-two months to continue after this time (v. 5); that is, the last three and one half years of the great tribulation period remain after this event.

Here is the order of events. As head of the revived Roman empire, the Antichrist conquers the world. His political dominion begins early in the tribulation period, just after the rapture, as he emerges the political genius at the head of the revived Roman empire. Near midtribulation period, he enters into a conflict with the prince of Rosh and defeats this foe from the far north (Ezekiel 38 and 39). This makes him a virtual world dictator, except perhaps for the Orient, which he meets in battle at the end of the great tribulation period. But there is another significant event which also seems to occur at midtribulation. The beast receives the death blow of a sword, from which he recovers. While in the state of simulated death, he is transported in spirit into the abyss where he is persuaded to give himself completely to Satan and thus is transformed into the beast.

The idea of a human being in league with the devil is not new. This theme has been repeated many times, outside the inspired Word, in the Faust legends centering around Dr. Johann Faust who lived in Germany during the sixteenth century. He is believed to have been in league with the devil and to have been able to do many feats of magic by the power of the devil. There is little doubt that a soothsayer by that name really lived in central Europe, and that he met his death in 1538. Few events of his life are certain, except most people believed that the devil possessed him. The *Historia von Dr. Johann Fausten,* first published in Frankfort in 1587, relates how he sought to acquire supernatural power and knowledge by a bargain with Satan. He signed a pact with his own blood and was given a demon, Mephistopheles, to serve him for twenty-four years. At the end of the twenty-four years, in the midst of an earthquake, the devil carried off Dr. Faust. This story became the theme of Sir Christopher Marlowe's great dramatic poem, *The Tragical History of Doctor Faustus,* 1588. The story became the theme of strolling actors in Germany, as well as Punch and Judy shows. At the beginning of the nineteenth century, Goethe raised the story to the level of a powerful drama. Charles Gounod's opera *Faust* was adopted from this motif and was performed for the first time in Paris in 1859. The theme also appeared in art, Rembrandt being one of the most famous painters to illustrate the legend.

From his Faustian experience in the abyss, the Antichrist will emerge to conquer the world spiritually, for those whom he has subdued by military force must now worship him as god. Israel has met this sort of spiritual madness before in Antiochus IV Epiphanes, who first conquered Israel militarily and then attempted to force a Hellenism upon the Jews in which he set himself forth as god, a part of the Greek Pantheon.

As a spiritual figure, the Antichrist is now brought into direct conflict with the saints of God. "And it was given unto him to make war with the saints, and to overcome them: and there was given to him authority over every tribe and people and tongue and nation. And all that dwell on the earth shall worship him, every one whose name hath not been written from the foundation of the world in the book of life of the Lamb that hath been slain. If any man hath an ear, let him hear" (Rev 13:7-9; cf. Dan 7:25).

The saints are those who receive Christ as Saviour during the tribulation period. Though the church is taken out of the world just before the tribulation begins, there will be many people who will receive Christ during the tribulation and be saved. Though they will not become regenerated members of the church, the body of Christ, they will be justified by faith, just as the Old Testament saints were. Among these saints there will be both saved Jews and gentiles. Largely the converts of the 144,000, these saints will be martyred by the Antichrist (Rev 7:13ff), though the 144,000 themselves cannot be slain (Rev 7:3-4; 9:4).

Running concurrently with the intense persecution of the tribulation period, there apparently is also a great revival, a spiritual awakening of profound magnitude. Revelation 7 presents a picture of multitudes saved during this time. Perhaps the world's greatest spiritual awakening is yet to come. It seems to be an axiom of revivals that they occur during times of crisis. There is usually a correlation between persecution and spiritual awakening. When persecution is most severe, spiritual devotion is also most keen. Since the tribulation is a time when Israel and the saints of God—the saints during the entire period, and Israel during the last half of the period—will suffer most intense persecution, the indications are that it might also be a time of great spiritual awakening. But what do the prophetic Scriptures indicate about this?

The New Testament teaches that just before the rapture of the church there will be a time of great spiritual dearth. The church age closes not in revival, but in apostasy. This is the consistent testimony of the New Testament.

> But the Spirit saith expressly, that in later times some shall fall away from the faith (1 Ti 4:1).
>
> But know this, that in the last days grievous times shall come. For men shall be lovers of self, lovers of money, boastful, haughty, railers, disobedient to parents, unthankful, unholy, without natural affection, implacable, slanderers, without self-control, fierce, no lovers of good, traitors, headstrong, puffed up, lovers of pleasure rather than lovers of God; holding a form of godliness, but having denied the power thereof (2 Ti 3:1-5).
>
> For the time will come when they will not endure the sound doctrine; but, having itching ears, will heap to themselves teachers after their own lusts; and will turn away their ears from the truth, and turn aside unto fables (2 Ti 4:3-4).

> Knowing this first, that in the last days mockers shall come with mockery, walking after their own lusts, and saying, Where is the promise of his coming? (2 Pe 3:3-4).

Even though revivals come in answer to prayer, there is nothing that the spiritual remnant in the church can do, either by prayer or the faithful preaching of the Word or by any other legitimate means that have previously produced revival to change the situation. This age will close in a great falling away (2 Th 2:3). This is a prophetic fact of Scripture that nothing can alter, for it is unalterably set in the counsels of God.

But what occurs spiritually just after the church age closes, inside the tribulation period, is another matter. For the same prophetic Scriptures that teach that the church age will close in a great spiritual decline, also teach that the tribulation period will begin in a great spiritual awakening. Joel 2:28 promises an outpouring of the Spirit upon all flesh. Simon Peter said that Pentecost was a fulfillment of this promise (Ac 2:16-21). However, two things indicate that Pentecost may not have exhausted the promise of Joel. First, Joel indicates that celestial phenomena would accompany the outpouring of the Spirit. This did not ocur at Pentecost. It may accompany the revival days during the tribulation (cf. Mt 24:29 and Rev 6:12f). Second, Joel spoke of the coming of the Spirit in a context of the former and latter rain (cf. 2:23). The former rain may have reference to the coming of the Spirit at Pentecost, while this latter rain may have reference to the spiritual revival of the last days. This is made more likely when we consider the fact that James unites the idea of a latter rain with the coming of the Lord. "Be patient, therefore, brethren, until the coming of the Lord. Behold, the husbandman waiteth for the precious fruit of the earth, being patient over it, until it receive the early and latter rain. Be ye also patient; establish your hearts: for the coming of the Lord is at hand" (Ja 5:7-8).

"With my soul have I desired thee in the night; yea, with my spirit within me will I seek thee earnestly: for when thy judgments are in the earth, the inhabitants of the world learn righteousness" (Is 26:9) . Since every born-again believer is taken out of the world at the rapture, and yet Revelation 7 presents a picture of multitudes of saints in the tribulation, it would appear that there must be a tremendous spiritual awakening during this period. The statistics are phenomenal. Among the Jews 144,000 will be saved. These will then preach the tribulation message composed of a call to repentance and to behold the Lamb of God. This is the same message that John the Baptist proclaimed. As a result of their ministry during the tribulation, an incalculable number, both of Jews and Gentiles, are saved.

> After these things I saw, and behold, a great multitude, which no man could number, out of every nation and of all tribes and peoples and tongues, standing before the throne and before the Lamb, arrayed in white robes, and palms in their hands; and they cry with a great voice, saying, Salvation unto our God who sitteth on the throne, and unto the Lamb. . . . And one of the elders answered, saying unto me, These that are arrayed in the white robes, who are they, and whence came they? And I say unto him, My Lord, thou knowest. And he said to me, These are they that come out of the great tribulation, and they washed their robes, and made them white in the blood of the Lamb (Rev 7:9-13) .

One hundred forty-four thousand Jews saved, plus a multitude which no man can number out of all the nations who have been washed in the blood of the Lamb! And all this within the limits of the tribulation period. What a revival! Neither Pentecost in the first century, nor the Reformation on the Continent, nor the evangelical revival in England, nor the Great Awakening in the Colonies, could match this spiritual awakening. Neither Luther, Wesley, Whitefield, Finney, Moody, Sunday, nor Billy Graham—individually or collectively—could muster such statistics as these. The world is yet in store for its greatest spiritual revival in which vast multitudes, beyond comprehension, will be saved. This is a phase of the tribulation period that has been little noted. Such emphasis has been put upon the horror of the tribulation that we have lost sight of the fact that it will also be a time of unprecedented revival.

While it is true that the tribulation will be a time of great spiritual awakening, it is also true that those awakened will be the object of the persecutions of the beast. It is for this reason that the prophetic Word seems to teach that, apart from the 144,000, most of those who are saved during the period will soon suffer martyrdom. This is why Revelation seven presents most of the tribulation saints not upon earth but in heaven (Rev 7:9). They have come out of the tribulation and

> Therefore are they before the throne of God; and they serve him day and night in his temple: and he that sitteth on the throne shall spread his tabernacle over them. They shall hunger no more, neither thirst any more; neither shall the sun strike upon them, nor any heat: for the Lamb that is in the midst of the throne shall be their shepherd, and shall guide them unto fountains of waters of life: and God shall wipe away every tear from their eyes (Rev 7:15-17).

In his great work *The Decline and Fall of the Roman Empire,* Edward Gibbon spoke of the attitude of Rome toward the religion of the various groups assimilated within the empire. He said, "The various modes of worship which prevailed in the Roman world were all considered by the people as equally true, by the philosophers as equally false, and by the magistrates as equally useful. And thus toleration not only produced mutual indulgence, but even religious concord."[3] The Roman empire tolerated all religions but Christianity. For example, Pliny the Younger, governor of Bithynia, wrote to the Roman emperor Trajan in A.D. 112 as follows:

> It is my rule, Sire, to refer to you in matters where I am uncertain. For who can better direct my hesitation or instruct my ignorance? I was never present at any trial of Christians: therefore I do not know what are the customary penalities. . . . I have hesitated a great deal on the question whether there should be any distinction of ages; whether the weak should have the same treatment as the more robust; whether those who recant should be pardoned, or whether a man who has ever been a Christian should gain nothing by ceasing to be such; whether the name itself, even if innocent of crime, should be punished, or only the crimes attaching to that name. Meanwhile, this is the course I have adopted in the case of those brought before me as Christians. I ask them if they are Christians. If they admit it, I repeat the question a second and third time, threatening capital punishment; if they persist, I sentence them to death.[4]

To this letter the emperor Trajan replied: "You have taken the right line, my dear Pliny, in examining the cases of those denounced to you as Christians, for no hard and fast rule can be laid down, of universal application. They are not to be sought out; if they are informed against, and the charge is proved, they are to be punished, with this reservation—that if anyone denies that he is a Christian, and actually proves it, that is by worshipping our gods, he shall be pardoned as a result of his recantation, however suspect he may have been with respect to the past."[5]

Trajan's attitude toward Christians in the second century A.D. was mild. His successors were to persecute the early church more and more fiercely. Why were Christians so universally hated and persecuted by the Romans, when no other religious group was? Edward Gibbon says that the Jews constituted a nation, and as such, were entitled to have their religious peculiarities. Christians, however, were a sect. And having no country, they subverted other nations from within. In addition, where the Jews were often active in Roman affairs when it was to their best interest, Christians withdrew from the mainstream of life, from responsibility in government, and from bearing arms in the defense of the government. It is for this reason, says Gibbon, that the Romans persecuted Christians.[6] Not so much for what *they did*, but for what *they were*. During the tribulation period the saints of God will again come under the power of the Roman empire. And again they will be persecuted, and for much the same reason. They will remain aloof from the kingdom of the Antichrist. They will be reluctant to cooperate with his political ambitions, and they will positively refuse to yield to his religious ambitions, for they will not worship him as god.

THE FALSE PROPHET

This is not another name for the Antichrist. The false prophet, the second beast out of the earth (Rev 13:11-18), is different from the Antichrist, though the two have been identified as the same person by some expositors. However, in the light of Revelation 19:20, which says, "And the beast was taken, and with him the false prophet that wrought the signs in his sight, wherewith he deceived them that had received the mark of the beast and them that worshipped his image: they two were cast alive into the lake of fire that burneth with brimstone," we must conclude that the two are not the same. In addition, Satan is also associated with these two. "And the devil that deceiveth them was cast into the lake of fire and brimstone, where are also the beast and the false prophet; and they shall be tormented day and night for ever and ever" (Rev 20:10). Here then is an unholy trinity that will dominate the earth during the end time: Satan, analogous to God the Father; the Antichrist, analogous to Jesus the Son; and the false prophet, analogous to the Holy Spirit. In both of these passages (Rev 19:20; 20:10) the definite article *the* appears before both "beast" and "false prophet." It is written "the beast and the false prophet," not "the beast and false prophet." In addition, the article is used before the word *devil,* indicating that all three—beast, false prophet, and devil —are definite personalities.

The false prophet is to the Antichrist what Menelaus was to Antiochus IV. Menelaus was responsible for enforcing many of the Hellenizing decrees of Antiochus IV upon his own people, the Jews. In addition, just as Antiochus IV was a gentile, and Menelaus, the high priest, was a Jew; so the Antichrist will be a gentile, while the false prophet seems to be a Jew. This is suggested by the fact that the Antichrist arises out of the sea (Rev 13:1), while the false prophet arises out of the land (13:11). The sea stands for "peoples, and multitudes, and nations, and tongues" (Rev 17:15). Thus the Antichrist, a gentile, arises out of the seething mass of humanity caught up in the world crisis precipitated by the rapture of the church. On the other hand, the false prophet arises out of the earth, or the land, which is Palestine. Apparently he is a Jew. He will mediate the will of the Antichrist to Israel, as Menelaus mediated the will of Antiochus IV to the people of Israel in his day.

The false prophet is characterized in his personal identity, by "two horns like unto a lamb, and he spake as a dragon" (Rev 13:11). These two figures immediately suggest the Lord Jesus Christ, the Lamb of God, and Satan, the dragon. The horns are visible. Thus, outwardly he reminds the world of the Lord Jesus Christ, but in counterfeit. But the voice of the dragon suggests that he is actually motivated by Satanic power. Just as the Holy Spirit is dedicated to bringing the world to know Jesus Christ, so the false prophet is dedicated to bringing all men into spiritual allegiance to the Antichrist. He does this in two ways. First, by mighty signs and wonders, and second, by the subtle deception of the image which he makes to speak.

"And he doeth great signs, that he should even make fire to come down out of heaven upon the earth in the sight of men" (Rev 13:13). This is the Elijah-sign of divine authentication (1 Ki 18:24; cf. Lk 9:54). The false prophet will be given the power to duplicate this sign. Jesus said that in the great tribulation period the Antichrist and the false prophet would emerge, "and show great signs and wonders; so as to lead astray, if possible, even the elect" (Mt 24:24).

Perhaps the false prophet does not come upon the world scene until midtribulation. This is suggested by several facts. First, he is associated with the beast. The Antichrist does not become the beast until his abyss-experience. During the first half of the tribulation the Antichrist is a political figure, the head of the ten-nation confederation that constitutes the revived Roman empire. His potential as an exclusive religious leader is subdued during the first three and one-half years because of the apostate world church and a resilient Judaism which thrives for the time upon the restored Levitical system in a rebuilt temple. As a political leader, the Antichrist does not need the assistance of the false prophet. However, at midtribulation, when the Antichrist emerges from the abyss, as the beast, having recovered from the death stroke, he will subdue both Judaism and the apostate world church. He will set himself up as the exclusive arbiter of religion. It is then that the ministry of the false prophet is needed to enable the beast to enforce his godmania upon the people.

So profound will be the false prophet's authentication of the Antichrist by his great signs and wonders that even the elect can be led astray by them. This does not mean that any of the tribulation saints—those who have accepted Christ as Saviour—will be tempted to believe in these signs. The elect here, as in all the prophetic Word, is the nation Israel, which is destined to accept Jesus as Messiah when he returns to earth a second time at the close of the great tribulation period. Unbelieving Israel can be tempted to believe these signs and wonders for they have not the spiritual stamina that the redeemed saints will have.

Israel, which is destined to receive Jesus as Messiah at his second coming, will enter into a greatly weakened state during the last three-and-one-half years, or great tribulation period. The cultural power of Judaism will have become only a faded idealism during this time. Israel will be stripped of all hope in both their ancient Levitical system as well as their Talmudic faith. However, it is this very emptying process which relieves Israel of her faith in Judaism, which will also prepare her to receive Jesus as Messiah. This is what the prophet Ezekiel means when he said,

> As I live, saith the Lord GOD, surely with a mighty hand, and with an outstretched arm, and with wrath poured out, will I be king over you: and I will bring you out from the peoples, and will gather you out of the countries wherein ye are scattered, with a mighty hand, and with an outstretched arm, and with wrath poured out; and I will bring you into the wilderness of the peoples, and there will I enter into judgment with you face to face. Like as I entered into judgment with your fathers in the wilderness of the land of Egypt, so will I enter into judgment with you, saith the Lord GOD. And I will cause you to pass under the rod, and I will bring you into the bond of the covenant (Eze 20:33-37) .

This emptying process of judgment will also make them, in the interim, very vulnerable to the deluding claims of the Antichrist. It is in this emptying process, then, that some in Israel will be tempted to yield to the Antichrist, especially since the appeals for allegiance to the Antichrist are made by a fellow Jew, the false prophet. This seems to be what Jesus meant when he said, "And because iniquity shall be multiplied, the love of the many shall wax cold. But he that endureth to the end, the same shall be saved" (Mt 24:12-13). The many in Israel who are tempted to yield to the Antichrist and his false system of religion, if they will but remain faithful to their historic culture, and to their spiritual propensities, will be saved when they see Jesus coming a second time (Ro 11:26), for then the remnant in Israel will receive him as Messiah.

In addition to the signs which he does, the false prophet also gives breath to the image which the people have made, "that the image of the beast should both speak, and cause that as many as should not worship the image of the beast should be killed" (Rev 13:15). It has been assumed that the Antichrist makes an image, sets it in the temple, and forces all to worship it. In addition, if anyone will not worship the image, the Antichrist has them killed. However, a close reading of these verses indicates that the people make the image, not the Antichrist. In Daniel 6 the prophet is cast into the den of lions because he had violated the royal decree. It is an interesting point of similarity that King Darius did not establish this edict. The presidents of the kingdom did, along with its deputies, satraps, counsellors, and governors (Dan 6:7). And they did so in order that they might have an occasion to accuse Daniel, knowing that he would put his faithfulness to Yahweh, the God of Israel, above any loyalty to the monarch (Dan 6:4-5). The pattern in Daniel 6 is threefold: Daniel is favored (6:1-3); Daniel is persecuted (6:4-18); and Daniel is delivered (6:19-28).

This is the same picture that we get of Israel during the tribulation period. Israel too will be favored during the first half of the tribulation period when the Antichrist has a covenant with her. However, during the last half of the tribulation period Israel will be persecuted. Then, finally, the faithful remnant in Israel will know deliverance at the end of the tribulation period when Jesus comes again. The persecution of Israel may be provoked by the same thing that caused the persecution of Daniel. Just as Daniel refused to obey the royal decree, so many in Israel will refuse to worship the image of the beast. However, just as the royal edict was the precipitating factor in Daniel's change from a place of favor to the place of the lion's den, so Israel may be removed from the place of favor to the place of persecution. And it may very well be that it is the image which precipitates the crisis in Israel's relationship to the Antichrist.

The exile cured Israel of idolatry. Never again would the people tolerate an image of any god. Tacitus, the Roman historian says, "The God of the Jews is a great governing mind, that directs and guides the whole frame of nature, eternal, infinite, and neither capable of change, nor subject to decay. In consequence of this opinion, no such thing as a statue was to be seen in their city, much less in their temple."[7]

One incident from Josephus will serve to illustrate the Jews' abhorrence of images. The Judean city of Jamneh had attracted many pagan settlers in the first century A.D. These heathen wished to worship idols; however, their Jewish neighbors would not tolerate any images in their city. When these pagan citizens of Jamneh learned that the Roman emperor Caligula (called Gaius by Josephus) thought himself to be a god, they erected an altar to him, which the Judeans promptly destroyed. When the emperor heard about this sacrilege he was outraged and ordered Petronius, the legate of Syria, to erect an enormous statue of the Roman emperor in the Holy of Holies in the temple of Jerusalem.

Petronius was deeply concerned over the imperial order because he knew that the Judeans would not tolerate the erection of such an image in the temple. Though he commissioned sculptors in Sidon to carve the statue, he also let them know that any delay would not be penalized. In the meanwhile, rumors about the statue leaked out and thousands of Judeans came to Petronius to plead with him not to carry out the emperor's decree. They even declared that they would rather be slain by his soldiers than to see the law of their forefathers violated. Petronius insisted that he could not ignore the order of Caesar. The Jews replied that just as he must obey the command of Caligula, so they must obey the command of God.

The Syrian legate was moved by the Jews' loyalty to their God. He wrote the emperor to explain the delay, asking not to be forced to put the statue in the temple until after the harvest, lest the Jews destroy it. The Roman emperor in a rage demanded that his image be immediately placed in the temple. Petronius went to Tiberias, probably to get advice from the family of King Agrippa—the king himself being in Rome—on how to avert the coming confrontation with the Jews. Again, as many as ten thousand Jews met Petronius in Tiberias, says Josephus.

Petronius, sensing a near rebellion, asked them, "Will you war then with the emperor, without considering his great preparations for war, and your own weakness?"

And they replied, "We will not by any means war with him, but we will die before we see our laws transgressed." Then they threw themselves down upon the ground, and stretched out their throats, and said they were ready to be slain. And they did this for forty days together, and in the meantime left off the tilling of their ground, though the season of the year required them to sow it.

"Thus firm did they continue in their resolution, and proposal to die willingly, rather than to see the erection of Gaius' [Caligula's] statue,"[8] says Josephus. The king's brother, joined by other members of the royal family, begged the Syrian legate to inform the emperor that the Jews were loyal to Rome, but that their religion would not permit them to tolerate an image in the temple, nor anywhere else in the land. Again Petronius wrote Caligula. This time the emperor suggested that Petronius commit suicide because he had dared disobey an imperial order. When Agrippa, who was at that time in Rome, heard of the emperor's order, Josephus says that he collapsed and was carried to his own home where he lay in a coma for thirty-six hours, for he knew that if the emperor succeeded in placing the image in the temple, there would be a general revolt in Judea. Philo gives an account of the outcome by saying that King Agrippa wrote a letter to Caligula, imploring him not to carry through his intent concerning the statue. Finally Caligula gave in and wrote to the legate of Syria, saying that if the statue had not already been placed in the temple then to forget it.

Josephus gives a different account of how King Agrippa accomplished this victory for his people. He says that Agrippa gave a banquet for the Roman emperor. In a merry mood, the emperor offered to grant any wish that he could for King Agrippa.

Agrippa replied, "Since, my lord, you declare, such is your liberality, that I am worthy of your gifts, I will ask nothing that will contribute to my own happiness, for what you have already bestowed on me has made me remarkable for that; I ask something which may make you glorious for piety, and render the Deity a helper of your designs, and may be an honour to me among those that hear of it, as showing that I never fail to obtain what I ask of you. Now my petition is this, that you will no longer think of the dedication of the statue which you have ordered Petronius to set up in the Jewish temple." (*Antiquities* 18.8.7). Caligula was assassinated on January 24, A.D. 41, twenty-seven days before the letter reached Petronius which implied that he should commit suicide. Thus the Syrian legate, as well as the Judeans, was saved from further bloodshed.

The Torah has declared, "Thou shalt not make unto thee a graven image, nor any likeness of any thing that is in heaven above, or that is in the earth beneath, or that is in the water under the earth: thou shalt not bow down thyself unto them, nor serve them; for I the LORD thy God am a jealous God, visiting the iniquity of the fathers upon the children, upon the third and upon the fourth generation of them that hate me, and showing lovingkindness unto thousands of them that love me and keep my commandments" (Ex 20:4-6). And since the exile had forever cured the people of Israel of their idolatrous tendencies, this abhorrence of images, carried over into the great tribulation, will cause the faithful remnant among the Jewish people to categorically refuse to worship the image of the beast. When they refuse, they will suffer the same fate as their ancient forefathers did in the days of Antiochus IV: "As many as should not worship the image of the beast should be killed" (Rev 13:15).

6

The Conflicts of the Antichrist

THE REIGN OF THE ANTICHRIST will come to an inglorious end amid a series of conflicts. The prophetic Word indicates that there are seven of these conflicts by which the Antichrist rises to power, in which he sustains himself in power, and through which he will meet his final doom. All of these occur within the limits of the tribulation period. Three of them are in association with an evil entity that the book of the Revelation identifies as Babylon (Rev 16:17—18:24). The Babylonian figure in the Bible stands for a world system of politics, religion, and commerce, which has left out God.

Though the origin of the Babylonian concept of civilization minus God is derived from the tower of Babel, in context here it is taken from the head of gold in Daniel's vision of the four successive world empires. Since Babylon was the first of these gentile world powers, it gives its name to the Satanic and materialistic character which is manifest in all succeeding empires, including the last one, the empire of the Antichrist. It is in this empire that the Babylonian system of politics, religion, and commerce is most dramatically presented.

The seven conflicts of the Antichrist are as follows. First, there is his conflict with political Babylon during his early rise to power as a new caesar at the head of the revived Roman empire. Second, his conflict with ecclesiastical Babylon shows itself as a manifest hostility against the great apostate church (Rev 17). Third, his conflict with commercial Babylon is his struggle against the predicted collapse of the world market and the economic conflagration which ensues (Rev 18). Fourth, there is the conflict with the foe from the far north. Fifth, Antichrist conflicts with the nation Israel during the last half of the tribulation, after he has broken the covenant with her. Sixth, he has a conflict with the Orient. And finally, there is the conflict with God at Armageddon. This general pattern, which has repeated itself in the career of every dictator in history, will characterize the career of the final world dictator. He arises amid conflict, maintains his dominion amid conflict, and then goes down in a final and great conflagration.

THE FIRST CONFLICT—THE RISE OF THE REVIVED ROMAN EMPIRE

Revelation 16:17-21 presents the fall of political Babylon, as the seventh bowl, containing the wrath of God, is poured out upon the earth. This is the end of the political power and world dominion of the Antichrist. This political dominion had its beginning just seven years prior to this time. It began as the final form of gentile world power, predicted in the book of Daniel, came into being. This final form of gentile world dominion is the revived Roman empire which is *separate,* but not *separable* from the ancient Roman empire which Daniel saw in two of his visions (Dan 2:40-43; 7:19-20). We have already noted that this climactic form of gentile world power is to arise again during the last days, for in each of Daniel's visions, this fourth gentile world power, Rome, is in existence at the second coming of Christ (cf. Dan 2:44; 7:21-22). In interpreting the prophetic Word, and in view of the fact that the ancient Roman empire has passed from this world scene and yet is in existence at the second coming of Christ, prophetic students have posited a revived form of the ancient Roman empire which must reappear in the tribulation period. The ancient Roman empire and its revived form are separated by the mystery age of the church which is unnoted by any of the Old Testament prophets, including Daniel in his two visions.

Every historian is aware of the dynamic of the Roman empire. Robert Payne says,

> The Roman empire perished and went on living. Long after the capital had become a small town outside the frontiers of the Byzantine empire and long after the last Roman legionary marched down the Flaminian Way, its civilization held sway in the West. The legacy of this most worldly of empires was to lie largely in the realm of ideas— in law, language, literature, government, attitudes, and styles. In innumerable ways, as century followed century, men's minds were to respond to a presence that was shorn of all the panoply of power while gradually becoming transfigured into a dominion of the spirit and of thought.[1]

The fact that ancient Rome lived on in spirit and even manifested itself in a revived form during the Renaissance, leads us to believe that it is not impossible for the ancient Roman empire to actually live again during the last days. The ancient empire of Rome took eight hundred years to reach its zenith, when in A.D. 117 the emperor Trajan had pushed its imperial boundaries to the Persian Gulf and to the Caspian Sea. It would live on for four centuries more, and the eastern divison for another thousand years after that. How different was the empire of Alexander the Great. It reached its limits in one decade of his life and then died when he died. Though historians assure us that the spirit of ancient Rome is very much alive today in the realm of ideas, it is the prophetic Word of God that assures us that the very structure of the ancient imperial empire will live again during the tribulation period; and that a new Caesar, more powerful than any of his ancient predecessors, will lead that revived Roman empire to universal political dominion.

One of the legendary founders of the city of Rome was named Romulus. Centuries later the empire was founded by Augustus. The last Roman emperor to reign in the west incorporated both of these figures in his name. He was the emperor Romulus Augustulus who vanished into obscurity in A.D. 476, after Rome had been sacked, robbed, burned, raped, and murdered by invaders from Europe. In addition to the reasons which Gibbons gives for the fall of Rome, it seems that there were several sets of circumstances which conspired to weaken and finally cause the collapse of the Roman empire.

The first of these circumstances were the three Jewish revolts which occurred during the first and second centuries. The fall of Jerusalem in A.D. 70, though a victory for Rome, was a costly one. Alexander the Great employed only 32,000 men to create a vast empire. Hannibal defeated the Romans with no more than 50,000 soldiers. Caesar had less than 25,000 legionnaires when he conquered Gaul and invaded Britain. But it took as many as 80,000 soldiers, and four years for the Romans to defeat the Jews. And this in contrast to the Jewish army which Josephus estimated at around 23,400 soldiers. On one occasion Titus had attempted to impress the Jews with Rome's might. He marched his entire army around the city—70,000 foot soldiers, 10,000 cavalry, and tons of equipment were pulled by the gates of Jerusalem. The parade lasted three days; however, this psychological warfare failed to impress the Jews who held out for another year. It was only after starvation, plague, and internal strife had so weakened the people that they finally were forced to surrender. But not until they had made a mockery of Roman military might did they capitulate. Though the Romans made a great show of victory in the inevitable triumphant parade, and though they struck coins to commemorate the defeat of Jerusalem, and though there still stands today in the Roman Forum the Arch of Titus, built to perpetuate the memory of the victory of Titus over the Jews, nevertheless, that victory was hollow. The Jews had demonstrated that the Romans were not invincible. The spirit of revolt spread in the Near East. Two more revolts of the Jews in the second century were also costly victories for the Romans. These also encouraged others to test the imperial strength of Rome. The empire began to feel the internal threat of rebellion, encouraged by the Jewish revolts which had cost the Romans not only in men and material but in prestige. The Jews had shown the world that the Romans were not unconquerable.

The Roman empire was also being weakened morally. Corrupt and unjust taxation, sexual looseness, the disintegration of the family, slavery, cruel and inhuman amusements, the eroding of the middle class, the disdain of work; all these and more conspired to corrupt the empire.

In addition, the empire suffered from the growing influence of Christianity. Because of the persecutions of the church by the empire, many of its Christian citizens had adopted an other-world outlook. Though Paul had tried to impress his Roman readers with Christian civic responsibility (Ro 13:1-7) , early Christians tended to live not for this world but for the next. This, in turn, led them to minimize civic duty and to disengage themselves from concerns with government. This overemphasis upon the hereafter led to a neglect of civic interests which increased as the number of Christians increased. It finally became a conspicuous factor in the deterioration of the empire.

The fourth ingredient in the fall of Rome was the most apparent—the invasions of the barbarians. These invasions began with the Goths in the third century, who were followed by wave after wave of invaders from northern and eastern parts of Europe. This was the most obvious cause of the fall of Rome. It will also cause the fall of the revived Roman empire in the last days. An invasion from the east, which will climax in the battle of Armageddon, will bring about the decline and fall of the revived Roman empire at the close of the great tribulation period.

The fall of ancient Rome was not final. One day a new caesar will arise, and with him a revival form of the ancient empire will reappear upon the world scene. John sees this in the Revelation. He says,

> The beast that thou sawest was, and is not; and is about to come up out of the abyss, and go into perdition. And they that dwell on the earth shall wonder, they whose name hath not been written in the book of life from the foundation of the world, when they behold the beast, how that he was, and is not, and shall come. Here is the mind that hath wisdom. The seven heads are seven mountains on which the woman sitteth: and they are seven kings; the five are fallen, the one is, the other is not yet come; and when he cometh, he must continue a little while. And the beast that was, and is not, is himself also an eighth, and is of the seven; and he goeth into perdition (Rev 17:8-11).

John sees five caesars (v. 10). These have already reigned. They may be the five emperors which were deified by an act of the Roman Senate: Julius Caesar, Augustus, Claudius, Vespasian, and Titus. "One is," John says, indicating the emperor Domitian who was even then on the imperial throne, for it was he who had banished John to the Isle of Patmos. "The other is not yet come," observes John. This is the last caesar to reign. It is the Antichrist who will reign over the revived Roman empire. John continues to observe that an eighth is also to come forth (v. 11). He is out of the seven, but somehow different enough to be designated an eighth. How? He is the same person as the seventh, for he is the final Roman caesar, the Antichrist, who is yet to come upon the world scene. However, as the eighth, he is different in that he becomes more than a ruler of the revived Roman empire.

He becomes god, not by legislative act, but by his own decree which will be enforced by Satan.

Here then is the evolution of this world ruler. The fact that this coming Caesar is designated by the number seven and eight, indicates *difference;* while the fact that the eighth is of the seven, indicates *similarity and relationship.* This is consistent with the prophetic word which presents the Antichrist during the tribulation period as the same person, yet with a Jekyll-and-Hyde personality. The differences are most clearly manifest in his relationship to Israel. During the first half of the tribulation period he is a new Roman caesar, head of the revived Roman empire, a world conqueror, and a political figure. His attitude toward the Jews is benevolent. However, at midtribulation period this same person becomes different. He is still the Antichrist and a political figure. But during the great tribulation period, or the last three and one-half years of the era, he becomes god. He breaks the covenant with the Jews, and as god he turns upon those Jews who will not worship him and severely persecutes Israel.

Thus the name *Beast* is reserved for the Antichrist during the last half of the tribulation period. Only after he has received his death stroke, which we have noted, and only after his complete capitulation to Satan, will he become the mad deity bent on coercing all the world, and especially the nation Israel, into worshiping him as god. Just as the revived Roman empire emerges in the last days from the roots of the old Roman empire, so the Antichrist emerges in the last days out of the roots of the imperial office of Caesar. A vital connection is seen, therefore, between both the physical empire in the last days and its imperial head, and the predecessors of each in the ancient Roman world.

When the rapture occurs and all born-again believers are taken out of the world then a predictable chaos results from the removal of many of the world's leaders in government, industry, business, and the professions. Ten kings quickly head up ten nations that are located within the geographical boundaries of the ancient Roman empire (Dan 2:42; 7:24). Though three of these kings offer some resistance (Dan 7: 24), the Antichrist quickly subdues them, and a ten-nation confederation forms the basis of the revived Roman empire. John says, "And the ten horns that thou sawest are ten kings, who have received no kingdom as yet; but they receive authority as kings, with the beast, for one hour. These have one mind, and they give their power and authority unto the beast" (Rev 17:12-13).

Revelation 6 may picture this initial struggle of the Antichrist to head the empire composed of the ten nations within the boundaries of ancient Rome, and which will occur just after the rapture of the church, at the beginning of the tribulation period. The amalgamation of these ten kingdoms into one empire occurs quickly, but with the exception of the three kings who put up some resistance, its cohesion is rapidly achieved by the Antichrist. However, it is opposition by these three kings which forms the first of the seven conflicts which the Antichrist will face. But with these three kings subdued, the revival of the Roman empire will be complete. When this occurs, then the secular and political history of Europe and the Near East will be right back where it was in the first century, when the prophetic time clock ceased in its movement, at the end of the sixty-ninth week of Daniel. The prophetic time clock will begin to tick off the last week of the times of the gentiles, under similar geographical boundaries and political circumstance to those which prevailed in Europe and the Near East when the time clock was stopped over two thousand years before.

While exploring a cave in the Judean wilderness in the spring of 1961, an archaeology team headed by Professor Yigael Yadin of Jerusalem's Hebrew University archaeology department found three beautifully executed glass dishes. The cave had been the last refuge of some Jewish zealots during the Bar Kokhba revolt in A.D. 135. Dr. Yadin wrote an account of the discovery in the *Illustrated London News,* and along with the article some pictures of the transparent glass dishes were printed. Some time later a noted British archaeologist, an expert in Roman glass, wrote to Dr. Yadin that there had been discovered at Richborough, Kent, a fragment of Roman glass which was very similar to what he had found in the Judean desert. Dr. Yadin comments in his recent book which deals with the second revolt, "The possibility should not be disregarded that the two bowls were actually manufactured in the same workshop. Strange are the ways of history! One bowl finds its way to a remote cave in the Judean Desert, and the other to Kent in England. But at that time, after all, the whole area was one Roman common market!"[2]

The Second Conflict—The Apostate Church

The second conflict which the Antichrist will encounter is the conflict with the apostate church (Rev 17:1-7). This conflict will begin at midtribulation period and is between the Antichrist and ecclesiastical Babylon.

Rather than being devoid of religion, the tribulation period will be one of the most religious periods of world history. We have already seen that it will be a time of worldwide revival. Possibly the latter rain of the Spirit will be even more potent than the former rain of the Spirit at Pentecost. But though there will be many who will be saved and become followers of Jesus, there will also arise during the tribulation a great apostate church. At first the apostate church will be an ally of the Antichrist. This is why John sees this apostate church under the figure of a whore, arrayed in purple and scarlet, and sitting astride the beast (Rev 17:3). This is a picture of a very wealthy (v. 4) state church (v. 2), which will be full of blasphemy (v. 3), and which will persecute the true saints of God (v. 6). During the first half of the tribulation there will be a repetition of the union between the institutional church and the Roman empire. Medieval history will repeat itself. This union between church and empire occurred in the fourth century A.D., and it will occur again during the tribulation period. The church of the tribulation period is an apostate church, of course, and not the redeemed body of the Lord Jesus Christ. For, after the rapture of the true church, there will come into being this apostate church, composed of unregenerate members, and made up of buildings, an ecclesiastical heirarchy, and empty ceremonies. It will be reminiscent of the institutional church of the Middle Ages when it was in its Pergamum force, in league with the government of the time, and thoroughly married to the world (Rev 2:12-17).

Therefore, the rise of the Antichrist is not only due to military causes; he also seems to use the religious forces that are available to him—notably, the apostate church and Judaism. The ancient Roman empire at first persecuted the church, then used it; the Antichrist will first use the apostate church, then persecute it. He will use it during the first half of the tribulation period for it will aid his rise to power. But when at midtribulation the apostate church is no longer needed, the Antichrist will turn upon it and persecute it.

> And the ten horns which thou sawest, and the beast, these shall hate the harlot, and shall make her desolate and naked, and shall eat her flesh, and shall burn her utterly with fire. For God did put in their hearts to do his mind, and to come to one mind, and to give their kingdom unto the beast, until the words of God should be accomplished. And the woman whom thou sawest is the great city, which reigneth over the kings of the earth (Rev 17:16-18).

Here then is the conflict between the Antichrist and ecclesiastical Babylon. The reason why the Antichrist turns upon the apostate church is obvious. He not only has no further use for it when he becomes a world dictator; but when he decrees himself god, he will tolerate no opposition.

THE THIRD CONFLICT—COMMERCIAL BABYLON

The third Babylon figure used in the book of Revelation has to do with the commercial world of the tribulation period (Rev 18:1-24). In this chapter John pictures the last days of the economic empire of the Antichrist.

It is important that we now note the perspective employed in the use of these three Babylonian figures, along with their precise focal points. Their focal points are politics, religion, and commerce, all three of which vitally concern the Antichrist during the entire seven years of his reign. John focuses upon them at three different points in the tribulation period, however. Though the final verses of Revelation 16 picture the termination of the political empire of the Antichrist, in connection with the seventh bowl of the wrath of God, political Babylon is emphasized during the first part of the tribulation period. This is when the political rise of the Antichrist is most dramatic. Ecclesiastical Babylon is foremost during the midtribulation period and the Antichrist's break with the apostate church. Commercial Babylon is prominent upon the close of the tribulation period and the complete collapse of the world economy. Therefore, the Babylonian figure—which is a symbol of this anti-God world system of politics, religion and commerce—covers the entire reign of the Antichrist during the tribulation period. But what concerns the Antichrist in his conquest of all the world—politically, religiously, and economically—shifts in emphasis as his confrontations change. At first they are political. At midtribulation they shift to religious issues. At the close of the tribulation period, the economy is the vital concern of the Antichrist in his attempt to maintain the stability of his empire. Of course, all three of these vital areas are about to fall into utter chaos at the end of the tribulation period. The war of Armageddon is just ahead. Yet the Antichrist will struggle to stabilize his world system of Babylonianized politics, religion, and commerce.

Since Babylon represents all civilization without God, this symbol can apply equally well to politics, religion, or even commerce, as it does in Revelation 18. Here the judgment of God is poured out upon the economy of the Antichrist. The reaction to the fall of commercial Babylon is presented from several viewpoints. The beast is not mentioned in this chapter, for he is not active in the destruction of commercial Babylon, as he was in the destruction of ecclesiastical Babylon. It is God who destroys the materialistic commercial society of the tribulation period (Rev 18:5). The beast is involved in this conflict between a materialistic society and God only because he is the administrative head of this economic structure.

Those who stand amazed at the fall of economic Babylon are, first, the kings of the earth (Rev 18:9-10). Who are these kings in relation to the Antichrist? In the ancient Roman empire there was one caesar, but there could be many kings reigning in the provinces at the behest of Rome. Herod the Great, for example, reigned as king in Judea when Augustus was caesar. Agrippa I was king in Iturea, Trachonitis, Galilee, Perea, Judea, and Samaria, while both Caligula and Claudius were Roman caesars. These kings who wail at the fall of Babylon are the provincial rulers who administrate the world empire of the Antichrist, and whose domains are affected most by the sudden disruption of commerce.

The second group which mourns the destruction of commercial Babylon is the merchants (Rev 18:11-17). They "mourn over her, for no man buyeth their merchandise any more" (v. 11). They are left with a vast inventory (vv. 12-13). As a result of the material values that motivated them, these merchants are utterly destroyed.

> And the fruits which thy soul lusted after are gone from thee, and all things that were dainty and sumptuous are perished from thee, and men shall find them no more at all.

> The merchants of these things, who were made rich by her, shall stand afar off for the fear of her torment, weeping and mourning; saying, Woe, woe, the great city, she that was arrayed in fine linen and purple and scarlet, and decked with gold and precious stone and pearl! for in one hour so great riches is made desolate (Rev 18:14-17).

A third group, the shipmasters, also mourns over the fall of commercial Babylon:

> And every shipmaster, and every one that saileth any whither, and mariners, and as many as gain their living by sea, stood afar off, and cried out as they looked upon the smoke of her burning, saying, What city is like the great city? And they cast dust on their heads, and cried, weeping and mourning, saying, Woe, woe, the great city, wherein all that had their ships in the sea were made rich by reason of her costliness! for in one hour is she made desolate (Rev 18:17b-19).

American history had its Black Friday, when the great financial panic occurred on September 24, 1869, as a result of the manipulation of the securities market by Fisk and Gould. October 24, 1929, is remembered as Black Thursday when the Great Depression began with the crash of the stock market. Just one week before the 1929 crash, Professor Irving Fisher of Yale University had announced, "Stock prices have reached what looks like a permanently high plateau." And then— sudden chaos. The eighteenth chapter of the Revelation notes over and over the suddenness of the economic crash that will come at the close of the tribulation period. "Therefore, in one day shall her plagues come" (v. 8); "for in one hour is thy judgment come" (v. 10); "for in one hour so great riches is made desolate" (v. 17); "for in one hour is she made desolate" (v. 19). Just as Roger W. Babson had predicted on September 5, 1929, "There is a crash coming, and it may be a terrific one," so the Revelation, with unerring and infallible prophetic accuracy, predicts the market crash of the closing days of the tribulation period.

Many of God's saints suffered through the aftermath of the 1929 crash during the Great Depression. The early 1930s were desperate years for everyone. But fortunately, the saints of God will not suffer the aftermath of the economic crash that is coming. For this economic collapse is a prelude to the immediate second coming of Christ. This is the reason why the fourth group of observers is called upon to rejoice. They are the saints, apostles, and prophets (v. 20). They are to rejoice because a new era of economic stability is coming.

Zechariah's vision of the woman and the ephah (5:5-10) may be a revelation of essentially the same truth. Prior to the exile, the Jews were an agriculturally oriented people. Their economy was a pastoral one. However, it was the exile that brought them into contact with the Babylonian economy and sowed the seeds of commercialism among them. Today we think of the Jews not as agricultural people but as merchants and other businessmen. In this vision—the seventh in a series, all of which have not only to do with the prophet's own day, but with the end time also—Zechariah is viewing the millennial earth. The theme of this seventh vision is that never again will the Lord permit the spirit of the Babylonian economic system to thrive. In this vision the woman is placed in an ephah (a dry measure which represents commercialism), and a heavy lead top is placed upon the ephah. She is then borne back to the land of Shinar—that is, back to Babylon where it all began. The prophet's message is this. If the spirit of greed, which is the human dynamic behind the Babylonian system of commerce, emerges among the unsaved of the millennial earth (Zec 5:5-6), it will be quickly and summarily dealt with (vv. 9-10). Therefore, the collapse of the Antichrist's economic structure puts an end to commercial Babylon. To its demise, Zechariah adds his epitaph: it will not rise again.

The Fourth Conflict—The Foe from the Far North

Ezekiel 38 and 39 record the conflict with the foe from the uttermost parts of the north (Eze 38:6, 15; 39:2). Daniel 11:40-43 describes the same invasion and in addition indicates that the Antichrist is involved in it, not as an invader, but as a protagonist of Israel. The foe is identified as being from the land of Magog. The leader of this northern foe is called Gog. He is further identified as the Prince of Rosh, Meshech, and Tubal (Eze 38:1-2). In addition, he has a number of allies (38:5-6). Many have identified the Prince of Rosh with Russia. Even if a philological identification between Rosh and Russia be rejected, geography would indicate that if the prophecy is fulfilled in modern times, the only major power in the far north, from Israel's standpoint, is Russia. In fact, Moscow is due north of Jerusalem. The identification is clear on geographical grounds. The foe from the uttermost parts of the north must be Russia.

Russia and her allies invade Israel at a time when Israel is resting securely and at peace. This is the only clue we have as to when this invasion occurs. But it is a clue that is most significant because of the uniqueness of the condition of peace and security in Israel. The prophecy has to do with the "latter days" (Eze 38:8, 16). It is clear that Israel is not today dwelling in peace and security—in "the land of unwalled villages" (Eze 38:11). Israel is an armed camp ready at a moment's notice for war. Soldiers at home on leave still carry guns with them at all times. The *Jerusalem Post* daily carries stories of vocal threats and overt acts of hostility from Israel's Arab neighbors who completely surround their country. Therefore, Ezekiel's prophecy does not have the present state of Israel in view.

In the future, during the great tribulation, Israel will not dwell securely and at peace. She will be severely persecuted by the Antichrist. Therefore, the only two periods in Israel's future when these conditions of peace and prosperity will prevail are, first, during the millennial reign of Christ, and second, during the first three and one-half years of the tribulation period. However, there can be no war in the millennium (Is 2:4); so this period is ruled out. The only other time is during the first half of the tribulation period when Israel dwells securely under the protective covenant made with the Antichrist. This covenant will be broken in the midst of the seventieth week (Dan 9:27); but before that time, for three and one-half years, Israel will be secure. It is during this first half of the tribulation that the Russian invasion of Israel will take place. Since the Antichrist has a covenant with Israel, which he has not at this point broken, he will be bound to protect her, just as the United States would probably come to the aid of Israel today if Russia attempted a direct invasion.

But this invasion of Israel not only will provide the Antichrist with an opportunity to destroy the northern confederacy—Russia and her allies—but it also will give to the Antichrist the opportunity for a takeover of Israel. This is his opportunity to defeat Russia and her allies, and at the same time an opportunity to divest himself of any further responsibility to Israel. In defeating Russia in Israel, he assimilates both countries under his ruthless rule. With the defeat of Russia, the Antichrist, who has reigned as Caesar over the revived Roman empire, now steps to a virtual world dictatorship. This comes as a direct result of his fourth conflict with the foe from the uttermost parts of the north.

The Fifth Conflict—The Nation Israel

"And there shall be a time of trouble, such as never was since there was a nation even to that same time" (Dan 12:1). "Alas! for that day is great, so that none is like it: it is even the time of Jacob's trouble" (Jer 30:7). "For then shall be great tribulation, such as hath not been from the beginning of the world until now, no, nor ever shall be. And except those days had been shortened, no flesh would have been saved: but for the elect's sake those days shall be shortened" (Mt 24:21-22). All of these passages indicate that the nation Israel will yet be exposed to a coming time of great trouble and sorrow. For their sake, those days will be cut to a minimum and allotted just enough time to accomplish the purging of Israel and the readying of the remnant to accept Jesus as Messiah. Those three and one-half years of great tribulation which Israel will have, will come as a result of the persecution of the Antichrist. This, then, is the fifth conflict in which the Antichrist is involved. This conflict will be with the nation Israel.

There are four groups within Israel with whom the Antichrist will enter into conflict: 1, Orthodox Jews who will not yield to the cult of the beast; 2, redeemed Jews who are spiritually saved during the tribulation; 3, the 144,000 Jewish missionaries who are invulnerable during this entire period; and 4, the two witnesses.

1. Daniel 9:27 indicates that in the midst of the seventieth week, three and one-half years into the tribulation period, the Antichrist will break the covenant that he has made with Israel. He will then plunge the nation into the last three and one-half years of suffering and sorrow, known as the great tribulation period (Dan 7:25; 12:7, 11; Rev 11:2, 3; 12:6, 14; 13:5).

After the rapture of the church, the Antichrist will use both the apostate church and Judaism as religious allies in his rise to power. But with the defeat of Russia and his assumption of his new role of world dictator, he needs neither of these religious allies anymore. In fact, they will become a competitive threat to his claim to be god. In order to be worshiped as god, he will permit no competition. Therefore, the apostate world church will be done away with, as we have seen, immediately at midtribulation. Then he will turn upon the Jews. Many will yield and worship him. Others will not worship him and will remain faithful to their ancient faith. It is this faithful remnant who will be the elect, and who will accept Jesus as Messiah at the close of the tribulation. It will also be this group of faithful Jews who will be severely persecuted during the great tribulation period because they will not acknowledge the beast as god.

Of course, Revelation 12 indicates that Satan is behind this persecution, as he always has been. He knows that Israel will produce the Messiah. Hence, his attacks began long before the great tribulation period.

> And a great sign was seen in heaven: a woman arrayed with the sun, and the moon under her feet, and upon her head a crown of twelve stars; and she was with child; and she crieth out, travailing in birth, and in pain to be delivered. And there was seen another sign in heaven: and behold, a great red dragon, having seven heads and ten horns, and upon his head seven diadems. And his tail draweth the third part of the stars of heaven, and did cast them to the earth: and the dragon standeth before the woman that is about to be delivered, that when she is delivered he may devour her child (Rev 12:1-4).

The child, the Lord Jesus Christ, is caught up into heaven. The mystery age of the church runs its course between Revelation 12:5 and 6. Then after the church is raptured, Satan's attacks continue in the great tribulation period.

> And the woman fled into the wilderness, where she hath a place prepared of God, that there they may nourish her a thousand two hundred and threescore days . . . And when the dragon saw that he was cast down to the earth, he persecuted the woman that brought forth the man child. And there were given to the woman the two wings of the great eagle, that she might fly into the wilderness unto her place, where she is nourished for a time, and times, and half a time, from the face of the serpent. And the serpent cast out

of his mouth after the woman water as a river, that he might cause her to be carried away by the stream. And the earth helped the woman, and the earth opened her mouth and swallowed up the river which the dragon cast out of his mouth (Rev 12:6, 13-16).

To this remnant in Israel who remain faithful to their historic faith, and who accept Jesus as Messiah when he comes again, Jesus gives instructions in his great prophetic discourse: "When therefore ye see the abomination of desolation, which was spoken of through Daniel the prophet, standing in the holy place (let him that readeth understand), then let them that are in Judaea flee unto the mountains: let him that is on the housetop not go down to take out the things that are in his house: and let him that is in the field not return back to take his cloak" (Mt 24:15-18).

The Talmud credits the Roman emperor Vespasian with the destruction of four hundred eighty synagogues in Jerusalem (*Megillah* 3.1.) Each town and city in Judea and in Galilee had a synagogue of its own, sometimes more than one. Tiberias at one time could boast of thirteen. As many as forty synagogues have been located by archaeologists, mostly in northern Galilee. Not a one of these dates from the first century A.D.,* but from the late second, third, and fourth centuries A.D. The reason is that all the first-century synagogues were destroyed by the Romans during the two rebellions of the Jews against Rome in A.D. 66-70 and again in A.D. 131-135.

In the terrible days which followed the fall of Jerusalem in A.D. 70, when all the synagogues had been destroyed in Galilee and in Judea, the rabbis gathered the faithful about them in caves and taught them. The Romans spent considerable time after the fall of Jerusalem, dislodging these pockets of pious resistance from the caves that surround the sea

---

*A first-century synagogue has recently been identified by Professor Yadin atop Masada. See Yigael Yadin's *Masada*, (New York: Random House, 1966).

of Galilee, as they did with the fortress of Masada down on the coast of the Dead Sea. The faithful who flee to the mountains during the great tribulation period may be in for an experience reminiscent of those days which followed the fall of Jerusalem in A.D. 70.

Twice in Revelation 12 it is noted that fleeing Israel has a place prepared by God for her refuge during the great tribulation period: "And the woman fled into the wilderness, where she hath a place prepared of God, that there they may nourish her a thousand two hundred and threescore days. . . . And there were given to the woman the two wings of the great eagle, that she might fly into the wilderness unto her place, where she is nourished for a time, and times, and half a time, from the face of the serpent" (Rev 12:6, 14). Many believe that this place prepared in the wilderness is the rock city of Petra. This city is located in ancient Nabataean territory, which prior to the fourth century B.C. was the land of Edom. This may be the reason why Daniel 11:41 says that Edom will be spared, along with Moab and Ammon. Perhaps all the Transjordan territory will provide refuge for the persecuted and fleeing Israel in those days. This will be a switch, for today, as in ancient times, this area (Edom, Moab, and Ammon) has been hostile to Israel (Eze 25:1-14). Two thirds of Israel will be killed during those closing days. But the Lord will preserve, perhaps in Petra, the third that comprises the faithful remnant. "And it shall come to pass, that in all the land, saith the LORD, two parts therein shall be cut off and die; but the third shall be left therein. And I will bring the third part into the fire, and will refine them as silver is refined, and will try them as gold is tried: they shall call on my name, and I will hear them: I will say, It is my people; and they shall say, the LORD is my God" (Zec 13:8-9).

Dr. W. E. Blackstone was so convinced that the rock city of Petra was to receive those fleeing Jews that he purchased thousands of New Testaments and had them hidden in the

rocks there so that fleeing Israel would have access to the
Word of the Lord in those days. The fact remains that the
remnant of Israel is to be preserved—whether in Petra, or in
other parts of Transjordan, or somewhere else. In fact, the
prophetic Scripture holds out a special blessing for those who
deal kindly with fleeing Israel in those days. This is the
meaning of the judgment of the nations in Matthew 25:31-46.
"Verily I say unto you, Inasmuch as ye did it unto one of these
my brethren, even these least, ye did it unto me" (v. 40). To
those who treat kindly Israel (the Lord's brethren according
to the flesh), the Lord promises a blessing (v. 34). Upon
those who do not treat Israel kindly during this time, the
Lord lays a curse (v. 41). Note carefully that both the blessing and the curse, predicted in this judgment of the nations,
is in fulfillment of the terms of the covenant made with
Abraham, "And I will bless them that bless thee, and him
that curseth thee will I curse: and in thee shall all the families
of the earth be blessed" (Gen 12:3).

2. During the great tribulation the elect in Israel will not
worship the beast. They will remain faithful to their historic
faith and will eventually receive Jesus as Messiah at the *close*
of the tribulation. But in addition to these, Satan will also
persecute those Jews who are saved *during* the tribulation.
"And the dragon waxed wroth with the woman, and went
away to make war with the rest of her seed, that keep the
commandments of God, and hold the testimony of Jesus"
(Rev 12:17). However, Satan does not mount a direct attack.
Rather, he uses the beast, who will severely persecute Israel
in his attempt to eradicate them.

Not only will the Antichrist face opposition which en-
genders conflict between him and the orthodox Jews—this
fleeing remnant who is the elect—but he also enters into conflict with those Jews who will accept Jesus as Saviour during
the tribulation. The former group will not be spiritually
redeemed until the *end* of the tribulation when they then

accept Jesus as Messiah. The latter group will be spiritually redeemed *during* the tribulation when they accept Jesus as Saviour. Both groups will be severely persecuted by the Antichrist.

There are two remaining groups of religious antagonists whom the Antichrist will face in his conflict with Israel during the tribulation. They are the 144,000 and the two witnesses.

3. The 144,000 are Jews who are saved *early* in the tribulation period. They are part of the great spiritual awakening that occurs just after the rapture of the church. Revelation 7:1-8 indicates that there will be 12,000 taken from each of the tribes of Israel. The listing of the twelve tribes has a strange omission of both Dan and Ephraim. In the case of Dan, as we have seen, many early expositors explained the omission on the grounds that the Antichrist was out of the tribe of Dan. Hippolytus, in his work *Concerning Antichrist*, says, "As Christ was born from the tribe of Judah, so will the Antichrist be born from the tribe of Dan." However, we do not believe that the Antichrist will be a Jew, and therefore this explanation, even though it is based on a rabbinic interpretation of Jeremiah 8:16, is not conclusive in explaining the omission of Dan. In the Old Testament the tribe of Dan was always associated with idolatry (Gen 49:17; Judg 18:30; 1 Ki 12:29). In rabbinic symbolism Dan stood for idolatry. It may be that his descendants are not permitted to stand among the 144,000 and against the Antichrist, as punishment for their perpetual idolatrous inclinations. In the case of the omission of Ephraim, Joseph is mentioned and may be a substitute for the name Ephraim.

In each case, exactly 12,000 are sealed and designated "servants of God" (v. 3). Does this mean that precisely 12,000 from each tribe are saved—no more and no less? No, for many more Jews, out of every tribe, will be saved during the tribulation; but exactly 12,000 from each are secured. Over them the Antichrist has no power. He is free, however, to martyr the rest of the redeemed Jews, along with all the gentiles, who are saved during the tribulation period as a result of the preaching of these sealed Jewish missionaries of the Word— the 144,000. So their sealing is not in view of their *salvation*, but it is in view of their *service* during the tribulation.

The 12,000 out of each tribe will be preachers of the kingdom gospel whom the Antichrist cannot harm. It is they who will carry the "gospel of the kingdom into the whole world for a testimony unto all nations" (Mt 24:14). The Antichrist will be antagonized at their preaching of the gospel, especially during the great tribulation when their preaching opposes his claim to be god. But he is powerless to harm them, nor can he silence them (Rev 9:3, cf. 7:3). They will win multitudes, both Jews and gentiles, to Christ during the time of their ministry. Their converts have not the seal of protection, however, which the 144,000 themselves have. As a result, the Antichrist will vent his fury upon their converts, and they will be slaughtered as a result of their profession of faith in Jesus Christ as Saviour and Lord. It is they who are pictured in Revelation 7:9-10: "After these things I saw, and behold, a great multitude, which no man could number, out of every nation and of all tribes and peoples and tongues, standing before the throne and before the Lamb, arrayed in white robes, and palms in their hands; and they cry with a great voice, saying, Salvation unto our God who sitteth on the throne, and unto the Lamb."

4. The last of the Jewish antagonists with whom the Antichrist has conflict are the two witnesses. These strange figures appear in the eleventh chapter of Revelation. The duration of their prophecy is 1260 days (Rev 11:3). This corresponds to the forty-two months mentioned in the previous verse in which the holy city will be trodden underfoot by the nations.

The 144,000 are active during the whole seven years of the tribulation, but the time of the appearance of the two witnesses is limited to the great tribulation period. Like the 144,000, they cannot be harmed during the appointed time of their ministry (v. 5). They will work miracles (v. 6). These miracles are reminiscent of those wrought by Moses and Elijah so that many believe that the two witnesses are actually these two great Old Testament figures returned to earth (cf. Mal 4:4-6). When their time of testimony is done, the beast will kill them (v. 7). Their bodies will lie in the streets of Jerusalem for three and one-half days (vv. 8-9), after which they will be resurrected and raptured (vv. 11-12). It is at the moment of their departure from the earth that the temple is probably destroyed.

> And there was given me a reed like unto a rod: and one said, Rise, and measure the temple of God, and the altar, and them that worship therein. And the court which is without the temple leave without, and measure it not; for it hath been given unto the nations: and the holy city shall they tread under foot forty and two months. . . . And in that hour there was a great earthquake, and the tenth part of the city fell; and there were killed in the earthquake seven thousand persons: and the rest were affrighted, and gave glory to the God of heaven (Rev 11:1-2, 13).

Measurements were often taken in the Bible in view of coming judgment. The temple has been desecrated beyond reparation. There will be no cleansing of it as there was in the days of the Maccabees when the temple was rescued from the abomination of desolation placed there by Antiochus IV. The tribulation temple will be destroyed and will be replaced by the millennial temple which the Lord himself will build for memorial services during the kingdom reign of Christ. Its destruction will occur at the close of the great tribulation period when two witnesses are caught up into heaven. Thus the worship of the beast is brought to an end with the conclusion of the ministry of the two witnesses. This means that the Lord will not permit the Antichrist to vaunt himself as god without the counterclaim of His two witnesses being heard during the entire course of the great tribulation. If any Jews yield to the cult of the beast and worship the Antichrist as god, they will do so in the face of the warning of the two witnesses.

In those days God will send two of his greatest servants: Moses, the liberator, the spiritual legislator of Israel; and Elijah, one of the greatest of the prophets. Each of these Old Testament figures saved Israel from bondage and idolatry during their respective days upon earth in Old Testament times. They will appear again to warn Israel and to keep many in the nation from total capitulation to the cult of the beast. The Antichrist will be powerless against them until the three and one-half years of their prophetic witness is finished. Finally he will be able to kill them—just as the antagonists of Jesus were powerless against his prophetic witness during the three and one-half years of his ministry on earth. When Jesus' ministry was finished, then his enemies could take him. But not before. When the witness of Moses and Elijah is done, then they will be killed. However, just as with the Lord Jesus Christ, they too will rise again and ascend into heaven. Their enemies will see them go into heaven. This public ascension, plus the ensuing earthquake in which a tenth part of the city is destroyed and seven thousand persons are killed, will also cause many to glorify God (v. 13). Therefore, just as he was enraged and frustrated by their life and ministry, so will the Antichrist be enraged at their death, resurrection, and ascension. All this will further weaken his claim to be god.

THE SIXTH CONFLICT—THE ORIENT AND THE BATTLE OF ARMAGEDDON

The termination of the Antichrist's kingdom will occur at the end of the great tribulation period. "And he shall plant the tents of his palace between the sea and the glorious holy mountain; yet he shall come to his end, and none shall help him" (Dan 11:45). The end of his reign will occur in Israel. It will come in association with the battle of Armageddon, after he hears tidings out of the north and east which trouble him (Dan 11:44). The picture seems to be something like this:

As a result of the midtribulation battle between the Antichrist and the king of the north, (Dan 11:40-43), the Antichrist will defeat Russia and her allies, including Egypt. He then will reign with uncontested sovereignty for the three and one-half years of the great tribulation period. Toward the end of this time there will come to him "tidings out of the east and out of the north" which greatly trouble him (Dan 11:44). The news will concern an uprising in the Orient and a vast army marching westward—as Atilla the Hun had done of old. Most historic invasions of the Holy Land have come from the north—as did the Assyrian invasion of the eighth century B.C., or the invasion of the Babylonians under Nebuchadnezzar, or the Seleucid invasions from Syria, or the Roman invasion in 63 B.C. Only Egypt invaded Israel from the south.

But no one ever invaded Israel from the west, because of the Mediterranean Sea, or from due east, because of the Arabian Desert. So if there is a land invasion from either Europe or from the Orient, it would naturally come from the north. But this invasion is not only from the north, it has its origin in the east. Thus the Orient will arise as the final foe of the Antichrist. "And the sixth poured out his bowl upon the great river, the river Euphrates; and the water thereof was dried up, that the way might be made ready for the kings that come from the sunrise" (Rev 16:12). These kings are Asians who are to cross the dried-up Euphrates river. They will round the Fertile Crescent and then will descend upon Israel from the north. Either the Antichrist never conquered the Orient in his midtribulation rise to world dictatorship, or the Orient is in insurrection against him when the end of the tribulation approaches.

It is an interesting parallel—the ancient Roman empire fell because of the invasion of barbaric hordes, whose unrest went back five hundred years to a crisis among oriental nomads in China. The kingdom of the Antichrist will fall due to a similar invasion of orientals. During the Chinese Han dynasty in the first century B.C., the rulers of China attempted to divest the country of all undesirables. A series of wars drove out of China all the itinerants who would neither settle down on farms nor take jobs in the cities. These nomads were called Huns after the Han dynasty which drove them out of China. As the Huns settled in India, Russia, and the Balkans, they drove out the previous inhabitants of these lands. These prior inhabitants were also nomads known as Visigoths, Vandals, and Ostrogoths. As the Huns were driven out of China, the Huns in turn drove from their homes the Visigoths, the Vandals, and the Ostrogoths, who migrated to Western Europe. Then from their new vantage point in Germany, Spain, France, and Italy, it was not long before these displaced nomads invaded Rome itself. The Visigoths were the first to do this. During the fifth century A.D., all had their turn at sacking the empire, including Atilla the Hun who came with his murderous band of cavalry into Italy but whose superstitious fear of Rome would not let him actually invade the city. Therefore, just as ancient Rome fell as a result of unrest in the Orient, so the revived Roman empire will also fall as a result of Oriental unrest.

There may be a description of this invasion in the sounding of the sixth trumpet

> And the sixth angel sounded, and I heard a voice from the horns of the golden altar which is before God, one saying to the sixth angel that had the trumpet, Loose the four angels that are bound at the great river Euphrates. And the four angels were loosed, that had been prepared for the hour

and day and month and year, that they should kill the third part of men. And the number of the armies of the horsemen was twice ten thousand times ten thousand: I heard the number of them (Rev 9:13-16).

The number of the armies of the horsemen is two hundred million men. Western Europe has always dreaded an invasion of Asiatics whose sheer numbers could inundate them. America also dreads a conflict with the raw hordes of Orientals apart from the protection of nuclear arms. Their numbers are awesome. Like the plague of locusts described in the first chapter of Joel, these people, if we did not have the deterrent of nuclear weapons, could swarm over the western world and deluge it with the sheer weight of their numbers. This seems to happen at the close of the tribulation. It may be that Joel begins his prophecy with the description of an actual locust plague. However, it is quite possible that his vision moves beyond some contemporary devastation by locusts to an invasion of Israel by an army, which he describes under the figure of locusts:

"Blow ye the trumpet in Zion, and sound an alarm in my holy mountain; let all the inhabitants of the land tremble: for the day of the LORD cometh, for it is nigh at hand; a day of darkness and gloominess, a day of clouds and thick darkness, as the dawn spread upon the mountains; a great people and a strong; there hath not been ever the like, neither shall be any more after them, even to the years of many generations. A fire devoureth before them; and behind them a flame burneth; the land is as the garden of Eden before them, and behind them a desolate wilderness; yea, and none hath escaped them. The appearance of them is as the appearance of horses; and as horsemen, so do they run. Like the noise of chariots on the tops of the mountains do they leap, like the noise of a flame of fire that devoureth the stubble, as a strong people set in battle array. At their presence the peoples are in anguish; all faces are waxed pale.

> They run like mighty men; they climb the wall like men of war; and they march every one on his ways, and they break not their ranks. Neither doth one thrust another; they march every one in his path; and they burst through the weapons, and break not off their course. They leap upon the city; they run upon the wall; they climb up into the houses; they enter in at the windows like a thief. The earth quaketh before them; the heavens tremble; the sun and the moon are darkened, and the stars withdraw their shining: and the LORD uttered his voice before his army; for his camp is very great; for he is strong that executeth his word; for the day of the LORD is great and very terrible; and who can abide it?" (Joel 2:1-11).

Therefore, at the close of the tribulation period, the forces of the Antichrist and the hordes of the Orient will enter into conflict. This will issue in the Battle of Armageddon. The setting of the battle is in the land of Israel. Several places are suggested. The fact that the location of the Battle of Armageddon is not limited to Galilee, but is also said to take place in the environment of Jerusalem, indicates that it might be better to speak of this final world conflagration as the War of Armageddon. Revelation 16:14 actually contains a word which means war, and the RV says, "to gather them together unto the war of the great day of God, the Almighty." As a war is made up of many battles, so Armageddon may be made up of many battles which roam over the entire map of Palestine. This is also suggested in Revelation 14:20; "And the winepress was trodden without the city, and there came out blood from the winepress, even unto the bridles of the horses, as far as a thousand and six hundred furlongs." This is roughly the approximate length of Israel from Dan to Beersheba.

Revelation 16:16 locates the battle in a place called in Hebrew, *Har-Magedon*. The name *Armageddon* may be derived from this Hebrew name which means mountain of

Megiddo. If this is the case, then the location of the final battle is the Plain of Esdraelon which lies below the ancient city of Megiddo. Megiddo was a Canaanite city which guarded the Pass of Megiddo. It was very strategic for this reason. It was refortified by Solomon and Ahab. Extensive archaeological investigations have taken place on this site and it is now one of the most popular tourist attractions in northern Israel. This ancient city has overlooked some of the world's most bloody battles which have occurred on the flat, triangular plain below the fortress.

While Israel was still in Egyptian captivity, in 1490 B.C. Thutmose III, pharoah of Egypt, defeated a confederation of the kings of Canaan, Syria, and the Mitanni, in the plain of Megiddo. This victory set the stage for Egypt's conquest of the entire Fertile Crescent. Pharaoh-necoh came up the plain of Sharon, cut across the Mt. Carmel range through the pass of Megiddo, and then out into the Plain of Esdraelon. Here King Josiah rode out to meet him in 609 B.C., and was killed in the ensuing battle. Pharaoh-necoh was crossing the land bridge between Egypt and Asia. This land bridge, called *Via Maris,* "the Way of the Sea," was the main artery between Egypt and Carchemish, where Pharaoh-necoh was going to engage the Babylonians in battle.

In this valley Hebrews and Canaanites have met in battle. Here also battles have occurred between Egyptians and Assyrians, between Babylonians and Greeks, between Seleucids and Ptolemies, between Romans and Arabs, between Crusaders and Turks. Here also the final battle of history between the Antichrist and the kings from the east will begin.

The Plain of Esdraelon is a triangular plain, bounded on the south by the Mount Carmel range. Megiddo is located about half way between Mt. Carmel on the apex of the triangle, and Mt. Gilboa, on the southeastern base of the triangle. Mt. Tabor is on the northeastern base of the triangle. Along the northern rim of the valley the city of Nazareth is located. Jesus often viewed this plain as he looked across the valley from Nazareth, on the north, to Megiddo on the south. The size of the plain is about fifteen by fifteen by twenty miles, with these three mountains roughly forming the three points of the triangle. This plain has access on the west to the Mediterranean Sea at the port of Haifa. It also has access to the Jordan valley through the Valley of Jezreel which is an extension of the Plain of Esdraelon on the east. The Pass of Megiddo gives access from the south via the Way of the Sea and across the Carmel range. The ancient route ran northeast from the plain to the Sea of Galilee, and from there into Syria and Mesopotamia, making possible an entrance to the plain from the north. Therefore, it can be entered from all four points on the compass. Possibly in this spot the Antichrist will first engage the invading hordes from the Orient. They will round the Fertile Crescent, cross the dried-up Euphrates river, pass through Syria, and then down into Israel, via the ancient trade route which empties into the Valley of Esdraelon. There below the ancient fortress of Megiddo the battle will be joined.

The prophet Joel indicates another spot for the final battle. Perhaps the fighting moves southeast, through the Valley of Jezreel, down the valley of the Jordan, up the Jericho road through the wilderness of Judea, to Jerusalem. Something like this is indicated, for both Joel and Zechariah, along with Jeremiah, pinpoint the battle in and around Jerusalem:

> For, behold, in those days, and in that time, when I shall bring back the captivity of Judah and Jerusalem, I will gather all nations, and will bring them down into the valley of Jehoshaphat; and I will execute judgment upon them there for my people and for my heritage Israel, whom they have scattered among the nations: and they have parted my land, and have cast lots for my people, and have given a boy for a harlot, and sold a girl for wine, that they may drink. . . . Proclaim ye this among the nations; prepare war; stir

up the mighty men; let all the men of war draw near, let them come up. Beat your plowshares into swords, and your pruninghooks into spears: let the weak say, I am strong. Haste ye, and come, all ye nations round about, and gather yourselves together: thither cause thy mighty ones to come down, O Lord. Let the nations bestir themselves and come up to the valley of Jehoshaphat; for there will I sit to judge all the nations round about. Put ye in the sickle; for the harvest is ripe: come, tread ye; for the winepress is full, the vats overflow; for their wickedness is great. Multitudes, multitudes in the valley of decision! for the day of the Lord is near in the valley of decision (Joel 3:1-3, 9-14).

Jehoshaphat means "the Lord judgeth." No one really knows where the Valley of Jehoshaphat is located; however, since the fourth century A.D. it has been identified with the Valley of Kidron which runs down the eastern side of Jerusalem, separating the old city from the Mount of Olives range. It is so named because a tomb there is called Jehoshaphat's Tomb. In the Kidron Valley, just below the sealed eastern gate into the old city, several tombs can be seen. This spot has been a favorite burial ground for Jews for thousands of years, for they believed that the trumpets of universal resurrection and final judgment would be sounded here. Some of the rabbis taught that it was necessary to be buried in the Holy Land in order to have a part in the resurrection which would precede the Messiah's reign upon earth. They even taught that the bodies of the righteous, no matter where on earth they might have been buried, would roll back, underground, to Israel and be raised there.

Thus for the Jew the most sacred burial spot on earth was this valley between the temple mount and the Mount of Olives. The tombs that mark this spot are several. The Pillar of Absalom, which dates from the time of the second temple, is there. There also are the Beni Hezir Tombs which are the burial places of a Herodian priestly family. Tradition has called these particular crypts the Tomb of St. James. Then there is also the Tomb of Zacharias, which dates to the first century A.D. However, behind Absalom's Pillar there is a large carved-out alcove, a burial cave which is decorated with an ornately carved frieze of acanthus leaves. This is the traditional Tomb of Jehoshaphat (king from 871-850 B.C.). Though these monuments are Greek in style and date from the Roman period, tradition identifies this area with the Valley of Jehoshaphat spoken of by the prophet Joel.

Jeremiah adds another fact to the cumulative picture of Armageddon. He identifies a spot a little further south of the Tomb of Jehoshaphat which he calls Tophet. He also says that this spot will be named the Valley of Slaughter.

> And they have built the high places of Topheth, which is in the valley of the son of Hinnom, to burn their sons and their daughters in the fire; which I commanded not, neither came it into my mind. Therefore, behold, the days come, saith the LORD, that it shall no more be called Topheth, nor The Valley of the son of Hinnom, but The Valley of Slaughter: for they shall bury in Topheth, till there be no place to bury. And the dead bodies of this people shall be food for the birds of the heavens, and for the beasts of the earth; and none shall frighten them away" (Jer 7:31-33, cf. 19:6 ff).

Tophet was probably the point, south of Jerusalem, where three valleys met. The Tyropoeon Valley which runs through the old city and down by the western wall of the temple mount, intersects here with the Valley of Hinnom. The Valley of the Sons of Hinnom sweeps around the western side of the city and turns east below the Ophel to meet the Valley of Kidron. All three of these valleys converge at the spot where ancient Israel offered sacrifices to the Ammonite god Molech (2 Ch 28:3; 33:6). Here also the field of Akeldama is located (Mt 27:7-8; Ac 1:18-19).

The Talmud places the mouth of hell in this place. It

says, "There are two palm trees in the Valley of Hinnom between which the smoke ariseth—and this is the door of Gehenna" (Sukkah, 32b) [3] The Arabs also call this lower end of the Hinnom valley, where it meets Kidron, at Tophet, the Valley of Hell. In Jesus' day the city garbage dump was located there. The fighting between Jews and Romans ended here in A.D. 70. As many as 600,000 bodies of dead Jews, slain in the defense of Jerusalem against the Romans, were carried out through the Dung Gate to be buried in Tophet. Jeremiah's words found fulfillment at that time. However, there is coming a greater fulfillment, when Tophet may well mark the spot where the Battle of Armageddon comes to its climax.

Jerusalem means city of peace. Yet more wars have been fought around and in this city, than almost any other city on the face of the earth. So earth's final battle will come to a close in Jerusalem and the city of peace will then know peace forever, for the Prince of Peace will reign there. Zechariah indicates in his prophecy that one of the final battles will occur within the city itself. "Behold, a day of the LORD cometh, when thy spoil shall be divided in the midst of thee. For I will gather all nations against Jerusalem to battle; and the city shall be taken, and the houses rifled, and the women ravished; and half of the city shall go forth into captivity, and the residue of the people shall not be cut off from the city. Then shall the LORD go forth, and fight against those nations, as when he fought in the day of battle (Zec 14:1-3).

The focal point of the Battle of Armageddon is the Holy Land. However, there is a vision in Zechariah which suggests that the judgment of Armageddon, while striking specifically in the Holy Land, finally becomes a universal one.

> And again I lifted up mine eyes, and saw, and, behold, there came four chariots out from between two mountains; and the mountains were mountains of brass. In the first chariot were red horses; and in the second chariot black horses; and in the third chariot white horses; and in the

fouth chariot grizzled strong horses. Then I answered and said unto the angel that talked with me, What are these, my lord? And the angel answered and said unto me, These are the four winds of heaven, which go forth from standing before the Lord of all the earth. The chariot wherein are the black horses goeth forth toward the north country; and the white went forth after them; and the grizzled went forth toward the south country (Zec 6:1-6).

The two mountains of brass out of which the four chariots emerge are two specific mountains. The expression in Hebrew is *the* two mountains, as the R.V. margin notes. This suggests two well-known mountains. Joel 3:2 speaks of the judgment of the nations occurring in the Valley of Jehoshaphat, as we have seen. From the time of Eusebius in the fourth century this valley has been identified as lying between the two mountains—Olivet and the temple mount. We have suggested that the Battle of Armageddon will come to its climax here in the environment of Jerusalem. However, Zechariah's imagery of the four chariots indicates that the judgment of God which occurs here in Jerusalem in the Valley of Jehoshaphat between Olivet and the temple mount will finally move out to issue in universal judgment. The four chariots will sweep out of the valley between the two mountains and move toward the north and the south. We have seen that the north and the south were the only doors of entrance into and exit from the Holy Land in biblical times. For this reason two chariots move toward the north and two toward the south. The inference is that while two continue north and south, the other two then turn east and west, fanning out to the four points of the compass, as "the four winds of heaven" (v. 5). Therefore, the judgment of Armageddon, which seems to contract in its focus upon Israel and Jerusalem, suddenly fans out, and the entire world is brought into judgment.

It is interesting that when Jesus sat upon the Mount of Olives and gave his great prophetic discourse, his view had command of all these areas. The Valley of Kidron, which may also be the Valley of Jehoshaphat, ran just below the hill where he sat with his disciples. To his left, a mile away beneath the pinnacle of the temple, was the place of Tophet, which Jeremiah says will become the Valley of Slaughter. Across the Kidron Valley, beyond the walls, was the temple mount, and then beyond that was the upper city itself. The scenes of the final battle must have been very real to Jesus, for he not only saw the very spot where Armageddon would end while he sat on the Mount of Olives, but he had spent his childhood and early manhood living on the hillside overlooking the Plain of Esdraelon where the Battle of Armageddon begins.

THE SEVENTH CONFLICT—THE SECOND COMING OF CHRIST

The nations gather in Israel to do battle with the Antichrist. However, both the forces of the invading kings from the East and those of the Antichrist, will finally come into battle with the Lord Jesus Christ. Jude says that Enoch, the seventh from Adam, saw this far off day and spoke of it. "Behold, the Lord came [past tense, but prophetic future] with ten thousands of his holy ones, [the Greek literally runs, "with His holy myriads"] to execute judgment upon all, and to convict all the ungodly of all their works of ungodliness which they have ungodly wrought, and of all the hard things which ungodly sinners have spoken against him" (Jude 14). Jude quotes from the apocalyptic *Book of Enoch*. His quotation does not endorse the whole *Book of Enoch* as inspired, as some of the early church fathers taught. It simply means that the Holy Spirit led Jude to recognize that this was a true statement, even in the midst of all the fantastic inventions found in this apocryphal work which is attributed to Enoch.

At the close of the great tribulation period a vast army will invade Israel from the Orient. Its purpose is to destroy the kingdom of the Antichrist. Hence, the battle is not between

Israel and the Orient. Israel is passive, having been subjected at midtribulation to the kingdom of the Antichrist. The battle involves Israel only because the Jews are a subject people who have been assimilated into the kingdom of the Antichrist. Of course, just as Israel would not readily assimilate into the ancient Roman empire but was always on the verge of revolt, so she will be a part of the revived Roman empire, but her identity will not be lost in this relationship. The Battle of Armageddon is between the revived Roman empire, with the Antichrist at its head; and his foes, the Oriental kings from the east. However, the battle occurs on holy ground for it all transpires—so far as the record goes—in Israel. Beginning on the Plain of Esdraelon, it moves south to Jerusalem. The nations that take part in this battle ravage Israel as a matter of course. It is then that the Lord takes a hand in the battle and brings it to a conclusion in order to protect his elect, the nation Israel.

> Come, my people, enter thou into thy chambers, and shut thy doors about thee: hide thyself for a little moment, until the indignation be overpast . . . In that day shall the Lord defend the inhabitants of Jerusalem; and he that is feeble among them at that day shall be as David; and the house of David shall be as God, as the angel of the Lord before them. And it shall come to pass in that day, that I will seek to destroy all the nations that come against Jerusalem . . . For I will gather all nations against Jerusalem to battle; and the city shall be taken, and the houses rifled, and the women ravished; and half of the city shall go forth into captivity, and the residue of the people shall not be cut off from the city. Then shall the Lord go forth, and fight against those nations, as when he fought in the day of battle (Is 26:20; Zec 12:8-9; 14:2-3).

Though the Battle of Armageddon begins as a conflict between the Antichrist and the Orient, it ends as a conflict between these two forces and the Lord. And the reason is that

God steps in to protect Israel who is being destroyed as the battle rages over the Holy Land. It is for this reason that Jesus says, "but for the elect's sake those days shall be shortened" (Mt 24:22). They are shortened when the second coming of Christ brings them to a close. It is in the midst of the Battle of Armageddon that the second coming of Christ will occur. The picture seems to be one of earthly hostility and battle, but the end is also accompanied with celestial disruption. The whole universe seems to be convulsed by this last struggle between the forces of evil and the returning Lord Jesus Christ.

> "But immediately after the tribulation of those days the sun shall be darkened, and the moon shall not give her light, and the stars shall fall from heaven, and the powers of the heavens shall be shaken: and then shall appear the sign of the Son of man in heaven: and then shall all the tribes of the earth mourn, and they shall see the Son of man coming on the clouds of heaven with power and great glory. And he shall send forth his angels with a great sound of a trumpet, and they shall gather together his elect from the four winds, from one end of heaven to the other" (Mt 24:29-31).

The prophet Joel also notes this. In Joel 2:29 the prophet promises the Holy Spirit to those who repent. This was fulfilled at Pentecost. The mystery age of the church which runs its course between Pentecost and the rapture, is unnoted by Joel between verses 29 and 30. This is consistent with all Old Testament prophecy as we have noted. Then Joel says, "And I will show wonders in the heavens and in the earth: blood, and fire, and pillars of smoke. The sun shall be turned into darkness, and the moon into blood, before the great and terrible day of the LORD cometh. And it shall come to pass, that whoever shall call on the name of the LORD shall be delivered; for in mount Zion and in Jerusalem there shall be those that escape, as the LORD hath said, and among the rem-

nant those whom the LORD doth call" (Joel 2:30-32). Simon
Peter quoted this entire passage at Pentecost (Ac 2:16-21).
However, the cosmic manifestation of God's power will not
be fulfilled until the second coming of Christ, for it obviously
did not occur on the day of Pentecost.

The second coming of Christ will bring to a close the times
of the gentiles. The times of the gentiles—in which Jesus
predicted that Jerusalem would be under the dominion of
gentile nations (Lk 21:24)—is to run its course beginning
in 605 B.C., when Jerusalem passed under the control of the
Babylonians, and it will end at the close of the great tribulation period. With but few exceptions, the city of Jerusalem
has been subject in turn to Babylonians, Persians, Greeks,
Ptolemies, Seleucids, Romans, Arabs, Seljuks, Crusaders,
Turks, and finally to the British under a mandate from the
League of Nations. During the first part of the tribulation
period it will be relatively free of gentile control, as it is
today, and has been since the Six-Day War. But during the
great tribulation period it will again be under gentile control
and remain so until the end comes. The second coming of
Christ will break finally and forever gentile control of the
Holy City. Many felt that the Six-Day War brought to a close
the times of the gentiles, for the city was freed from gentile
dominion for the first time in 1,832 years. However, Jerusalem's liberation in June, 1967, is no more significant than
it was in 165 B.C. when the temple was cleansed and the subsequent Hasmonean dynasty brought the city for a while
under Jewish rule, apart from any gentile suzerainty. But it
was not permanent.

In 63 B.C. the Romans came, and though the Hasmoneans
continued their rule until 37 B.C., the Romans ended all that
the Maccabean revolt and the subsequent reign of the Jewish
kings had promised. The city was back under gentile dominion. For a few years, during the first Jewish revolt against
Rome, 66-70 A.D., the city was free of gentile dominion. But

even then, hostile Roman forces were just outside the walls. When Bar Kokhba's rebellion began in A.D. 132, the Romans were taken by surprise. They had not expected the Jews to have the heart to engage in another war with Rome. Hadrian ordered his best general, Julius Severus, from Britain where he was engaged in putting down a revolt of the Celts. Severus entered Israel at the head of thirty-five thousand crack troops. But Bar Kokhba's inferior army dealt the imperial force a mighty defeat.

For two years Jerusalem was free of gentile control, except that the Romans were outside the city burning and destroying every living thing in Israel that the army itself could not use. Men, women, children, and cattle all were mercilessly butchered in the wake of the Roman advance. Finally in the year 135, Bar Kokhba's forces yielded and the Romans once again took over Jerusalem. Jerusalem was then declared off limits to Jews.

In 1947 the British, who had ruled Palestine under a mandate from the League of Nations since the end of World War I (actually since 1922), brought the Palestine question to the United Nations. The special Committee on Palestine recommended that Palestine be partitioned into independent Jewish and Arab states. Jerusalem was to be under international control—still in gentile hands. On May 15, 1948, the British mandate ended. However, just a few hours after the proclamation of Israel's independence, the armies of Egypt, Jordan, Syria, Lebanon, and Iraq, along with Saudi Arabian contingents, invaded Israel. When an armistice agreement was signed after seven months of fighting, Jordan wound up in control of the Old City of Jerusalem. The city remained divided until the Six-Day War of June, 1967. Then a unique thing happened. For the first time in history Jerusalem was taken from the east and the Israeli army passed into the Old City through St. Stephen's Gate which overlooks the Valley of Kidron, across from the Mount of Olives.

From that day in June, 1967, until today, Jerusalem is no longer under submission to the gentiles. But it will not last. The Jewish population in Jerusalem is 283,100 (1970), far outnumbering the Arab population of 72,000. The capital of Israel is Jerusalem, where the Knesset, a unicameral legislature, sits. The parliamentary democracy of Israel has invested supreme authority in the Knesset which is housed in Jerusalem. All of this attests to complete Jewish dominion of the city. However, this will not endure. When the end comes, Jerusalem will be under the control of the Antichrist.

Thus the times of the gentiles will not come to a permanent conclusion until the second coming of Christ. This is what Daniel declares in his imagery of the smitten colossus.

> As for this image, its head was of fine gold, its breast and its arms of silver, its belly and its thighs of brass, its legs of iron, its feet part of iron, and part of clay. Thou sawest till that a stone was cut out without hands, which smote the image upon its feet that were of iron and clay, and brake them in pieces. Then was the iron, the clay, the brass, the silver, and the gold, broken in pieces together, and became like the chaff of the summer threshing-floors; and the wind carried them away, so that no place was found for them: and the stone that smote the image became a great mountain, and filled the whole earth. . . . And in the days of those kings shall the God of heaven set up a kingdom which shall never be destroyed, nor shall the sovereignty thereof be left to another people; but it shall break in pieces and consume all these kingdoms, and it shall stand for ever. Forasmuch as thou sawest that a stone was cut out of the mountain without hands, and that it brake in pieces the iron, the brass, the clay, the silver, and the gold; the great God hath made known to the king what shall come to pass hereafter: and the dream is certain, and the interpretation thereof sure (Dan 2:32-35, 44, 45).

The times of the gentiles included the four great world empires: Babylon, Medo-Persia, Greece, and the ancient Roman empire. The latter will merge into the revived Roman empire, which was always latent in the fourth empire. Therefore, the prophetic word has declared that there will be only four world empires. All other dreams of world conquest are destined to failure. The next world kingdom that will be set up is that of the millennial kingdom over which the Lord Jesus Christ himself will reign. And this he will achieve just after the nations are subdued, during the final battle, in the midst of which the Lord Jesus Christ will return to the earth.

> And I saw the heaven opened; and behold, a white horse, and he that sat thereon called Faithful and True; and in righteousness he doth judge and make war. And his eyes are a flame of fire, and upon his head are many diadems; and he hath a name written which no one knoweth but he himself. And he is arrayed in a garment sprinkled with blood: and his name is called The Word of God. And the armies which are in heaven followed him upon white horses, clothed in fine linen, white and pure. And out of his mouth proceedeth a sharp sword, that with it he should smite the nations: and he shall rule them with a rod of iron: and he treadeth the winepress of the fierceness of the wrath of God, the Almighty. And he hath on his garment and on his thigh a name written, KING OF KINGS, AND LORD OF LORDS (Rev 19:11-16).

The last act initiated by the Antichrist will be his attack upon the armies of the Lord. "And I saw the beast, and the kings of the earth, and their armies, gathered together to make war against him that sat upon the horse, and against his army" (Rev 19:19).

The devastation of the Lord's enemies will not be wrought with physical weapons. "And out of his mouth proceedeth a sharp sword, that with it he should smite the nations" (Rev 19:15). Once before Jesus had shown the power of His spoken word, but without fatal results. The temple guards had come to the Garden of Gethsemane to take Jesus. "When therefore he said unto them, I am he, they went backward and fell to the ground" (Jn 18:6). The power of his word caused his captors to fall prostrate before him. That time they recovered and took him. But the next time he speaks to his enemies the sword of his mouth will utterly slay them.

Revelation 19:17-18 presents a picture of absolute carnage resulting from this final battle. The Antichrist is not killed in this battle. Daniel 11:45 speaks of his coming to his end between the sea and the glorious holy mountain, that is, in Israel; however, this must be the end of his reign, and not of his life. Revelation 19:20-21, says that the Antichrist, along with the false prophet, are "cast *alive* into the lake of fire that burneth with brimstone: and the rest were killed with the sword of him that sat upon the horse, even the sword which came forth out of his mouth: and all the birds were filled with their flesh." Just as two Old Testament saints, Enoch and Elijah, went alive into heaven without death; so these two will go alive into the lake of fire without seeing death. After the millennial reign of Christ, a thousand years later, they will be still there, for Satan will join them at that time. "They shall be tormented day and night for ever and ever" (Rev 20:10). There is no hope of annihilation.

The times of the gentiles climaxes in the judgment of the nations. "But when the Son of man shall come in his glory, and all the angels with him, then shall he sit on the throne of his glory: and before him shall be gathered all the nations" (Mt 25:31-32). The nations will be judged and will receive a blessing or a curse according to the way they have treated Israel. Specifically, the nations' treatment of Israel during the tribulation will be at issue. How did the nations treat Israel during the time of great tribulation, when she was fleeing from the severe persecution of the Antichrist? Did the nations provide a refuge for Israel? If so, "inasmuch as ye did it unto one of these my brethren, even these least, ye did it unto me" (Mt 25:40). According to the Abrahamic covenant they will be blessed (Mt 25:34). Or did the nations reject fleeing Israel, and expose them further to the wrath of the Antichrist, refusing to protect and shelter them? If so, "Verily I say unto you, Inasmuch as ye did it not unto one of these least, ye did it not unto me" (Mt 25:45). According to the Abrahamic covenant they will be cursed (Mt 25:41).

If the nations are to be blessed or cursed, according to their treatment of fleeing Israel during the Antichrist persecutions of the great tribulation period, what about Israel herself? What is the prophetic destiny of the people themselves who have suffered under the reign of the Antichrist? Two things are indicated concerning the future destiny of those Jews who suffered either martyrdom in the case of the saints, or persecution in the case of the Jews who remained faithful to their ancient faith and who do not yield to the cult of the beast. The former group, the saints, will be resurrected. The latter group, the elect nation, will be regathered and regenerated.

The saints are those Jews, along with the gentiles, who accept Jesus as Saviour during the tribulation. Most, if not all, of them are martyred as soon as they are spiritually saved. Since the resurrection and the rapture precede the death of those martyrs, occurring at the beginning of the tribulation, what is the program of God for the tribulation saints who are martyred? When will they be raised?

The resurrection which occurs along with the rapture is a unique church event. Only the church, the body of Christ, is included in this resurrection. Paul says "the dead in Christ shall rise first" (1 Th 4:16). The term *in Christ* refers to a distinctive group in the theology of Paul. It designates only those who are born again during the church age. It does not include the Old Testament saints. Nor does it include the tribulation saints. But when are the Old Testament saints and the tribulation saints raised from the dead? Daniel 12:2 indicates a resurrection which takes place after the tribulation, "And many of them that sleep in the dust of the earth shall awake." Isaiah speaks of this same event. "Thy dead shall live; my dead bodies shall arise. Awake and sing, ye that dwell in the dust; for thy dew is as the dew of herbs, and the earth shall cast forth the dead" (Is 26:19). These are among the few resurrection passages in the Old Testament, and both refer to that time at the close of the great tribulation period when the Lord will raise the Old Testament saints.

And then will come that glorious day in Israel's history, just before the millennial reign is established on earth, when the nation Israel will accept the Lord Jesus Christ as the Messiah. "And I will pour upon the house of David, and upon the inhabitants of Jerusalem, the spirit of grace and of supplication; and they shall look unto me whom they have pierced; and they shall mourn for him, as one mourneth for his only son, and shall be in bitterness for him, as one that is in bitterness for his first-born . . . In that day there shall be a fountain opened to the house of David and to the inhabitants of Jerusalem, for sin and for uncleanness" (Zec 12:10; 13:1).

This is the day of which Paul spoke when he said "and so all Israel shall be saved" (Ro 11:26). This is the day that the prophet Ezekiel had in view when he saw the Spirit of God move upon a valley of dry bones and the whole house of Israel came to life.

> Then he said unto me, Son of man, these bones are the whole house of Israel: behold, they say, Our bones are dried up, and our hope is lost; we are clean cut off. Therefore prophesy, and say unto them, Thus saith the Lord GOD: Behold, I will open your graves, and cause you to come up out of your graves, O my people; and I will bring you into the land of Israel. And ye shall know that I am the LORD, when I have opened your graves, and caused you to come up out of your graves, O my people. And I will put my Spirit in you, and ye shall live, and I will place you in your own land: and ye shall know that I, the LORD, have spoken it and performed it, saith the LORD (Eze 37:11-14).

This too is the fulfillment of the new covenant, of which both Ezekiel and Jeremiah spoke.

> Behold, the days come, saith the LORD, that I will make a new covenant with the house of Israel, and with the house of Judah: not according to the covenant that I made with their fathers in the day that I took them by the hand to bring them out of the land of Egypt; which my covenant they brake, although I was a husband unto them, saith the LORD. But this is the covenant that I will make with the house of Israel after those days, saith the LORD: I will put my law in their inward parts, and in their heart will I write it: and I will be their God, and they shall be my people: and they shall teach no more every man his brother, saying, Know the LORD; for they shall all know me, from the least of them unto the greatest of them, saith the LORD: for I will forgive their iniquity, and their sin will I remember no more (Jer 31:31-34).
>
> For I will take you from among the nations, and gather you out of all the countries, and will bring you into your own land. And I will sprinkle clean water upon you, and ye shall be clean: from all your filthiness, and from all your idols, will I cleanse you. A new heart also will I give you, and a new spirit will I put within you; and I will take away the stony heart out of your flesh, and I will give you a heart of flesh. And I will put my Spirit within you, and cause you to walk in my statutes, and ye shall keep mine ordinances, and do them. And ye shall dwell in the land that I gave to your fathers; and ye shall be my people, and I will be your God. And I will save you from all your uncleannesses: and I will call for the grain, and will multiply it, and lay no famine upon you (Eze 36:24-29).

Thus the days of Israel's suffering and spiritual blindness will be over. The times of the gentiles and the persecutions of the Antichrist are finished. The long-awaited Messiah of Israel has come. He, whom Israel rejected in his first coming, will be accepted as Messiah in his second coming, and a nation shall be born in a day. "And I saw thrones, and they sat upon them, and judgment was given unto them: and I saw the souls of them that had been beheaded for the testimony of Jesus, and for the word of God, and such as worshipped not the beast, neither his image, and received not the mark upon their forehead and upon their hand; and they lived, and reigned with Christ a thousand years" (Rev 20:4). It is this reign of Christ as Israel's Messiah which the prophet Isaiah described.

> The word that Isaiah the son of Amoz saw concerning Judah and Jerusalem. And it shall come to pass in the latter days, that the mountain of the LORD's house shall be established on the top of the mountains, and shall be exalted above the hills; and all nations shall flow unto it. And many peoples shall go and say, Come ye, and let us go up to the mountain of the LORD, to the house of the God of Jacob; and he will teach us of his ways, and we will walk in his paths: for out of Zion shall go forth the law, and the word of the LORD from Jerusalem. And he will judge between the nations, and will decide concerning many peoples; and they shall beat their swords into plowshares, and their spears into pruninghooks; nation shall not lift up sword against nation, neither shall they learn war any more (Is 2:1-4).

APPENDIX

A Chronology of the Times of the Gentiles

605 *The Babylonian Period.* The times of the gentiles begin with Nebuchadnezzar's conquest of Judah. Jerusalem is taken and the first wave of Jews carried into captivity, Daniel among them. Jerusalem will henceforth be trodden down of the gentiles as the times of the gentiles runs its course between the Babylonian captivity and the end of the great tribulation period. The Babylonian dominion of Israel is the head-of-gold period (Dan 2:36-38; 2 Ki 24:1; 2 Ch 36:5-6; Dan 1:1-2; Lk 21:24).

597 King Jehoiachin is carried captive by Nebuchadnezzar and the second wave of Jews is taken into Babylon, Ezekiel among them (2 Ki 24:10-16; 2 Ch 36:10; Eze 1:2).

587 Zedekiah rebels against Nebuchadnezzar. He is blinded and taken to Babylon where he dies. Zedekiah is the last king in the line of David to reign in Israel until the Messiah reigns during the millennium (Eze 34:23-24; Jer 23:5; 2 Ki 24:18—25:21; 2 Ch 36:13-21; Jer 39:1-8).

539 Cyrus, having established himself in control of the Medo-Persian empire in 549 B.C., captures Babylon, and the second world empire to dominate the Jews during the times of the gentiles comes upon the world scene. This is the breast-and-arms-of-silver period (Dan 2:32, 39; 6:1-3).

538 The edict of Cyrus opens the way for the Jews in Babylon to return to the land (Ezra 1:1-4).

515 The second temple is dedicated in Jerusalem (Ezra 6:15-18).

537-334 *The Persian Period.* The Jews are in the land but are under the control of the Persians (Josephus, *Antiquities* 11.7).

445 Artaxerxes decrees the rebuilding of the walls of Jerusalem, thus beginning Daniel's seventy weeks (Dan 9:24; Neh 2).

334-167 *The Hellenistic Period.* The Jews, in the land, are under the successive dominion of the Greeks, then the Ptolemies of Egypt, and then the Seleucids of Syria. This is the third great world empire to dominate the Jews during the times of the gentiles. It is the belly-and-its-thighs-of-brass era (Dan 2:32, 39; Josephus, *Antiquities* 11.7—12.6; Dan 11:2-20).

175-163 The reign of Antiochus IV Epiphanes whom Daniel saw as a type of the coming Antichrist (Dan 8:1-2; 11:21-35; Josephus, *Antiquities* 12.5-9; 1 Macc 1:10—6:16; 2 Macc 4:7—9:28).

167-63 The Maccabean revolt and subsequent Hasmonean dynasty in Judea. A short time of Jewish independence. This is the little-help period of Dan 11:34. (Josephus, *Antiquities* 12.6—14.4).

63-A.D. 70 *The Roman Period.* This is the fourth great world empire to dominate the Jews in the times of the gentiles. It is the legs-of-iron-and-feet-part-of-clay era of Daniel 2:33 (Josephus, *Antiquities* 14.4—20.11).

A.D.

29/30 The Messiah Prince is cut off on the cross, and the sixty-ninth week of Daniel's prophecy ends. The prophetic time clock stops for Israel and will not resume again until the tribulation (Dan 9:26).

29/30 The first Pentecost after the death and resurrection of Jesus sees the coming of the Holy Spirit to create the church by baptizing believers into the body of Christ (1 Co 12:13). The age of the church runs its course within the times of the gentiles between Pentecost and the rapture. This is the great parenthesis. The age of the church is never seen in the Old Testament. The course of the church age is pictured in Matthew 13 and Revelation 2-3. The close of the church age is seen in 1 Timothy 4:1-3; 2 Timothy 3:1-5; 4:3-4; and 2 Peter 2:1-3; 3:3-4.

63-70 The time of Israel's travail (Mt 24:4-8) includes the great revolt against Rome, the coming of the people of the prince, and the fall of the second temple (Dan 9:26; Mt 24:2; Josephus, *Wars* 2:17—7:11) .

132-135 The revolt of Bar Kokhba against Rome.

135-1948 The second exile of the Jews.

395-636 Byzantine rule in Palestine.

636 Beginning of Arab rule in Palestine.

691 The Dome of the Rock is completed on the temple mount where the Jewish temple previously stood. Until this day it dominates the only spot on earth where sacrifices can be offered according to the Torah.

1099 The Crusaders take Jerusalem. Christians rule in Palestine intermittently from 1099 to 1244.

1517 Ottoman Turks conquer Palestine. The present walls that surround the old city of Jerusalem are built.

1897 The first Zionist Congress meets in Basel.

1897-1948 This is the great era of Zionism's aliyahs in which many Jews return to the land—but in unbelief.

1917 The British capture Palestine from the Turks in World War I.

1922-1948 The British rule Palestine under a mandate from the League of Nations.

Nov. 29, 1947 The United Nations General Assembly adopts partition plan for Palestine, providing for the establishment of a Jewish state.

May 14, 1948 The new state of Israel is proclaimed. Open immigration now permits vast numbers of Jews to return to the Land. The second exile ends (Eze 11:14-17) .

June, 1967 *The Six-Day War*. Jerusalem is liberated from Jordanian control and for the first time in nearly two thousand years the Jews are in complete control of Jerusalem.

FUTURE EVENTS

The rapture of the church. The dead in Christ are raised and the generation of living believers is translated. The judgment seat of Christ is set and rewards are given to believers for faithful service (1 Th 4:13-17; 1 Co 15:51-54; 2 Co 5:10-11).

Daniel's seventieth week begins as Israel enters the tribulation period (Dan 9:27).

Israel's time of tribulation (Mt 24:9-14). This is the first three and one-half years of the seven-year period comprising Daniel's seventieth week (Rev 6:1—9:12).

World chaos occurs as a result of the rapture of the church and makes possible the rise of a new world leader, the Antichrist (Rev 6:1-16).

The ancient Roman empire revives as the Antichrist arises out of the midst of the ten-nation confederation. This is the feet-part-of-iron-and-part-of-clay period of the times of the gentiles (Dan 2:33, 41-42; 7:24).

A world-wide spiritual awakening during the first part of the tribulation period, the latter rain of the Spirit, (Ja 5:7-8; Joel 2:23; Zec 10:1; Hos 6:3). During this time the 144,000 Jewish missionaries are saved and sealed (Rev 7:1-8); they preach the gospel during the entire tribulation period (Mt 24:14). Many others, both Jews and gentiles, are saved and make up the saints of God who are martyred by the Antichrist (Dan 7:21, 25; Rev 7:9-17).

A covenant is made between the Antichrist and Israel. The temple is rebuilt and the Levitical system of priesthood and offerings begins again (Dan 9:27).

The apostate church flourishes during the first half of the tribulation period (Rev 17:1-7).

Israel is secure under the protection of the Antichrist's covenant until she is invaded at midtribulation by Russia. The Antichrist comes to Israel's defense. Russia is defeated and the Antichrist becomes a world ruler (Eze 38-39)

At midtribulation the Antichrist breaks the covenant made with Israel and the great tribulation period begins. (Dan 9:27; Mt 24:15-28; Rev 11:1—18:24).

Antichrist receives the death stroke from which he recovers. He is now manifest as the beast. His image is set in the temple and he demands worship as god (Mt 24:15; 2 Th 2:4; Rev 13:1-10).

The false prophet appears to aid the beast and cause the earth-dwellers to worship him as god (Rev 13:11-18).

The apostate church is destroyed (Rev 17:1-6).

The two witnesses appear and prophesy during the great tribulation period, until they are killed at the close of the period, after which they are resurrected and raptured. (Rev 11:1-12).

Israel, faithful to her orthodox faith, is severely persecuted by the Antichrist during the great tribulation period (Jer 30:5-7; Dan 12:1; Zec 13:8; Mt 24:21-22).

Many in Israel flee and are protected by the nations (Mt 24:15-20; Rev 12:6, 13-17).

The fall of commercial Babylon toward the close of the great tribulation (Rev 18:1-24).

The kings of the Orient invade Israel and hostilities erupt between them and the forces of the Antichrist. The battle of Armageddon and the doom of the Antichrist (Dan 11:44-45; Rev 16:12-16; 2 Th 2:8; Rev 19:19).

The second coming of Christ ends the times of the gentiles (Dan 2:44; 7:9-13, 22-28; Rev 19:11-16).

Antichrist and the false prophet are cast into the lake of fire. (Rev 19:20—20:10).

The gentile nations are judged on the basis of their treatment of God's covenant people Israel, during the times of the gentiles (Mt 25:31-46).

Notes

CHAPTER 1

1. Alexander Roberts, ed., *Ante-Nicene Library,* vol. 1, p. 106.
2. Norman Cohn, *The Pursuit of the Millennium,* p. 54.
3. Ibid., p. 18.
4. Ibid., p. 59.
5. Arnulf, quoted by A. F. Villemain, *Life of Gregory the Seventh,* vol. 1, p. 175.
6. Christopher Hill, *Antichrist in Seventeenth-Century England,* p. 18.
7. Ibid., p. 186.
8. Ibid., p. 40.
9. Salmon, quoted by T. Francis Glasson, *His Appearing and His Kingdom,* p. 40.
10. Ibid., pp. 40-41.
11. Oswald J. Smith, *Is the Antichrist at Hand?* [tract]
12. Francis A. Wight, *The Beast, the False Prophet, and Hitler* (Butler, Ind.: F. A. Wight, 1941), p. 6.
13. Jeanne Dixon, *My Life and Prophecies,* pp. 178-80. Used by permission of the publishers, Wm. Morrow & Co.

CHAPTER 2

1. Jerome, *Commentary on Daniel,* trans. Gleason L. Archer, p. 136.

CHAPTER 3

1. Norman Snaith, *The Jews from Cyrus to Herod,* p. 45.
2. Solomon Zeitlin, *The Rise and Fall of the Judean State,* vol. 1, p. 318.
3. Otto Morkholm, *Antiochus IV of Syria,* pp. 144-45.
4. Jerome, *Commentary on Daniel,* p. 86.
5. Zeitlin, ibid., vol. 1, p. 92.
6. Edwyn Bevan, *Jerusalem Under the High Priests,* p. 83.
7. Ibid.
8. Josephus, *Antiquities* 7.5.4.

CHAPTER 4

1. Theodor H. Gaster, trans., *The Dead Sea Scriptures* (New York: Doubleday, 1957), pp. 61-62.
2. E. R. Bevan, *The House of Seleucus,* vol. 2, p. 171.
3. Solomon Zeitlin, *Rise and Fall,* vol. 1, p. 89.
4. Robert Payne, *Ancient Rome,* p. 73.
5. R. H. Charles, *The Apocrypha and Pseudepigrapha of the Old Testament,* vol. 2, p. 257.

CHAPTER 5

1. R. H. Charles, *The Revelation of St. John,* vol. 1, p. 350.
2. Ibid., vol. 2, p. 80.
3. Edward Gibbon, *The History of the Decline and Fall of the Roman Empire,* vol. 1, pp. 250-51.
4. Pliny, quoted by Betty Radice, *The Letters of the Younger Pliny,* p. 293.
5. Ibid., p. 295.
6. Max I. Dimont, *Jews, God, and History,* pp. 147-48.
7. Arthur Murphy, *The Works of Cornelius Tacitus,* (Philadelphia: Thomas Wardle, 1844), p. 500.
8. W. Hersey Davis and Edward A. McDowell, eds., *A Source Book of Interbiblical History,* p. 542.

CHAPTER 6

1. Robert Payne, *Ancient Rome,* p. 11.
2. Yigael Yadin, *Bar-Kokhba,* p. 205.
3. I. Epstein, ed., *The Babylonian Talmud* (London: Socino, 1938), p. 142.

A Selected Bibliography

Anderson, Sir Robert. *The Coming Prince*. London: Pickering and Inglis, 1909.

Andrews, Samuel. *Christianity and Antichristianity*. Chicago: B.I.C.A., 1898.

Appian. *Roman History*. Trans. Horace White. 4 vols. The Loeb Classical Library. Cambridge, Mass.: Harvard U. Press, 1912-13.

Barclay, William. *The Revelation of John*. The Daily Study Bible series, vols. 1-2. Philadelphia, 1959.

Baron, David. *The Ancient Scriptures and the Modern Jew*. Findlay, Ohio: Dunham, n.d.

———. *Christ and Israel*. London: Morgan and Scott, n.d.

———. *A Divine Forecast of Jewish History*. London: Morgan and Scott, n.d.

———. *Israel's Inalienable Possession*. London: Morgan and Scott, n.d.

———. *The Visions and Prophecies of Zechariah*. London: Marshall, Morgan, and Scott, n.d.

Bede. *Historical Works*. Trans. J. E. King. The Loeb Classical Library. Cambridge, Mass.: Harvard U. Press, 1930.

Berry, P. "Antiochus IV Epiphanes." *The Journal of Biblical Literature* 24 (1910) :126-138.

Bevan, A. A. *A Short Commentary on the Book of Daniel*. Cambridge: Cambridge U. Press, 1892.

Bevan, E. R. *A History of Egypt Under the Ptolemaic Dynasty*. London: Methuen, 1927.

———. *The House of Seleucus*. 2 vols. London: E. Arnold, 1920.

———. *Jerusalem Under the High Priests*. London: E. Arnold, 1920.

———. *The Legacy of Israel.* Oxford: Clarendon, 1927.

———. "A Note on Antiochus Epiphanes." *The Journal of Hellenistic Studies* 20 (1900) :26-30.

———. "Syria and the Jews." *The Cambridge Ancient History* 8 (1930) :495-533.

Bickerman, E. *The Maccabees.* New York: Schocken, 1947.

Bousset, Wilhelm. *The Antichrist.* Trans. A. H. Keane. London: Hutchinson, 1896.

Bunyan, John. "The Antichrist and His Ruin: And of the Slaying of the Witnesses." *The Works of John Bunyan.* Edited by George Offor, vol. 2, pp. 41-82. London: Blackie & Son, 1854.

Caird, G. B. *The Revelation of St. John the Divine.* New York: Harper, 1966.

Charles, R. H. *A Critical History of the Doctrine of the Future Life.* London: A. & C. Black, 1913.

———. *Daniel.* The Century Bible series, no. 11. London: Caxton, n.d.

———. *Religion's Development Between the Old and the New Testaments.* London: Butterworth, 1934.

———. *The Revelation of St. John.* The International Critical Commentary, nos. 1-2. Edinburgh: T&T Clark, 1920.

Cohn, Norman. *The Pursuit of the Millennium.* London: Secker & Warburg, 1957.

Cooper, David L. *The Antichrist and the World-Wide Revival.* Los Angeles: Biblical Research Society, n.d.

———. *Is the Fig Tree Cursed Forever?* Los Angeles: Biblical Research Society, n.d.

———. *The Grand March of Empire.* Los Angeles: Biblical Research Society, n.d.

———. *The Image Vision of Daniel Two.* Los Angeles: Biblical Research Society, n.d.

———. *The Invading Forces of Russia and of the Antichrist Overthrown in Palestine.* Los Angeles: Biblical Research Society, n.d.

———. *Messiah: His Glorious Appearance Imminent.* Los Angeles: Biblical Research Society, 1961.

———. *Messiah: His Final Call to Israel.* Los Angeles: Biblical Research Society, 1966.

———. *The Seventy Weeks of Daniel.* Los Angeles: Biblical Research Society, 1941.

———. *When Gog's Armies Meet the Almighty in the Land of Israel.* Los Angeles: Biblical Research Society, 1970.

Culver, Robert D. *Daniel and the Latter Days.* Chicago: Moody, 1954.

Cumont, Franz. *The Oriental Religions in Roman Paganism.* Chicago: The Open Court Pub. Co., 1911.

Curtius. *History of Alexander.* Trans. John C. Rolfe. The Loeb Classical Library. Cambridge, Mass.: Harvard U. Press, 1946.

Dagut, M. B. "Second Maccabees and the Death of Antiochus IV Epiphanes." *The Journal of Biblical Literature* 72 (1953) :149-157.

Davis, W. Hersey, and McDowell, Edward A., eds. *A Source Book of Interbiblical History.* Nashville: Broadman, 1948.

DeHaan, M. R. *The Jews and Palestine in Prophecy.* Grand Rapids: Zondervan, 1950.

Dimont, Max I. *Jews, God, and History.* New York: Signet, 1964.

———. *The Indestructible Jews.* New York: Signet, 1971.

Dio Cassius. *Roman History.* Trans. Earnest Cary. 9 vols. The Loeb Classical Library. Cambridge, Mass.: Harvard U. Press, 1914-27.

Diodorus Siculus. *Library of History.* Trans. C. H. Oldfather, C. L. Sherman, C. Bradford Wells, Russel M. Greer, and Francis Walton. 12 vols. Loeb Classical Library. Cambridge, Mass.: Harvard U. Press, 1933-63.

Dionysius of Halicarnassus. *Roman Antiquities.* Trans. Earnest Cary. 7 vols. The Loeb Classical Library. Cambridge, Mass.: Harvard U. Press, 1937-50.

Dixon, Jean. *My Life and Prophecies.* New York: Morrow, 1969.

Downey, Glanville. *A History of Antioch in Syria from Seleucus to the Arab Conquest.* Princeton: Princeton U. Press, 1969.

Driver, S. R. *The Book of Daniel.* The Cambridge Bible for Schools and Colleges. Cambridge: Cambridge U. Press, 1901.

Eddy, S. K. *"The King Is Dead": Studies in the Near Eastern Resistance to Hellenism.* Lincoln: University of Nebraska Press, 1961.

Elliott, Russell. "The Antichrist." *Our Hope* 54 (1947) :335-38.

Eusebius. *Ecclesiastical History*. Trans. Kirsopp Lake and J. E. L. Culton. 2 vols. The Loeb Classical Library. Cambridge, Mass.: Harvard U. Press, 1926-32.

Fereday, W. W. "Armageddon." *Our Hope* 47 (1940) :397-401.

Freehof, Solomon. *A Treasury of Responsa*. Philadelphia: Jewish Pub. Soc., 1962.

Furfey, P. H. "The Mystery of Lawlessness." *Catholic Biblical Quarterly* 8 (1946) :179-91.

Gaster, Theodor. *The Dead Sea Scriptures in English Translation with Introduction and Notes*. New York: Doubleday, 1957.

Gibbon, Edward. *The History of the Decline and Fall of the Roman Empire*. 6 vols. Philadelphia: John D. Morris, n.d.

Glasson, T. Francis. *His Appearing and His Kingdom*. London: Epworth, 1953.

Glover, T. R. *The Conflict of Religion in the Early Roman Empire*. London: Methuen, 1909.

Herodotus. *Histories*. Trans. A. D. Godley. The Loeb Classical Library. 4 vols. Cambridge, Mass.: Harvard U. Press, 1920-25.

Hill, Christopher. *Antichrist in Seventeenth-Century England*. London: Oxford U. Press, 1971.

Hunlingford, S. *The Apocalypse*. London, 1881.

Ironside, H. A. *The Great Parenthesis*. Grand Rapids: Zondervan, 1943.

———. "Looking Backward over a Third of a Century of Prophetic Fulfillment." *Miscellaneous Papers,* vol. 1. New York: 1945.

Jerome. *Commentary on Daniel*. Trans. Gleason L. Archer. Grand Rapids: Baker, 1958.

Josephus. *Antiquities*. Trans. H. St. J. Thackery, Ralph Marcus, Allen Wikgren, L. H. Feldman. Loeb Classical Library. Cambridge, Mass.: Harvard U. Press, 1930-65.

———. *The Life. Against Apion*. Trans. H. St. J. Thackery. The Loeb Classical Library. Cambridge, Mass.: Harvard U. Press, 1926.

———. *The Jewish War*. Trans. H. St. J. Thackery. Loeb Classical Library. Cambridge, Mass.: Harvard U. Press, 1927.

Keil, C. F. *Biblical Commentary on the Book of Daniel*. Grand Rapids: Eerdmans, 1949.

Kincaid, C. A. "A Persian Prince—Antiochus Epiphanes." *Oriental Studies in Honor of Crusetji Erachji Pavri.* London, 1923.

Kopecky, Donald. "Salvation in the Tribulation." *Bibliotheca Sacra* 109 (1952) :266-270.

Leupold, H. C. *Exposition of Daniel.* Grand Rapids: Baker, 1969.

Livy. *Livy.* Trans. B. O. Foster, F. G. Moore, Evan T. Sage. A. C. Schlesinger. Loeb Classical Library. Cambridge, Mass.: Harvard U. Press, 1919-67.

Logsdon, S. Franklin. *Profiles of Prophecy.* Grand Rapids: Zondervan, 1970.

Louvish, Misha, ed. *Facts About Israel 1971.* Jerusalem: Keter Books, 1971.

McCall, Thomas S. "How Soon the Tribulation Temple?" *Bibliotheca Sacra* 128 (1971) :341-51.

McClain, Alva J. *Daniel's Prophecy of the Seventy Weeks.* Grand Rapids: Zondervan, 1940.

Montgomery, James A. *A Critical and Exegetical Commentary on the Book of Daniel.* The International Critical Commentary. Edinburgh: T & T Clark, 1927.

Morkholm, Otto. "The Accession of Antiochus IV of Syria." *The American Numismatic Society Museum Notes* 11 (1964).
———. *Antiochus IV of Syria.* Copenhagen: Gylendal, 1966.

Newman, John Henry. "The Protestant Idea of the Antichrist." *Critical and Historical Essays,* vol. 2. London: Pickering, 1871.
———. "The Patristic Idea of the Antichrist." *Discussions and Arguments on Various Subjects.* London: Longman & Green, 1899.

Oesterley, W. O. E. *The Jews and Judaism During the Greek Period.* London: S. P. C. K., 1941.

Pache, Rene. *The Return of Jesus Christ.* Chicago: Moody, 1955.

Payne, Robert. *Ancient Rome.* New York: American Heritage, 1970.

Pentecost, J. Dwight. *Things to Come.* Grand Rapids: Dunham, 1964.
———. *Will Man Survive?* Chicago: Moody, 1971.

Pink, Arthur W. *The Antichrist.* Swengel, Pa.: Bible Truth Depot, 1923.

Pliny the Younger. *Letters and Panegyricus.* Trans. Betty Radice. Loeb Classical Library. Cambridge, Mass.: Harvard U. Press, 1969.

Plutarch. *The Parallel Lives.* Trans. B. Perring. Loeb Classical Library. Cambridge, Mass.: Harvard U. Press, 1922-27.

Polybius. *The Histories.* Trans. W. R. Paton. Loeb Classical Library. Cambridge, Mass.: Harvard U. Press, 1922-27.

Price, Walter K. *Jesus' Prophetic Sermon.* Chicago: Moody, 1972.

Procopius. *History of the Wars.* Trans. W. R. Paton. Loeb Classical Library. Cambridge, Mass.: Harvard U. Press, 1914-26.

Rankin, O. S. *The Origin of the Festival of Hanukkah.* Edinburgh: T & T Clark, 1913.

Reeves, Marjorie. *The Influence of Prophecy in the Later Middle Ages.* Oxford: Clarendon Press, 1969.

———. "Joachimist Influence on the Idea of a Last World Empire." *Traditio* 17 (1961) :323-370.

Roberts, Alexander, ed. *Ante-Nicene Christian Library.* Edinburgh: T. & T. Clark, 1864.

Rostovtzeff, M. *The Social and Economic History of the Hellenistic World.* 3 vols. Oxford: Clarendon Press, 1941.

Rowley, H. H. "Menelaus and the Abomination of Desolation." *Studia Orientalia J. Pedersen Dicata.* Copenhagen, 1953.

Scofield, C. I. "The Last World Empire and Armageddon." *Bibliotheca Sacra* 58 (1951) :355-362.

———. "The Times of the Gentiles." *Bibliotheca Sacra* 58 (1951) : 343-355.

Scroggie, W. Graham. *Prophecy and History.* London: Morgan & Scott, n.d.

Seiss, Joseph A. *Voices from Babylon.* Philadelphia: Cook, 1879.

Smith, J. B. *A Revelation of Jesus Christ.* Scottdale, Pa.: Mennonite Pub. House, 1966.

Smith, Oswald. *Is the Antichrist at Hand?* Toronto: Tabernacle, 1926.

Smith, Wilbur M. *You Can Know the Future.* Glendale, Calif.: Gospel Light, 1971.

Snaith, Norman H. *The Jews from Cyrus to Herod.* Surrey: The Religious Education Press, 1949.

Strabo. *Geography.* Trans. Horace L. Jones. Loeb Classical Library. Cambridge, Mass.: Harvard U. Press, 1917-32.

Strauss, Lehman. *The Book of the Revelation.* Neptune, N. J.: Revell, 1967.

———. *The Prophecies of Daniel.* Neptune, N. J.: Revell, 1969.

Suetonius. *The Lives of the Caesars.* Trans. J. C. Rolfe. Loeb Classical Library. Cambridge, Mass.: Harvard U. Press, 1913-14.

Swain, J. W. "Antiochus Epiphanes and Egypt." *Classical Philology* 39 (1944) :73-94.

Tacitus. *Histories.* Trans. Clifford H. Moore. Loeb Classical Library. Cambridge, Mass.: Harvard U. Press, 1914-37.

Talbot, Louis T. *The Prophecies of Daniel.* Wheaton, Ill.: Van Kampen Press, 1940.

Tarn, W. W., and Griffith, G. T. *Hellenistic Civilization.* London: E. Arnold, 1952.

Techerikover, V. *Hellenistic Civilization and the Jews.* Philadelphia: Jewish Pub. Soc., 1959.

Townshend, R. R. "Antiochus Epiphanes, the Brilliant Madman." *The Hubbert Journal* 11 (1913) :819-29.

Villemain, A. F. *Life of Gregory the Seventh.* Trans. James B. Brockey. London: Richard Bentley, 1874.

Walvoord, John F. *The Church in Prophecy.* Grand Rapids: Zondervan, 1964.

———. *Daniel.* Chicago: Moody, 1971.

———. *Israel in Prophecy.* Grand Rapids: Zondervan, 1962.

———. *The Nations in Prophecy.* Grand Rapids: Zondervan, 1967.

———. *The Revelation of Jesus Christ.* Chicago: Moody, 1967.

Williamson, G. A. *The World of Josephus.* London: Secker, 1964.

Wright, Francis A. *The Beast, the False Prophet, and Hitler.* Butler, Ind.: Francis Wright, 1941.

Wright, John. *The Play of the Antichrist.* Toronto, 1967.

Yadin, Yigael. *Bar-Kokhba.* New York: Random House, 1971.

Young, Edward J. *The Prophecy of Daniel.* Grand Rapids: Eerdmans, 1949.

Young, Karl. *The Drama of the Medieval Church.* 2 vols. Oxford: Clarendon, 1962.

Zeitlin, Solomon. *The Rise and Fall of the Judean State.* 2 vols. Philadelphia: Jewish Pub. Soc., 1962.

Subject Index

Abomination of desolation, 55-56,
130, 136-37
image of Beast, 96-97
its identity, 94
set up at midtribulation, 61-62,
188
Adonai, 13
Adso, 30, 31
Alabaster, William, 35
Alexander the Great
advent of, 79
comes to Jerusalem, 65-66
conquers with Hellenism, 102-8
Daniel's prophecy concerning,
101
death of, 80
empire of, short-lived, 172
four generals succeeded, 78
strategy of Hellenization, 103
Ames, William, 36
Ante-Nicene era, 21-22
Antichrist
antagonist of church and Israel, 9
appeals to all as god, 133-34
breaks covenant with Israel, 186-
87
career and the last days of, 11
career of, ends at second coming,
22, 78
church will never know, 44
claim of, to be god, 98-99
conflict of, with apostate church,
178-80
contends with four groups in Israel, 187-94
covenant of, broken with Israel,
56
Daniel's picture of, merged with
Antiochus, 87
death stroke of, 137, 145-47
desires to be worshiped, 10

dictator-savior, 122-24
early rise of, 49
expectation of, 20, 33
four basic views of, 16-17
identification of, 15
and Israel's false Messiah, 132-33
a Jew? 74
John's use of the term, 150-52
"king of fierce countenance," 45-
50
medieval view of, 31
not a false Messiah, 132
person of evil, 7
related to Israel and nations, 44
reported as dead, 127-28
revealed after rapture, 44
review of career of, 154
rise of, 177
seven conflicts of, 170-71
spirit of evil, 7
spirit of, and gnosticism, 151-52
under Satan's control, 147-48
Antiochus IV, 18
contrasted with Antichrist, 47
Daniel previews reign of, 67-70
Daniel's prophecy concerning,
101-2
empire of, 83-84
encourages worship of himself,
91-92
Epiphanes, 75, 91
false rumors about death of, 88,
127
Hellenizing edicts of, 69
history of, 84-86
identified as little horn of Daniel,
8, 78-86
interest of, in Judah, 82
madness of, 97-98
magnifies himself as god, 97-99
meaning of the name, 84

232

Scripture Index